THIS IS LONDON

ᵒˢˀ 16 - 5 - ᵞ/22

'Work of this sort really is necessary; this is the stuff we must think about if we are ever to get to grips (assuming it's not too late already) with what lies ahead for our cities . . . more than I can possibly say, I admired its author's pluck, determination, compassion and refusal to judge – and I'd like him to know that some of the stories he told will haunt me for a long time to come'

Rachel Cooke, *New Statesman*

'An exhilarating account of the British capital . . . His writing is visceral, and at its best echoes the immersive style of the great Polish reporter and author Ryszard Kapuściński . . . He treats his subjects with great sensitivity . . . an important, unflinching piece of reportage. Judah digs deep into parts of London that a less adventurous journalist would avoid, unearthing some of the many tragic narratives shaping a city at the turbulent forefront of globalisation'

The National (Scotland)

'Judah's epic account of contemporary London . . . is reportage, not a moral tract; Judah wants to tell it like it is, with I-am-a-webcam neutrality, not preach or harangue . . . It's when Judah sits down with someone and listens that the book really takes off. He is brilliant at getting people to speak . . . Judah gets so close to his protagonists that he writes as if from inside their heads, in the manner of W. G. Sebald'

Blake Morrison, *Guardian*

'Ben Judah is an excellent foreign correspondent . . . Here, he turns the skills he learnt abroad to his home city . . . he listens to the stories of those normally forgotten . . . it is these stories that make the book so timely . . . Judah has succeeded in opening readers' eyes to the hardships experienced by many and ignored by most'

Independent

BEN JUDAH

THIS IS LONDON

LIFE AND DEATH IN THE WORLD CITY

PICADOR

First published 2016 by Picador

This edition published 2016 by Picador
an imprint of Pan Macmillan
20 New Wharf Road, London N1 9RR
Associated companies throughout the world
www.panmacmillan.com

ISBN 978-1-4472-7627-2

9 8 7 6 5 4 3 2

A CIP catalogue record for this book is available from the British Library.

Printed and bound by CPI Group (UK) Ltd, Croydon, CR0 4YY

CONTENTS

VICTORIA COACH STATION

I have to see everything for myself. I don't trust statistics. I don't trust columnists. I don't trust self-appointed spokesmen. I have to make up my own mind. This is why I am shivering again, in Victoria Coach Station, at 6 am.

I am being pushed around. Automatic doors slide and close. Crowds are dazed with arrival. African men in hoodies and pleather jackets rub their eyes. Polish meatheads grip onto huge toolboxes as they make for the street. Arab men in body warmers and fleeces pull out throwaway phones, and dial those they know.

I have been coming to the coach station every morning now for weeks: counting the buses, and pacing up to strangers – first dozens, then hundreds – recording what they say into my phone. Again, I am hung-over. I am cold. Again, the freeze steams every pane, and the damp air kneads itself into my clothes.

Wheels crash through dirty water as coaches, bleeping and reversing, unload Paris, Bucharest and Rome. Pigeons flutter and ventilators moan. Hard rain patters the vaulting glass over the grubby terminal like a baby's rattle. My hands sting red as I key rapid notes into my screen: this is what life is like, morning after morning, at our miserable Ellis Island. The point from which our society is changing.

This cramped hall, lined with grimy old payphones, echoes with languages I cannot understand: Sinti, Turkish, maybe Swahili. Tiles shine with electric light. Now Eurolines empties. A Romanian woman in a grey shell suit pulls off her hood, smiles timidly, a step away from a stocky man, and flicks her long glossy, brown hair back and forth. An oily, unshaven boy, in all-black hoodie and puffa

jacket, drags a sports bag and stares blankly into the squiggling colours of the tube map.

I am standing in the damp again, keying in what I can see.

Because I only trust what I can see. I was born in London but I no longer recognize this city. I don't know if I love the new London or if it frightens me: a city where at least 55 per cent of people are not ethnically white British, nearly 40 per cent were born abroad, and 5 per cent are living illegally in the shadows. I have no idea who these new Londoners are. Or even what their London really is.

This is why I keep coming here.

Paris bleeps in. Wheelie bags click-clack, tugged by French metrosexuals in drainpipe jeans, chirping and gossiping. They wipe the rain off their moisturized faces and brown horn-rimmed glasses. A tall, masculine girl, with a slothlike frame and a jean skirt, pulls herself up to the tiled wall and leans on it for a moment, closing her eyes, until a harried African cleaner in Day-Glo, clutching a mop, accidentally, thwacks her shoulder, and apologizes. But she hardly registers, as my fingers quickly input her reactions: like that Day-Glo is on an invisible man.

Now Cologne bleeps in. Two Bulgarian toughs with lined faces and puffy eyes, in matching sky-blue ski jackets, unload charcoal rucksacks, packed with pneumatic drills. They both scowl as the belly of the coaches empty, as frumpy, squabbling Roma in forest-green headscarves and long black skirts snipe at each other as they haul bin bags, stuffed to bursting with torn blankets and mouldy duvets, over the mirroring puddles. They are following a yawning man under a black leather cap clutching only a scratched violin case.

Making sound recordings of the murmuring din, I lose count of the coaches. Every week two thousand migrants unload at Victoria Coach Station. This is where tens of thousands of migrants arrive every year, the equivalent of a whole city, the size of Basildon or Bath. They are all part of the same thing: the new London.

There is now a little light.

The cold tingles my nerves. I am here because I don't understand this city.

I shove my phone into my pocket. You never learn it all just watching. You never learn it all from the numbers. You have to go up and talk to people: completely, utterly different people from you. I want to talk to those three Roma. I refuse to let someone else tell me what they think.

I follow them into first light.

Three Polish labourers crouch at the entrance, over crinkled plastic bags, gesturing they want to cadge some fags from French flops in beige macs. But here, these are too expensive to share.

Yelling and cursing, and waving to their stragglers, the three Roma trudge forcefully out into the hissing rain. They are all pushing granny trolleys, each massively overloaded with plastic weave sacks, and half a dozen crutches.

They look like they know where they are going.

I pace behind them in scuffed trainers like a thief, keying in what they see: thundering traffic, watery light, the ornate red-brick Edwardian mansion offices, with column porticos, or the monumentally flat, blue glass office fronts, where by the vents the tramps are still sleeping. Around Victoria Station sleeping bags are everywhere. Tramps sleep in the arches, they sleep in the shuttered gates, they sleep in the stone carved colonnade, they sleep by the vents of the dismal space-age mall, they sleep at the bus stops, and in dozens, they sleep on newspaper beds.

I notice the three Roma linger and glance at the tramps huddling all along the porticos of the fantastical, cross-dressing facades on the road to Buckingham Palace.

I count the street-sleepers behind them: six, seven, eight. Twice, I watch them pause, as if looking for friends. The further I follow them, the sooner I realize the Roma are looking for someone, in the sleeping bags curled up on the manky steps of these studied fantasies in stone, these drag queens in fancy dress who long to be ancient Greek and English at the same time, as the road curves round sinister spear-like railings, built to keep the poor out of dark dripping garden squares.

Who are they looking for under these overweening buildings?

They push on past curved lintels and fleshy balustrades – overblown geometries, and cornices – buildings sculpted with that lurid,

time-melting imagination which gripped the English when they were powerful. The Roma are eyeing the tramps waking up until they reach the hurtling traffic and begin to traipse along by a dirty low brick wall, sealing off the bare crowns of chestnut trees, topped with black spikes and barbed wire. These are the battlements of the gardens at Buckingham Palace.

The three Roma glance back, worried.

They know they are being followed now.

This is Hyde Park Corner. Rimmed with enormous pretensions. The stern classical palace – its columns and preening pediments, fantasizing it is the Acropolis – was once a hospital. But now the Union Jack flutters over the most expensive hotel in London, where every guest has at his disposal a personal, perfectly trained butler. I stand in dim light and imagine the valets in tails throwing open towering old doors – once for wheelchairs, patients and nurses – to sheikhs, oligarchs and plutocrats. But there is no change in the limestone pudding over the road impersonating a Corinthian temple. This is the old palace of the Duke of Wellington. And his aristocratic progeny still use the upper floors above a fusty museum.

I am running along the pavement now.

I lose them at the mouth of a dingy underpass. The Roma women have scuttled below ground as fast as they can. This is where I hover. Then I see the Fiddler coming out of the tunnel gloom. I can instantly tell he is just like them.

'When did you come to London?

His brow creases, shocked.

'Why have you come to London?'

We are surrounded by money. Two men in flannel suits rush past us chattering in Russian towards the offices of J.P. Morgan's private wealth management division. Outside the Lanesborough Hotel a black cab unloads perfumed Arabs in flowing robes, like priests of pure money. The Fiddler drops his case to his feet.

He is looking at me like I am about to arrest him.

'Please talk to me, I'm not a policeman.'

His lips slowly relax. The Fiddler is shaved with brown wrinkled eyes, and a brush-thick moustache; he wears a black leather cap

with goofy sheepskin ear warmers. He is standing in a black raincoat with a crumpled Remembrance Day poppy, rummaged somewhere along his way. He speaks very softly, and as he clutches his scratched violin case his mumbles are almost drowned out by whooshing double-deckers.

'The harvest was bad. This was my last chance.'

He looks at the floor like a guilty man. I know he wants to leave but I won't let him. I have power over him for a few seconds. And I want him to speak.

'I've come to London to fiddle and beg.'

I switch on the recorder. He says the crops in northern Romania sold for nothing. He says two weeks ago his fridge went empty and when his children mewled like pregnant cats from hunger he knew he had no other choice but to go to the Roma loan sharks. He says he quivered as he went in. The Fiddler knew he was useless to them: he had never been abroad before, speaks less than five words of English, and has no skills appropriate for a contract.

His voice rubs against the traffic in the recording.

'They told me these were the richest streets in the whole world. They told me these were the streets of the Arabs . . . The lenders told me that if I came here I would have to sleep with the beggars on the street. And that would be a bit cold . . . But there were rich Arabs walking around everywhere who would give you some money if you beg . . . or some coins if you fiddle here and there for them.'

He looks at me as if to go: can I show you?

I nod and he unfastens the gold painted locks. He proudly lifts his violin out of the scuffed box. Then clutches it. This is how he is going to try and pay back his debt-collectors. But he is not really a musician. He has played the fiddle a bit in the orchestra at the village church. But as he saws at the strings, and his eyes roll heavenwards, the screeching betrays him.

'What the hell are you trying to do?' The Fiddler sneers at me incredulously. 'You're never going to understand anything like this. You think all you have to do is come and ask me a few questions? You're an idiot, then . . . You'll never get anything about what it means to be a beggar until you've slept on the streets.'

My heart sinks. I know he's right.

'But won't it be ridiculous to only sleep there for a few days?'

He grins as he packs away the fiddle.

'The first few days are the ones you never forget.'

Then he turns his back on me, and descends into the dinge of the underpass.

PARK LANE

His voice gets inside my head.

I can hear him. I can hear the Fiddler as I count the tramps.

I can hear him as I mark this spot [X] in my notebook. I can hear him as I scrawl down exactly what I can see: six beggars, four men, two women – Roma – sleeping in front of the glare of an estate agent's window on Park Lane. I get down what two of them are saying. One youngish man, with pinched green eyes, pleads he came to be a tramp but dreams he is a film maker. The other, a hunched, crippled midget, says traffickers mauled him with a flick knife to beg for them here. As they talk, they stand in front of the illuminated glass, where electric screens shimmer behind them with house prices: five million, two bedrooms, six million, eight bedrooms. This prime vendor has been locked shut for hours but the sterile white lights are left on.

This light makes the beggars feel safe.

I fold my notebook closed and keep going. It's close to 11 pm.

Night after night, I have been pacing up and down the harsh, polluted motorway of Park Lane, trying to map the street sleepers. My first [X] is at the very top of the surging traffic. There are six Roma who sleep in front of a Sainsbury's local. Their damp-stained duvets are shoved right up against a glass wall plastered in an enormous print of glossy fresh baguettes. The second [X] is just across from the traffic lights: an English tramp, a crack-head, who shouts, 'Those Gypsy scum came and beat us out of the places us English had been in for years. They'll rush you, mate.' My third [X] is the benches by Speakers' Corner under the enormous tree crowns of Hyde Park: twelve Roma sleep there, one a smack addict with a

scraggly ginger beard, his face slanting to a point, who sits on a blue shell suitcase.

At first the map seemed hopeless. Impossible. I gathered figures out of the darkness, recorded their voices, and then watched them disappear, dark figures swarming towards the glowing mouth of the Underground, the cars' lamps twirling red and yellow round the traffic island at Marble Arch.

This is street life: disorientation, a jumble of snatched faces, and car noise. But then slowly the flow hardens into patterns. The jumble of faces becomes clear, then repetitive. Night after night, I begin to map the turns and circles the beggars make, like clock-work. Now I can mark a [X] where the working girl stands smoking on the hour at the beginning of Edgware Road. Now I can see the rhythm in the streets.

Tonight is the same as all other nights.

After-dinner couples are strolling along Park Lane. Slavic blondes with sad-making eyes drift past on the arms of perfumed Saudi men; euphoric smokers in long coats, suits and tuxedos, with whisky breath, come out of the hotels. When the one newsagent locks up, under the overhanging colonnade where the Fine & Country estate agent glows, the Bangladeshi boys working there toss out buckets of foul water. I record their contemptuous voices: 'The beggars they sleep here like mice. We have to keep the thieves away. This water means they can't sleep until it dries.'

There is only one [X] I still have to cross.

I need to know what it feels like to be invisible. I need to know what it means to become unseen on plutocratic boulevards. I need to know what it is like to be glared at like a mangy half-man. This is why I am wearing beggar's clothes: worn out, third-hand brogues, thin joggers, a torn puffa jacket and a tight woolly hat.

The couples flinch and avoid me in the flow.

I hover in the shadow of a lamp and flick through the pages of my notebook. My catalogue of invisible nightwalkers. Yesterday, I met a black crack addict in a blue hoodie who attacked the pay phone for some pieces, and then ran away sobbing, like the stick-man in the shadows. Two days ago, I talked with a pair of Roma flower girls – their skin was soft, waxy – in black headscarves, pacing up and down clutching roses. They told me they were fourteen. Tonight, a Roma knife-peddler came up to me, his moustache curling over his lip, and began to tell me the story of the binding of Isaac and where the prostitutes are. Then he stumbled off to hawk his knives and disappeared.

The last [X] on my map is the hardest: I need to sleep rough.

I have been meeting the Fiddler here for a week. With a [*] at both ends of Park Lane he has shown me where he scrapes his instrument. He has allowed me to plot his territory. With his finger he has run a line across my map, showing the route he takes up and down after coins.

His comments, I've written at the bottom in biro.

'Everything looks like chaos here but it is not. Each [X] is an encampment of Gypsies from a different village in Romania. The debt-collectors pay for the tickets. They are being charged 100 per cent interest on their loans. That's how it works.'

There is a question of mine the Fiddler won't answer. 'Do the debt-collectors have enforcers on Park Lane?'

Tonight, I am waiting for the Fiddler in sodium light outside the Fine & Country estate agent. Cream-cake mansions with colonnades flicker in and out of a dozen screens. I glance at my phone; he promised he would be here. The Roma are homing in to sleep; they shuffle and stumble on crutches and sticks, sniffling for coins in Russian, Arabic, and French, with gnarled fingers pinched onto outstretched paper cups. They wheel their belongings in granny trolleys under the bare trees of Hyde Park, and cross their legs under these preposterous, belittling buildings, pleading with their eyes, for fifty pees and pounds. The shape of the Fiddler moves into the light. With a flick of his leather cap he gestures at me to follow him.

'We are not from this village. I hate those Gypsies. They are thieves. Our village is down at the bottom of Park Lane. At the edge of the streets of the Arabs.'

The Fiddler laughs at my map as the traffic swirls past in a static hiss, screened with the immense, winter-dead plane trees in the darkness of Hyde Park. He chortles quietly as we pass an illuminated Americana of boasting concrete, glass and stucco ultra-luxury hotels, overlooking the Serpentine.

The Fiddler stops, and stares at a gleaming Mercedes, where in the white space of a supercar showroom, the lights never go out, be it day or night.

'What struck me first when I came to London, two weeks ago now, were the lights. There are no lights in my village. There are no buildings wrapped in lights. There are no rooms where white lights never go off. The whole two nights on the coach from Romania I was depressed. I curled up and saw my children in my head. The ones I can't feed. But when we arrived in London and the night came and we saw the lights, I felt we had, maybe, a chance to pay back the debts.'

As we walk I think to myself how Park Lane is like a seaside promenade. These washed-up people and hotels staring into the darkness – kilometres of park – lightless like the night sea. The car drone replacing the waves. I am listening to the Fiddler talk about the first time he played in London. He says he stood right in front of a huge florid department store, the brightest building he could find in all these streets, and began to scrape the violin into a Gypsy melody, up and over, as manicured Arab men, in black tailored coats, gold watches glinting from their wrists, and impossibly leggy Russian women, clutching black leather handbags that shone like gems, passed by Harrods, laughing with each other, in another world. Fiddler was amazed: his eyes were full of this outlandish red building baubled in lights.

'These bright, bright buildings . . . They are so beautiful. But that night when I went back to the tunnel where we sleep I began to feel scared. I'd made no money and the others were telling me . . . The night before there was a Polish attack. They said that three drunk builders came into the tunnel and started beating them. They were sleeping when the attack happened. And that night the others had seen those three Poles coming off a building site nearby.'

The Fiddler looks me cold in the eye.

'Are you sure you are ready? Are you sure you want to sleep with our village? The life of the people of the street is dangerous and not easy. Sometimes the Arabs also attack us. They kick us. And there are people down here who are not from our village. They are mad, crazy, drug people and they scream at night.'

The Fiddler takes me into the underpass.

The encampment from Slobozia is under Hyde Park Corner. The chi-chi stucco and glistening Maseratis are out of sight. We enter subterranean tunnels of cream white tiles. They shine with clinical white lights embedded into the ceiling. These are long and low tunnels. And they are covered with thin line-drawings of the glories of Victorian London. Walls of men in top hats and ladies in flowing frocks. Tiles painted with cavalry charges and country houses. And, in places, if you look closely, they are smeared with blood and shit.

'Those English . . . They scare me.'

The Fiddler points. This is where the smack-heads are. They are mostly northern. And they are dying. There is a girl with a blue sleeping bag who sits under the tiles of the golden coach and horses. She barely looks human, and she hides this in a thick waterproof hood, because her neck has pinched and vanished, and her eyes have swelled up, all glassy and black, on a bulbous head which has lost its hair, so she looks more like an Anunnaki, or an alien. Fiddler says she hardly sleeps.

'All of us from Slobozia are frightened of her.'

He says they always choose the tunnel furthest away from her, with the pastel-coloured sketches of the garden wing of Buckingham Palace, when they camp down, ripping up and laying down their scavenged cardboard boxes.

'Here we are. This is where we sleep. The rubbish of London.'

Fiddler is exhausted and confused as the village beds down in the tunnel. He says they have to keep walking until this late, when they are almost faint, otherwise they get told to move on. He says around now is the time the police stop caring. The Fiddler scratches his stubble and his eyes turn to me, sombre. There are sixteen of them here in the tunnel; throwing down what mishmash they have

– worn peach and yellow blankets, patterned like summer flowers, between damp duvets.

'I'm worried I am going to be stuck here begging for ever. Here where there could be a Polish attack. Here in the tunnels where people come and go. And the tramps blabber like crazy people.'

The Fiddler stares at the others. The villagers all look different. There are gaunt faces and sunken eyes. There are some caked in dirt and others still smooth and bright. Their skin is a yellowish ivory or a tanned brown. And they plead with me to find them work in the stables. The Fiddler starts asking questions for them.

'Is it true that the Queen of England has given an order that the Romanians may never work with her thousand horses? Is it true that the Queen hates us and she thinks we will steal her horses? Please tell her . . . we can make ironwork, their horseshoes, we can leatherwork the reins. We can do anything with horses.'

The pubs are emptying.

There is a giddy, expectant thrill in their laughter as the drinkers cross the tunnel. They are playful, almost happy, like children. The Fiddler has one last chance for a pound or two. He holds his violin in his right hand: with the thick muscular fingers of a farmer. Along each knuckle is a thin scratch, in an old black ink tattoo, and in the flesh of his thumb and forefinger are five black dots, like the fifth face of a dice. As his eyes swell, the wail of the violin echoes in the underpass.

Drunk eyes linger on us. A white man, stubbling, slick black and grey fringe, with a red cravat, turns to the thick-lipped, dark Asian woman on his arm, with curly black hair, in a long brown flannel coat, and points at the Fiddler. She turns to him, as they pass, playfully stunned by what they see. But fumbling through her green leather bag, she finds only copper change.

This enrages the Fiddler.

'I can't take it any more. Today I only made fifteen pounds. All day I went trying to play the music for the Arabs and they gave me nothing. I saw them coming in and out of the golden places but they gave nothing. They couldn't even see me.'

The Fiddler is distraught about the police. They have shocked him. They are white. They are brown. They are even black. And they keep coming up to him and confiscating his money. But there is nothing he can do when he loses a day of fiddling for coins. He barely knows how to say, 'Hello, Bye,' in English.

'They keep on stealing our money. There was this big black man . . . I did not believe there could be a black man who was a policeman at first. But I was wrong. He came up to me and said I am not allowed to beg and took my money. Why does the Queen of England allow this to happen to us?'

I write this all in my notebook.

The Roma never sleep alone. I am in an invisible village – with its saints, thieves, confusion and fools. My eyes run along the line of faces in the tunnel: some are dozing, some are sleeping, others are still begging, some I cannot quite make out. There are now more than thirty-five thousand Roma in London. And thousands are living like this.

Fiddler pads himself down. The villager next to him is too exhausted to talk. The beggar's face is sunken, veined and clings to his cheekbones, as his chewed lip hangs open. His beady black eyes try to focus on me under a moth-nibbled hood, before falling asleep, bedded into the side of Fiddler, to keep warm.

'This city has no snow but this damp it gets under your skin.'

The Fiddler yawns. There is not much to eat. The villagers have been bin-rummaging, once again. And they only found a few sandwiches being thrown out round the back of a Pret a Manger. They have foraged some stale Arabic flatbreads and chew them with a squishy processed sausage. There are a few pieces of cheese too, but these are gone quickly.

Fiddler does not eat. He covers his face with his tattooed hands and starts talking to me about having been an alcoholic. Things have not turned out the way they should. Fiddler says he has always lived his life in and out of brawls. Tucked into his pocket is a scuffed and thumbed New Testament. But he doesn't want this. What Fiddler wants is a dictionary. There is no other way to make back the debt.

'If I had a dictionary I could do everything. But I'll do anything.

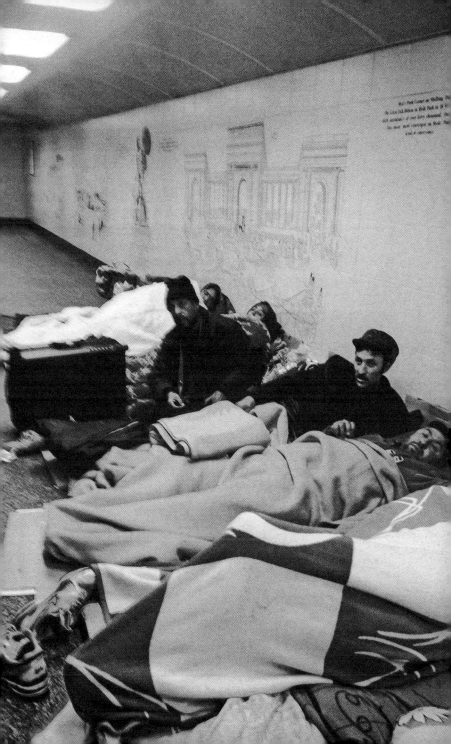

I'll sweep. I'll labour . . . I can work as a smith, I can beat iron, I can work as a locksmith . . . My loan to come here to fiddle is at a hundred per cent interest. And I have to make the money. Because I have three children in Slobozia.'

My eyes drift over the village making their beds.

But the Fiddler is already gone. Asleep with his head craning upwards, mouth open onto white perfect teeth. Looking at him, I suddenly realize no one has my back. This worries me as I bed down, a metre or two along, next to Pale Eyes. His skin is a khaki yellow and he has big cheeks and a flat forehead. His eyes are a thick green pallor, the kind of iris you only ever see amongst the Roma. He wears a woollen peaked cap to the side of his head and a bobbled blue fleece. Pale Eyes is desperate, even his smile is contorted by his anguish.

I can tell he is coming close to theft.

'I have five children . . . and debts, and debts.'

Pale Eyes has chewed off his nails. He speaks a few words of Spanish, but everything has gone wrong since the olive-growing season. The harvest was not so good this year. And they threw him out. And when he got back to Romania the harvest was worthless there, too. He is gabbling.

'I've never been on the street before . . . I've never been in this confusion before. When I was in Spain I always had accommodation included.'

Pale Eyes says he is scared. He is scared of the dying English tramps in the tunnel. He hears them babbling at night and when their sleep-shouting echoes, it chills him. He is frightened they could get up and stab him in one of their shrieking episodes. Or one morning, he will wake up, and see those zipped-up sleeping bags no longer squirming, now rigid and still. Beginning to smell.

'They could grab me . . . I can't speak the language. I can't understand what is going on. I could get a disease. I could get kicked by one of the drunks. I could not make enough money to pay the debt . . . And then my children, they will hurt my children.'

Pale Eyes is not intelligent. His mouth hangs open slightly at all times. And he has trouble getting his ideas across. But that does not stop him trying. As he offers me a piece of mouldy flatbread he tells me that he likes Indiana Jones movies and really loves watching Bollywood singing. Because the Indians sing so nicely.

'I can't read.'

As the hour drags on I meet the other villagers: their figures become voices and stories. The wife of Pale Eyes smiles at me. Her lined face is in its twenties. Her hair is covered in a black kerchief and she buries herself into Pale Eyes when she sleeps. She is younger. Her smile plays with being feminine. And she has five children already, back with the debt-collectors, in Slobozia.

'Babies. That's why I can't read.'

The sixteen villagers bundled up into these rancid blankets begin laughing and joking. That she can make two thousand pounds in a day. Because this is how begging works. They say that a cripple is a real juicer. And that if you can't find a cripple you have to equip your crew with crutches to mimic a cripple. A woman is the second best, unless she has a baby, in which case she makes even more than a cripple. Then an old woman can make a fair bit, whilst the lowest is the least likely to elicit pity – the regular man.

'She makes the most . . . She's the best.'

Pale Eyes grips onto his wife. His eyes flash with his torment: hunger, humiliation, maybe how the condemned feel. I keep glancing back at the sleeping Fiddler for reassurance as the others begin to turn in. But he lies face covered with his tattooed hands. The glare of the tunnel lights never dims. They are burying themselves into each other under the urine-reeking jumble of flowery cream and checked blankets they have, to recycle every bit of body heat.

Pale Eyes is hoarse.

'When I dream in the tunnel . . . I dream of all kinds of things. I think my dreams are random. But I dream of my children. I dream of my house. I dream of their faces. I dream of the debt. I dream, I dream . . . of not being here.'

Pale Eyes doesn't sleep easily. He trembles and turns. He lies there looking at the grille along the roof of the tunnel: its dot-dot-dot pattern laid out in the Euclidian brutality of something that is not meant to be looked at. Another man is shouting.

'I was deceived . . . I was deceived like so many others by the television . . . I was deceived, by the double-decker buses. And all the television of the London state.'

As I lie here, I start to feel the burn of contemptuous passing glares.

This is when I meet the Lawyer.

The villagers have rejected this man. He speaks not from his throat but mumbles from his lips. His eyes are slanted and brown under thick eyebrows. There is desperation and lager on his breath. His nostrils flare, encrusted with blood. And waving a police memo and a prosecution form, spluttering a little, he comes as close to my face as he can.

'I was deceived . . . And I was broken by the London state . . . And I was broken by the policemen of this cruel London state, who when they confiscated my money they forced me, a lawyer, a theologian and a priest, to rummage in bins . . . and to commit such heinous crimes.'

The Lawyer does not look me in the eye. The streets, or the hunger, are fast lining his sinking, jaundiced cheeks, glinting with weeks of encrusted sweat. He looks askew onto the pastel drawings of the top hats and gentlemen and, waving his left hand for flourish, begins to deliver a soliloquy about his crimes, to the chagrin and grimace of the villagers, with the stop-start rhetoric so beloved of Romanian politicians.

'I did not rob the florist . . . What kind of beast? What kind of animal in the whole world would rob a florist?'

The logic of desperation has taken over.

The Lawyer babbles, his voice cracking, as he lists the robbery of a laptop, the theft of a thousand pounds, the assault of a florist, and then denies them all furiously. And, referring to himself, over and over, as a lawyer and a priest, he begins to talk about the Roma, and the state of Romania.

'My country, my country is good country . . .'

Then he bursts into tears, waving his hands, at the sixteen sleepers in the tunnel under the sketches of Buckingham Palace, cursing – 'I'm not with them' – and after blubbing a little, mumbles how frightened he is of the Irish tramp who is zipped up in the tunnel to the left. Then the Lawyer blunders off, shouting, 'I'm not like the other,' to build himself a bed out of cardboard boxes, which he also uses to build a barrier between him and the blue sleeping bag, firmly zipped over the sleeping head of the Irish tramp, who frightens him so much.

'He moans, and shouts all night.'

I write in the notebook, the unease in my skin.

I have to hold on to the villagers. They are all I have.

If they reject me like the Lawyer I will have to sleep with the smack-heads in the other tunnels. I can feel stress tightening in my chest. The cold is starting to chafe. But I need to keep recording. I need to talk to every villager I can. Because I need to answer the question the Fiddler refused to answer: are there enforcers from the debt-collectors in Hyde Park Corner?

The jangle of change runs through the tunnels. Two stragglers arrive at camp with deeply creased little plastic bags weighed down with their coins. Both are still phony limping on crutches as they enter the tunnel, but as they reach the bedding, they chuck down these props ahead of them. They are no longer needed.

These two villagers are in their early twenties.

The first to reach the blankets is Ciprian, who smiles like a toddler under a pea-green hoodie. His two front teeth were kicked out by a horse. His moustache shines, black and healthy, because he is only twenty-one. But he seems stupid. He has the slurry voice of a child. Unlike the others, he does nothing to hide the begging money, and without thinking, he rummages through the torn duvets until he pulls out a velvet box the size of a biscuit tin.

Ciprian opens it, tips in his coins, and looks radiantly into around £90 in round little pounds and silvery fifty pees. He smiles at me toothlessly happy and gestures at his friend to tip all the money he has into the velvet box.

This is how I meet Prince. He enters the tunnel second, with a slow, unhurried walk, wearing a cheap branded fleece from some garage, and a baseball cap with muffy earflaps. Prince is twenty-four, with a swarthy, rounded head, a healthy black beard quickly

covering his still boyish skin. His voice is both childish and power-less. His posture flaccid and resigned. And when he looks at me it is with the glassy eyes of an early stage heroin user. Prince never eats. And his mood never seems to change.

'Why do the English hate Romanians?'

After Prince tips his begging money into Ciprian's velvet box, as tinkling the coins pour, we talk as he beds down next to sleeping Pale Eyes. He looks vacantly at those passing us through the tunnel. But there is nobody this night who does not give the beggars emotional looks. There is not one hour when the click-click of heels ever stops. This is what Prince sees.

'Either pity . . . or hate.'

I watch too, from the bedding. Those who notice, the invisible village, lock their eyes ahead on the end of the tunnel, refusing to see. There are those whose glance is full of shock and anger. There are those whose eyes swell with horror and move on. And there are those who comment and shout.

'But this is Hyde Park Corner, bruv!'

Fiddler shivers, asleep. This is Friday night and the drinkers are out. The tunnel echoes with voices becoming louder, and laughs turn to cackles, as the night creeps to closing hours. And then those that become angry as I talk with Prince in the tunnel.

'But this is Hyde Park Corner, bruv!'

Four Asian boys in blue hoods and pressed jeans march through the tunnel with looks of disgust. They pause, on the edge of earshot, their voices craving to vent their anger at the villagers sleeping rough.

'This is bare rough, man.'

Footsteps give way to footsteps. There are four more boys, around sixteen: their faces painted with mouse whiskers who had been shouting so loudly – 'And so it begins, and so it begins' – who, shivering from the cold, go silent as they walk into the tunnel, with looks that rapidly turn from fear, to pity, to shame, as one, with a tiny nod, grimaces slightly.

'Salaam aleikum.'

The eyes of the man who shouts this are red with drink. He is an old man, Lebanese most probably, and he taps his walking stick ahead of him, but can barely walk in a straight line, brushing slightly on the pastel Buckingham Palace on the tunnel walls. Prince shouts back.

'Aleikum salaam.'

But the drunk in the red-checked shirt gives him nothing. Prince does not react. Instead he talks a little as the others began to sniffle and snore. Prince mutters there is nothing more useful to the beggar than languages. You have to know phrases in Arabic, or in Turkish, and French, if you want to be a Knightsbridge beggar.

'If they are Muslim . . . talk like a Muslim.'

I write what I see: there are drunk women, confident, and happy, on the arms of men, who shout in the tunnel the way drunk people do, what they really think about these poor people, as their heels click and clack, and they sway slightly.

One glares at me, clutching her man, then hollers.

'You may be a beggar . . . But you've still got a Moleskine!'

Prince lets his eyes follow her wobbling ass.

'They look good. But all English girls are alcoholics. Just look at them . . . They drink like pigs. They drink until they can hardly walk. They disgust me . . . They are loose and wild.'

The villagers are almost all asleep.

This is when Bright Eyes appears. He is lean and wiry and lets off a pulsing energy, of paranoia, animosity and implied violence. He is in a Barbour jacket covered with envelope pockets, with a grey hoodie underneath. He is shaky, like a man on cheap speed, and his lips are upturned, the way the mouths of those who only speak with violence can sometimes seem to freeze.

Bright Eyes is the debt-collector's enforcer in Hyde Park Corner.

He saunters along the tunnel, with one of the crutches his beggars pretend to use, hitting and poking his sleepers with it, until he finds who has the velvet money box. His nasty, unsettling energy of someone who is used to being feared shakes the sleepers upright. Fiddler jolts with a fright. Poking them some more, he begins to count the money, and when he is done he clicks his tongue, and waves around his crutch like a light-sabre toy, chuckling.

'Who are you?'

Bright Eyes has a sneer, and the whitest skin of all of them. And his ears stick out, either side of his piercing thick grey-green Roma eyes, which bore into me with nervous, shivering, energy. He is in his late twenties. He is also simple and jumpy and moves his hands like he holds a blade.

'Why are you here?'

Those eyes dig into me and try to make me leave. They dig into me with an implied stabbing. There are two dirty and chubby faces behind him in grey sports coats and joggers. The rounder, ruddier-faced one mopes in a Harvard hoodie, smeared with mud. Both beefcakes hold beer cans. They are his enforcers, and Bright Eyes flits his head between them as backup. I look around: the beggars all tremble, squint and cower. I make eyes at Fiddler. But he turns away. There are no best friends on the street.

'Are you a policeman?'

And then, Bright Eyes thinks maybe something else.

'Speak Gypsy!'

He sneers expectantly. There are only Roma beggars and policemen in his world. I can only be one or the other. Bright Eyes throws his useless crutch down with a clatter and keeps boring his pupils into me. His light blondish stubble has been recently shaved. He does not hunch his back like a street-sleeper.

'I'm frightened of foreigners,' he lisps.

'Why did you come abroad then?' I puff.

'When I'm with my big brother I'm frightened of nobody,' he snarls back, lifting up his jacket to shown an enormous scar lacing his stomach, and paces off, his twitching hands dug into the front pockets of the Barbour.

Bright Eyes is gone. Both his sidemen too. And the tunnels lose his menace. Polish builders in Timberlands stomp through the passageways glaring at the sleepers. African men, mumbling with pity, are the only ones who give the beggars some coins, coming to a total that night of 82p.

Fiddler is trying to sleep.

Prince is thinking.

'The English, they are the meanest . . . They never give anything.

They give the littlest. The Arabs and the Moroccans, they shout at us and they swear at us. But the black men, they are the most generous. They give the most . . . The Chinese, they sometimes give something.'

The Fiddler stirs and flicks his tattooed hand.

'That's rubbish. The Chinese give up nothing.'

Prince is in debt. And he tries, a bit, to pretend the money is being collected in the velvet box to make it easier to wire to Romania, and Bright Eyes the enforcer poking them with crutches is only a friendly joker. But it is a lacklustre attempt at a lie, and he gives up, and lets his mind wander.

'Why do the English hate the Romanians so much? Is it because the Romanians were allied to Hitler in the Second World War? Will they never forgive us for being an Axis power? Why have they not moved on?'

Prince turns to the Old Man scrunched up next to him. He wears a sheepskin kaftan and has a gnarled and gullied face of sharp points and missing teeth. His flaking jaw hangs leathery and covered in black and white stubble. His thick lips hang in an exhausted, degenerating way.

'Prince is right. I think the English hate the Romanians because we fought with Hitler in the war . . . And that's why they won't give us a pound. And they come up to us. And shout, "Fuck you . . . Gypsy."'

The Old Man worked on the collective farms and keeps on mumbling that if the revolution against Romanian communism hadn't happened he wouldn't be here begging in the tunnel for his eight children. His tiny body is thin and spindly and his white hair has gone from the crown of his head. He is fifty-four.

'This is my last chance. Begging is my last chance.'

The Old Man likes to joke, and to laugh a little at any moment he can, and he tells me that his favourite movies are those of Jackie Chan. But he says London is the last roll of the dice for him, and all the rest of them in the tunnel. And he knows that not having a winter coat is sucking him dry. He is becoming weaker, he feels, with every night on concrete.

'I want work . . . I want work. I want to feel like a man again. I'll be a painter, a decorator, a sweeper, an animal feeder, anything. I can't keep sleeping here like a rat. I want an address, I dream of an address, and then I want to have a pension . . .'

The Old Man waves his hands in the air and curses.

'Then what about Bright Eyes?'

There is a chuckle and a puff of mocking dismissal from the beggar beside him. He is the twentysomething, with a lustrous moustache and a black bonnet, who shares the same checked yellow-on-white duvet, with Prince and the Old Man.

'The Old Man's rubbish. We're not looking for work. We're all here to beg.'

After he throws away the lie, this beggar keeps looking at his own reflection in a little metal cigarette case, now his fags are gone, opening and closing it, licking his moist, healthy moustache as he adjusts the collar of his grizzled black fleece.

They sometimes call him Cigarette Box boy. He keeps talking.

'We're all here to beg to work off our debts. We give the enforcers all the money. They told us to come here. But we are never going to make back the loans they gave us to come here. We're trapped. And they have our children in Slobozia.'

That's when it hits me, who I am sleeping with.

The beggars are virtual slaves – unseen on the streets of Knightsbridge.

'We bin-rummage to save what we have and hand it over to them.'

I look at them and feel a rush of nerves fizzing up my spine. The grille is pulled over the Tube at the end of the tunnel and those walking through the glare and the pencil drawings of redcoats and coach and horses become hurried, and drunker still, as the women turn paranoid.

Four or five times I hear the click-click of heels come to the end of the tunnel, and then the shape of a woman hovers and turns back. There are many tweedy men, whose faces turn to guilty smiles, or turn-away eyes, and strange looks, impossible to read, like the swarthy man with the shoulder bag who winks and grins at us, lingers, then walks on.

Prince looks straight at me.

'I'm frightened of the Gypsies up at the top of the streets of the Arabs . . . the ones at the end by the brightly lit hotels. They are all from Suceava. And they have hand tattoos . . . I was begging there at the start of Oxford Street . . . and I saw the demon tattoo. And I saw those Gypsies have the Satan tattoo.'

I ask him what the Fiddler's tattoos mean.

I can see them as he sleeps with his head wrapped in his arms.

'The five dots mean you were in prison . . . The four dots are the walls and the dot in the middle is you. And the dots on the knuckles means you were in federal prison. These are the tattoos that came from Russia, and we live close to that country.'

Prince frowns and looks at me.

'You look like a Gypsy with that hat on. But your face looks like a Russian, it is not like an English. This is why the English can't see you any more.'

The beggars are all sleeping.

Only Prince watches the women in stilettos teetering as fast as they can through the tunnels tiled with the sketches of gentlemen on penny-farthings and the victories of the Duke of Wellington. Only he sees the two Asian boys in T-shirts, sweating, their eyes like saucers, bellowing about drum and bass.

There is never silence in the underpass. And sleep here is shallow for the slaves. The engines of the sports cars roar and pop, the lorries rattle, and never far away sounds the clack-clack-clack of passing feet.

'I'll fuck your cunt . . .'

Only when I try and sleep do I hear the tramp that terrifies the beggars. They speculate he was once a rich man who has lost everything. Because of what they hear him shout at night. In the next tunnel, white hair and long beard over his face, all blotchy whites and beaten reds, he lies, his arm tattoos exposed, half undone from his blue sleeping bag, gabbling and groaning his *Finnegans Wake*, mouthing the sounds of bullets as he sleeps, tossing and turning in the tunnel, babbling in and out of sense.

'And you want to have sex with me . . . And I'll fuck you . . . and give you a right . . . I'm not, I'm not going anywhere . . . This was supposed to happen . . . You slut . . . You fucking slut . . . I'll get you back.'

The glare never dims.

Prince talks to me about God. He says God is like an angel or a spirit, he isn't quite sure. And when he walks down the long street full of glinting Arabs with white smiles and furred Russian blondes, fakely limping on his stolen crutch, Prince feels the presence of this angel.

'It feels like a shadow.'

This is when I sleep.

That morning we wake in the stench. It is thick, sweet, like sweat, and piss – which is what it is. The roar of the whirling traffic above drowns out everything. The beggars bundle up their duvets and try to shove them into granny trolleys and backpacks before the police arrive to kick them on. The women have gone to wash in the Serpentine.

'I have debts, I have debt . . . I have five children.'

Pale Eyes woke distraught, gesticulating, a slave one step closer to theft. Prince is numb. But, as he walks out of the tunnel, I hear him praying.

PECKHAM HIGH STREET

I need to see every story from the other side.

This is why I am on the 136 bus into black London. I need to record successes. I need to record failures. I need to record the beggars. And I need to record the police.

The bus bleeps and stops.

They call this Frontline Peckham, where the red-brick police station, with its slate roof, and long-defunct chimneys and white-rimmed sash windows, glowers into the cramped little concrete balconies of the council estate, over a white-van-congested road. A black addict, in a grey shell suit, smeared with street dirt, rummages around in the bins, ripping through the cardboard boxes.

He turns and screwfaces me, with my notebook outside the station. A few steps back, two tense Afghans in fleece jackets, hands in pockets, hover behind their fruit tables outside the newsagent, readying to scuffle with him if he tries his luck.

This is 8 am. The rain becomes heavier, until you can feel it patter on your coat. For a second or two, it catches the weak sun; and the fall shines in white light. One after another, double-decker buses unload angry-looking school children in sky-blue uniforms, almost all of them black, in front of the locked betting shops, the opening money transfers, the shuttered African fabric shops, the Payless cash-and-carries and the broken cashpoint, its screen flashing static lines. I take four street photos, outside the off licence, and linger, under wet blinds running with water, lettered all along in a fading print plastic, JESUS IS LORD PHIL . . . 2:11.

Before going in I count the faces coming out of the police station. The tooth-grinding grimace on the black youth, with a fake-fur-rimmed parka hood, rubbing his right fist. The squint coming from the blubbery face of the Pole in a red fleece and ski jacket, biting his crusty lip. The veined eyes on the exhausted African mama, with messed-up braids, scanning, unsure where to go, shaking in a green padded body warmer. And the light-stunned, knuckle-rubbed stare of the Roma in an unzipped leather jacket, morose, gaunt and blinking, into this grey morning along Peckham High Street.

'They all behave differently when you handcuff them.'

His voice is hoarse and he shakes my hand in front of the faded and ignored photograph of Princess Anne in the hallway. The Policeman is coming off the night shift, and fidgety from coffee and exhaustion, he guides me through fire doors, into the interview room. The officer pulls up a chair, flips over a paper witness state-ment on the plastic table, and with a ching-ching, begins playing with his handcuffs.

'The Romanians, they are always very crafty. They come in here and they go to you, "I don't speak English . . ." But the moment they go out again they are chatting freely. Now the Africans, when the boys come in who have stolen some mobile phones, the mothers come and find them. And they are shouting, and screaming and slapping them in custody, because they are religious, and the sons have brought shame on the whole community. The Pakistanis, when they are terrorists, you would never know they are terrorists, they are just like you and me . . . and they keep trying to draw you on politics, trying to make you talk. "Don't you hate this government for this, or don't you hate this government for that . . ."'

The Policeman pinches red puffy eyes. But he seems too caffein-ated to stop jittering. One minute he slouches forward. The next minute he slouches back. He is wearing a worn golden wedding band and a strong slightly sweet perfume. He throws his palms up and out as he explains how to handcuff someone. You have to pre-tend to shake their hand. He smiles and laughs at odd moments. But there is no way you can talk comfortably in a police station. The closed space of this interview room is dotted with cameras and recording signs. But it is only when he starts running his hands backwards and forwards over the interview table that I begin to make out the smudges of handprints on the creamy walls.

'But the Polish, when they come in, they go, "Give me food, give me tea, can I have some more, now let me sleep . . ." because they are sleeping on the street, and when they come in here they no longer care, and they know that we have to feed them.'

This man is not like the other policemen. He speaks like a doctor with a sad, mournful voice. He is uncomfortable answering questions, and as he talks, he keeps touching a chewed biro on the interview table, fingering it, bit by bit snapping off little pieces off its plastic case, before mindlessly arranging them in a line in front of him.

'Last night we got a call, to one of the estates near the river, dem ones that look over the blocks, into the lights of the Canary Wharf . . . just there over the river. Because there was a Pole sleeping in the bin chutes. He was begging me, "Arrest me, arrest me," trying to provoke me, going, "Please arrest me for being drunk and disorderly." But I looked at him and went, "Mate, I'm not arresting you to give you a place to sleep."'

He makes no eye contact. But squints into the switched-off television screen. The sticker explains this is used for language translation. And that with a press here and a click the screen will read out the witness statement. You could not be a policeman here without it. There are more people in London with little to no English than live in Newcastle.

'The English are vanishing. London is no longer an English city at all . . . London is a patchwork of ghettos. Right here is Peckham, you have the Africans, over the river in Whitechapel we have the Bengalis, further east from there we have the Pakistanis, and west from here in Brixton we have the Jamaicans. I could go on, and on, and on.'

He moves an empty cup of tea, for no reason, and picks up the overturned witness statement, and makes sure this paper runs parallel to the lines on the table.

'There is a crime wave right now . . . Because we have opened up to the EU. The Romanians they are begging, and pickpocketing,

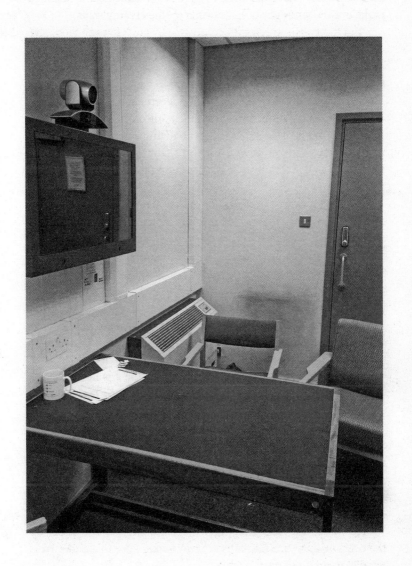

and moving around the streets with the little trolleys stealing the clothes left outside charity shops. They are squatting and telling us they are hungry . . . There is a flood coming in.'

The Policeman scans me, and says what he thinks.

'The English are dying. The English are declining and they are declining fast . . . You can see it on the streets. In the markets, there used to be only English people there screaming, in the cockney accent. But they've gone now . . . and all the English pubs, they are boarding up, and the English churches, they are being rented out to the Africans. The Anglican Church is disappearing . . .'

The Policeman is black. He is Nigerian. Immigrant in London since 1989. But he does not tell me this in the police station. The plasticated notice on the wall says we are being recorded. And there are things in London you can and cannot say about race when you are being overheard. As I gather up my papers in the interview room, to leave, he looks at me, and says: 'I don't come to work to punish people.'

I meet the Policeman again.

I am on the double-decker bus heading south, from the concrete and towers at Elephant and Castle, empty on the top deck except for a crumpled fried-chicken box, filled with little brown bones. The road is drab: scuffed-up launderettes, dimly lit betting shops, dead bingo halls, and twirling doner kebabs. Drizzle wets the tarmac. I count two daytime white drinkers, scuttling into a scruffy locals-only pub.

Nobody is about until the road meets a small park, bushes blossoming with plastic litter: white and blue bags, hanging crinkled on railings, caught in the spring trees. I know this green. Like so many others, in South London, it is a gathering place for the tramps and the hoodies, who sit around smoking skunk on the damp benches, overlooked by African churches in defunct seventies office buildings. These high-street windows are covered in thick red curtains, to cover the prayer hall in the dingy open plan, where finger-wagging Nigerian preachers warn of the demons amongst us.

The electronic voice chimes: 'Camberwell Green.'

There is a whole African city in London. With more than 550,000 people this would be a city the size of Sheffield. And it has grown almost 45 per cent since 2001.

African London is rich and poor: a city where I have seen Mayfair champagne fights and single mums rummaging through food banks. A city to fill a thousand notebooks. But for the most part the hundreds of stories I hear are from a poor city: of scrubbers and security guards. They tell me African London began here, in the estates between Peckham and Camberwell Green, right back in the 1990s, when this was the first little patch of London Nigerians and Sierra Leoneans felt was really their own.

I jump off the bus and rush. The Policeman is waiting.

The whole McDonald's thumps with low-level beats and happy music. I am meeting the Policeman upstairs. I look over the tables: African men slump back, worried, maybe waiting, whilst a wet Afghan, in a thick coat, hovers around the toilet. The main table is taken. Plugged into music a black guy is emitting a vibe not to get too close. He slouches wearing thick gold-rimmed shades and mouthing the words to his song.

The whole place smells of frying fats and cleaning fluids. But this is neutral space: the kind of place people can talk, where migrants can take calls, receive friends, and generally be unmolested after a 99p espresso. And this is the place where a wasteman comes, sits back and enjoys his buzz for a little while. Nobody bothers anyone upstairs at the Camberwell McDonald's.

The Policeman is waiting. His police jacket is under a black mac covered in tiny watery beads from the rain. Sitting there, he looks more like a security guard with twitching bug-like eyes. He has carefully trimmed himself a circle beard, but his mouth droops with exhaustion. All morning, he has been on patrol – stopping and searching, every block, every street, every park, every cul-de-sac, all the way from here to the Old Kent Road. He is the man in charge. But he still triggers a grin.

He can't lose that accent.

'Good ta meet ya, man . . .'

Policemen are not normally black. Minorities make up 55 per cent of London. But they are only 10 per cent of its police. Policemen are rarely immigrants. Not normally men who began right at the bottom, without the right papers.

'I wasn't always in the force.'

The Policeman sips some tap water. And tells me he used to be one of those melancholy African men muttering round the other tables, swapping work tips for cigarettes in the back corner of McDonald's, worrying as the rain patters away.

'When I landed . . . this city was another place.'

He looks searching into me: why do I want this story, why am I interested in him and not some politicians. And then, warily, calmed that in the McDonald's everything is recorded on multiple CCTV, in case this is some sting, he begins to tell me, slowly and stoically, everything that has happened. Comfortable, because these clunky cameras do not record well enough to make out sound.

'My London began in 1989 . . .'

The plane was landing. He wriggled in his seat. He was about to discover a vast, almost imaginary city where freedom and suffocation are a daily occurrence, an endless ritual, a constant dance. His hands were shaking. This was the beginning.

'I felt . . . pumped. I was ready to go. Like my life was about to begin. This was London, my London . . . And I thought the streets would be paved with gold. I thought the money would be growing on trees. And that I would be there . . . picking it easy.'

Through passport control his thoughts raced manically. He thought his dream business would soon be milking it. Money would soon be flowing back home. He thought he might become a millionaire, or even more: the next big one.

Those first few days were vertiginous and free. He wandered breathless along supermarket aisles. He marvelled at uncountable brands and choices. His eyes swelled with the giddying sophistication of the Bakerloo Line and Green Park station. His heart fluttered at the electro-shimmering adverts in Piccadilly Circus. He knew, instantly, everything was possible, everything was permitted, in this bombastic city of stucco and glass. Be it money – or love.

'Six months later I was crying myself to sleep . . . I was homeless.'

London was glinting, giving nothing up.

He clasped his hands together in the African church on Camberwell Green. There was nothing for it. He mumbled to angels as the gospel grew louder. He was ashamed. The women were singing louder and louder. But this was not how he was supposed to live. He hated pulling little tricks to find a bed to sleep in: little pieces of cunning, like calling up his friends, ones he barely even knew, and inviting himself round, eking out the evening until the Tubes were shut off, before suggesting, with his eyes on the floor, it was too late to schlep home.

The glass walls of the McDonald's whisper with tiny impacts. The Policeman flicks his eyes onto these windows lashed with thousands of rushing rain beads. His face hardly budges except for his mouth. There is no emotion there. It is all in his voice, with its pauses and quivers, as he hesitates, now this all seems so far away.

'I was ashamed and embarrassed and upset . . . I was lost, I was broken, I was ready to do anything . . . to stay in this city, to stay in this world. So, that meant becoming not the businessman I had wanted to be. It meant becoming a kitchen boy.'

The first work he found was in Liverpool Street serving bankers. He felt tiny in this canyon of jagged glass. The financiers ate decorative food off porcelain plates, whilst in the backrooms he pulled encrusted grease off a cauldron with a paint scraper. The dishwashers could smell his misery. The bankers would snap their fingers. The waiters uncorked hundreds of wine bottles. They raked it in. But, back in the kitchen, the Irish manager barked and snarled at the Africans that one broken porcelain plate was one week's wages.

'It was almost like accepting the hierarchy. I was an African person. And these were the white people. Like naturally that's how it should be. There were a lot of Irish and Australian chefs . . . But the kitchen boys were all Nigerians and Ghanaians. That was when I realized, that's the pecking order . . .'

Here was the golden city he dreamt of in African shanties. He was finally here. But he was discovering that migrants like him

clean, wait and guard the golden city. Never really to enter. Here he was swilling down the tenderloin-steak plates of hedge-funders and commodity-hustlers. As close as he could get: but hardly there.

'I hated myself.'

The kitchen boys told him there was work in a hotel in rich man's Chelsea. Laundry work. Down in the basement. But good money. Those ten years were nothing but steam. Nothing but the whirring machine and the smell of soap. Hours where his hands would sort through piles of stained sheets. They kept on coming, but there was one joy towards the end: when Mariah Carey was in residence he found her knickers. Pinning them up on the notice-board, he became a hotel hero.

'Since we did that every other person started looking for dem stars' underpants. Everyone was wow . . . and wanted to touch them.'

He lets out a sad laugh, and looks around him, the way police-men do, at the old African man in glasses and a tweed suit peering at some scribbles on a piece of paper, squinting so hard, and at the two Polish tracksuits, gobbling and ignoring each other, the way only exhausted boys in the building team can do, and his eyes linger for a moment on the sallow black crack addict mumbling to an empty packet of chips on the table in the corner. And then, he blinks, and we go back into his story.

'Things were the same in that hotel.'

He kept seeing the hierarchy. The room service and the wait-resses, the people who touched the food, they were mostly white. Not from England, but the whites who were coming in. Australians, by and large. The receptionists, those who greeted the guests, and keyed things in for them, were Irish, with singsong voices, who swore at him there was no work for people like them back home. The cleaners, humming, always humming, between the floors and the corridors, with their trolleys and sprays, they were Africans, or a few that had very strange faces, which he thought must be South American.

They were always moaning in the steam of the laundry room. They were Nigerians and Ghanaians, the lot of them. And, bundling and folding, they would curse the tricksters who brought them here, or the ones who counterfeited their visas, or passports, and left them in this lurch, in the hidden city of illegal workers.

'Nobody asked me if I wanted to do this. They just put me there . . . And I was there. Lifting out more and more linen. And they even made me a laundry boss. So, one day they tell me this man is crying . . . And I go to find him. And he was weeping, so loudly in the laundry room – a grown man.

'And he was telling he had met this woman in Lagos and she had brought him to Peckham. But he'd come on a fake passport she had. But now she had thrown him out . . . And he was crying, "Now I cannot even work, what am I going to do. I'm homeless and she kept the passport." In the end I had to let him sleep on my couch for a whole month . . .'

Again, a surprise. Hotel management lifted him out of the laundry room: he became a valet. And for five years he stood at the whirling entrance door. Rich men – Americans, Russians, Arabs – would toss their cars keys at him and he would park those splendid cars. Fantastically dressed in servants' attire he would attend to them. He would bend down to tie their shoelaces and take their orders. The hotel was adamant: silence must he held towards any insult.

'The celebrities would ignore me. Be on their phone. They were minted . . . y'know. And I was there tying up the shoelaces. No. I did not feel angry. I felt I was privileged. Like I was rising up. That one day when I made it . . . When I'm back in Africa, when I'm having my pleasure . . . There would be boys bending down doing this for me.'

Now he was a valet-boy he was on call from reception at all times. There were mornings where he found the mirrors smashed and the rooms trashed. The mini-bar door swinging wide open. There were times when those in residence were violent: there were times when they were also mad. Men like the unhinged aristocrat who would hand him a fifty-pound note every time he came to his room. Real madmen, the kind you have to speak slowly to, like a baby.

'He would come out in his underpants back to front into the corridor. Or sometimes with his underpants over his trousers. But being mad, he was not crazy violent . . . but more autistic and mental-health issues. He would chuck underpants and Visa card at me and order me . . . go to the Harrods to buy new underpants. Every day . . . It was really bad. You feel you work hard and you will never get to that level. He was not the one who made the money. It was his family that made the money . . . And I felt, well, that's the way money is.'

Sirens went off, outside round Camberwell Green, in the rain, with that short turnaround howl, which the urban kids say isn't about fighting crime at all, but keeping the criminals frightened, and for a moment the story snaps. There is a flinch to his muscles as he sits, a tension ripples in the shoulders, and his eyes suddenly flick to the windows, the way this sound can only dog-whistle to the feds and thieves, in this town, and then we are back in the hotel.

'My previous job it was completely different . . . Y'know the posh drunks they would come in and then vomit there. And you are almost pre-programmed to just clean it up with a smile. And the celebrities they would come in and break the nice vases, and smash the nice flowers and throw the nice cushions . . . and you would only smile and pick it up for them. Now I would just arrest them.'

He was scrubbing the vomit off the marble floor when the fantasy began, or maybe it was when he found the mirrors smashed, all over again, in the master suite. This was when the valet-boy began to fantasize about handcuffing people. Nigerians had passed the word on: the police wanted black men. And now there was no getting the image of him in a constable's helmet out of his head.

The valet-boy thought about it picking up sheets. He thought about it running after room service. He thought about the little baton and the shining fluorescent vest. He kept thinking policemen don't go, 'Good morning, sir,' to swearing alcoholics with red-wine stains dappled over their shirts. Policemen don't let mumbling women with spirits on their breath and mascara smears round their eyes swear at them about the room service.

The valet-boy began applying, over and over again.

'Y'see, when I got here . . . I accepted it . . . the pecking order.

'Like that's the way. Then I stopped. London can crush you . . . Or London can transform you. You can rise up here. The white people they are not stopping you. But it's difficult, very difficult, because . . . of the way London is. You need so much ammunition – knowledge, money, everything – to jump to the next level. Most they don't. They can't . . . and they sink into London.

'For me, I got blessed. I saw a door opening and I jumped through it.'

There was no more steam. There were streets to his life now, no more long, gloomy, interminably carpeted corridors. He had been in London little more than ten years. But the city had a surprise for him. He was patrolling up and down the Old Kent Road now, checking what was happening, between the halal butchers, the money transfers, the pavement fruit stalls and the boarded-up pubs. He took it all in.

'I loved putting on the uniform . . . that beautiful uniform, for the first time.'

Slowly it began to creep up on him, in the faces, and along the shop fronts, how much London had changed since 1989. He kept noticing, the English, they were becoming more emotional. You could see it when they were driving, more and more of them would unfurl their window, become all red-faced and start shouting and spittling. The streets were changing too. The Irish were disappearing, and so too were the little English shops. Those grubby units were more Kashmiri, Arabic and Turkish now, sometimes owned by people he could hardly even place. Cockney old London had shattered into a thousand dazzling, inscrutable shards.

'This is not where I landed . . . The whole make-up, the whole thing, the whole of London changed. Back then, the hierarchy, it used to be the higher you go the whiter you become. But the make-up is changing. The make-up is different now. The whites used to be Irish and English. Now there are many, many whites who are not English . . . The split now is more: immigrants and natives. And there are millions and millions of them . . . flooding in.'

The Policeman keeps on seeing the hierarchy.

He has been on patrol for more than fifteen years now. But this is what you see as a policeman. Like the time he was called out to the Burger King on Rye Lane on rapid response. The car was swerving up when the skinny man first saw him. He saw the police and just ran. He bolted past the fried-chicken shops. He bolted past pound shops.

'He was running . . . like a man on a mission.'

This was suspect behaviour. The police made chase. But he wouldn't stop. He started jumping over fences. He was leaping through gardens. He was smashing through hedges. He was going like Mo Farah. The police set the dog squad after him. Then a helicopter with its infrared. He was whimpering, and covered in bruises, when the Policeman finally cuffed him.

'Me . . . I could understand where he is coming from. Man . . . I felt so bad. He was not gonna get away. He was not gonna get away from the dog unit. We thought it was drugs or maybe an illegal weapon. But he was an illegal immigrant. Which is why he saw police . . . and ran. I empathize with him. I'm human. I know where he is coming from. Y'know, I only hope he empathize with me.

'He was a Nigerian.'

He noticed little things on his patrol. The crimes that were more daring, with a bit of punching or running, they were mostly done by the black boys. They were plucky, the ones who were born here, and they wanted their mobile phones. The Policeman often wondered what they did with so many mobiles, hundreds and hundreds of them, until one of the senior officers explained the way it worked to him: they were selling them on to those surly Afghans with the shifty electronics shops.

'They are not Afghan Taliban . . . that's a myth. They are very high-tech. They will always be there behind the counter with a laptop or a tablet. They are fixing them and unlocking them for the robber boys. That's the business . . . and dem Afghans . . . they are very much involved, a lot of them are very criminally minded.'

The Policeman clears his throat.

'I'm gonna be straight with you. Black people tend to get involved in street crime, it's more confrontational. Those boys,

IF YOU ▓▓▓▓▓▓▓▓ ▓▓
UKBA OF▓CERS IN THE S▓▓ ▓.
(UK Border ▓gency / Immigration ▓ice

DON'T PANI▓ **KNOW YOUR R**

- You are <u>FREE</u> ▓ <u>▓VE</u> at any time
- You <u>DO NOT</u> ha▓ ▓nswer any questions
- You <u>DC NOT</u> hav▓ ▓ive your name and add ▓
- Y▓ ▓ ▓▓ ▓OT ha▓ ▓ow them a▓ ▓cume
- ▓ ▓T h▓ ▓t th▓ ▓ear ▓ou

they are dem lost boys . . . their parents are too poor in time for them . . . working double . . . so when they are teenagers, and they come home, there is no mummy or daddy. So they hug the block.'

He eyes me for a second.

'I'll be honest, I say this without prejudice. The white community tends to get more involved in burglary. These ones, they are mens. Y'see, crimes that require a little more planning, like the burglary, those crimes . . . are white. The white community, they are not so daring, but they are more criminal-minded, they do . . . the proper thinking . . . They are coming into the homes with the screwdrivers and the tools and everything. That's why with the drugs, cannabis – black; crack and cocaine – white. The higher the drug the whiter the criminal.'

His eyes flick behind him.

'But being frank, when I became a policeman first in the nineties . . . You used to have kids, black people, the West Indies, who were high in crime and at the bottom of things. But that is changing . . . it's the way London is moving . . . but now most of our burglaries, thefts, robbery is coming from the new entrants . . .'

It was more complicated than black and white now.

'There is a problem, y'know . . . with East Europeans. They are making me more and more work . . . it's the street drinking, it's an epidemic. They are mostly old guys . . . they are drinking a lot, tramping a lot. And now they are getting more and more into the burglary. This, right now . . . is the flavour.'

His voice has changed: he is finally speaking freely.

'Y'see this happens when it comes in floods . . . in the fifties and sixties the flood was from the West Indies, then Asians it was in the seventies. And then in the eighties, it was coming from Africa. Now we are having the time of the Europeans, they are the ones who are coming in . . .'

A hoarse crack addict interrupts us.

'Bruv . . . allow us some change.'

The thirtysomething almost looks normal. He is young, black and unshaven. But his voice already has that demented, repetitive junkie's ring.

'Bruv . . . allow us some change.'

Policeman and addict ignore each other in the McDonald's truce.

'The worst case I got called to . . . I got a call to Peckham. There was a naked woman in the rain. And like wow, everybody wanted to attend to that call. They was all going, "Is she fit?" Because it was a naked woman running around in the rain in Peckham . . . we all wanted to go in there. So we drove. Almost every unit in Peckham. Almost every unit racing. And we got there . . . and she was naked.

'And yes, she was fit.

'One of the girls took her raincoat off to wrap her, and preserve her dignity, and took her to the house. But as soon as we opened the door . . . smoke . . . everywhere. She was shouting . . . "What's happening? What's happening?" And she started to cry.

'"Where's my baby? Where's my baby?"

'What she had done is she had put the baby in the oven. And put it on. She was having a schizophrenic episode. We crashed . . . it was from high of the highs to the lowest depths . . . A three-weeks-old baby. It was charred. It was burnt.

'She was suffering from schizophrenia . . . she was West Indian.'

He flinches, touches his plastic cup, and carries on.

'I'm gonna level with you . . . Y'see in London you've always had the Africans at the bottom of the pile along with the West Indians. I don't mean West Indians like who flew in yesterday from Jamaica but I mean the second generation of West Indians. They are the bottom too . . . Then you get some Afghans. Then the Eastern Europeans coming up. The East Europeans are above us Africans . . . because they are more acceptable. Because of the likeness of the race. There is a commonality in Europe of the ethnicity . . . you know? That's the way it is.

'Then you get the Asians . . . Then you get the Irish. Then you get the white . . . And at the very top you get the rich . . .

'Where there is no race.'

NEASDEN LANE

I circle the city.

Days, hours, on random routes that lead nowhere.

Searching.

Rain dapples on the car windscreen into Neasden. Wipers squeak and squeal. The road north from White City unwinds in the colours of a Lowry painting. The curving tarmac is suddenly over-cut with vaulting, spectacularly swooshing motorways, as it slices through bleary-eyed depots and railway junctions. Grasping trees thickly border the edges of deserted warehouse service roads; grim perimeters ringed by rusting wire fences and littered shrubs.

Neasden is where row after row of Victorian London finally ends. The mellow Georgian mansions and little cottage-pie lanes in Shepherd's Bush have suddenly gone. Harlesden's endless ladder of cramped, pompous Edwardian terraces, dotted with defunct gin palaces, has given way to bogus Tudor drives. And this is where gentrification ends, too. The English currency of status in this city is Victorian brick – and these niggling suburban semis are far from what the wealthy English dream for in London.

John Betjeman had it in for Neasden. This was the loneliest village in London. The home of the average citizen and the garden gnome. Neasden was Britain in its pebble-dashed conformity. The poet took the train through Metroland. This was his England. The kingdom of the privet hedge and the net curtain. The heartland of the garden shed and the fumbling suited commuter. I took the car.

There is trouble in Metroland. Betjeman's people have gone. The men who went on about Spitfires are mostly dead. Their sons were the ones who hated the suburbs: boys who grew their hair long, resentfully strummed guitars, and only came back for those cold awkward teas and finally to clear out the family house.

The English don't want to live in this borough any more. Betjeman would never recognize Brent. The white British population is now around 18 per cent. South Asians make up 33 per cent. The black population, roughly 19 per cent. Between 2001 and 2011 the white British population of Brent tumbled: losing almost 30 per cent.

These net curtains now hide urban poverty. The garden gnomes have gone. The old terraced slums ringing Victorian London from Brick Lane to Frontline Peckham now have soaring wealthy white populations and matching rents. The sexually frustrated children of Neasden want to be close to Shoreditch not the M40 to the Cotswolds. They want to be central, they want to cycle – they want the city.

I think of Betjeman as I park outside a Hindu temple brooding over a car park. Thin lead clouds smear over the blue skies. There is a muggy heat. These are the last days in spring. The cars have begun to pass with windows down. You can sense people are becoming uncomfortable in their clothes. There are a few hours, here and there, when people unzip in the northern sun, but then shiver cold again in the drizzle.

The Neasden outdoors has an indoor gloom: obscuring the temple's hallucinogenic intricacies chiselled into reaching limestone domes. There is a slight smog. Through purring open doors, a chubby, satin-robed man with radiant green eyes stands holding out a pillow topped with a porcelain sleeping Ganesh. Waxed mahogany beams support the ceilings. These folds of wood are woven with frenzied dancing figures, racing animals and psychedelic flowers. Their humming rhythm begins to tingle powerfully inside the heart.

Crippled women slouch towards the sanctum. Dribbling men are lifted out of wheelchairs. This shimmering space contains pure calm. Carved white limestone swirls like a rising whirlpool into the dome. The carving is of such intensity that the whole dome vibrates with colour: hints of soft electric green, blue and red light wash over the point of mystery. This is the most beautiful room in London I know.

But this dome is an exception. Instead of allowing Muslims and Hindus to make dingy terraces sing with minarets and cupolas, planning permission is frustrated at every turn. Ostentatious Oriental designs are blocked by the councils. This means the other London mostly prays in basement mosques, converted cinemas and damp bingo halls, where the lighting is dim and the carpets are scuffed, where the pipes whine and the electricals hum, and every draught creeps in.

'They never wanted us to build this here, but we never gave up . . .'

A flake-skinned temple guard clutches me in the car park. He waffles he came north from Croydon because he was pulsed by six heart attacks and paralysed from the neck down; but the temple sanctum has blessed him back to health. The guard shakes his head, wobbling huge drooping ears, and peers expectantly.

'The locals were opposed, of course. But now they think our temple is a great beauty . . . They know how powerful it is. This temple has been sending out its energy waves out . . . and reducing drugs and crime all over Brent.'

The guard shoves his hands in his pockets. Then sighs.

'But England has changed you know . . . When I first came to England much more people were going to church . . . now they are not going. I think this very bad. But some whites now come to this temple . . .'

I drive further into Neasden. Behind the temple loom two seemingly industrial chimneys backing onto two schools. One, cubic, eighties red-brick, is run by the temple. The other, a fusty old red-brick craning its head into the class system, is not.

Neasden was built mostly in the 1930s. It was somewhat fashionable, even prosperous, for a while. It was the suburb of birdwatchers and Sunday bridge clubs. This was the life sold all over London. They sold it in pamphlets as thatch-cottage serenity, and in posters of rustic bliss, and country rambles – the new-build escape from the infested back-to-back warrens of Whitechapel. This was an architects' urban dream: a middle-school imagination that fetishized the cosy above all else.

But dreams change.

I am driving through a failed suburbia of PVC doors and plastic windows. The hedge-clippers and the lawnmowers are silent. The privets are mostly gone. So are the rose bushes and the rhododendrons. The driveways are cracked with weeds and covered in little mounds of broken electricals: I see a smashed old box TV, shoved into the silvery mouth of a scratched washing machine, its hatch door lopped off.

Betjeman's dream is dead. And this is changing the suburbs. Migrants now land at the edges. Poverty now accumulates out of sight. Gabled semis are turning into clammy tenements. Every time Nan dies in Neasden her house gets passed over to a key-jangling landlord. Illegal rentals and overcrowding abound. The fire brigades are worried. Polish builders are hutching-up four or more to a room. Bunks are thrown into Grandad's musty old garden shed and bandit extensions are built on the unkempt lawns. The old working-class suburbs are turning into slums.

> Neasden Is A Slum!
> It's not so strange that someone gets beaten up there
> – that's everyday life.
>
> London: Poles wounded in a night brawl.
>
> The two Poles were wounded in knife fights in London's
> Neasden. Most likely a group of five Englishmen got into
> a scuffle with two Poles.
>
> I lived in Neasden where 15 Poles lived in the same house.

This is what the Eastern Europeans think. And this is not hard to find out. To know what Poles really think read their online forums. These are posts stuck up on the newspaper site Gazeta.pl. The thread: *Neasden is a slum!* But there are others too. Threads about overcrowding. Threads about beatings. And accidents at work.

> So what that fifteen people live in a tiny room, that's not
> normal. Let immigrants from Africa or Bangladesh live like
> that, but not people from Europe!

The rain droplets are warm as I wander along Neasden Lane.

Black hoods hang around the Quality Fried Chicken. Their empty boxes at their feet. Down the lane urban believers in Nikes, puffa jackets and air-fresh white jubbah robes saunter in and out of the London Fatwa Council by the glowing Kashmiri grocers. I watch the hoodies come in here with their paranoid shuffle. There are some preachers who will only ever carry those Nokia throwaway phones. Because they are always listening: to every sermon, and to every charity appeal.

My notebook is full of their stories.

The boys tell me there are informers wherever there are Muslims. But they say no informers do it for free: there are some who do it for the passports, some who do it for English lessons, but that anyone will do it for a council flat – all you have to do is call MI5 and answer their questions. Who went to Syria? Who raised what money?

They come in themselves sometimes, the watchers, into the basement mosques, and the shisha bars, with little leaflets explaining what the law is and what they have a right to request. They wink at the owners. We know who has right to remain and who doesn't in the family. We know who is here illegally. So, if anyone we are looking for comes in we are going to hear from you. OK?

I stand outside a clapped-out corner shop. The glass wall inside plastered in forty biro-scrawled little notes. Rooms available only for Europeans, Sikhs or Hindus. There is work for carers and mobile digits to call. There is work in a massage parlour and the number of the pimp. There is a protest for Gaza.

I wander the lane collecting stories. The walls are plastered with posters to call home. Romania 1p. Pakistan 4p. Poland 1p. The loneliest village in London has become heavily Eastern European. Two Polish village boys in black baseball caps strut up and down clutching after-work beers. A Romanian guy in a fake Armani jacket and joggers does the same. They wear cheap aftershave, but still stink of booze, and sweat slightly with the sudden bursts of sun.

The machines in the Romanian kiosk breathe throatily, cooling dozens of meaty sausages. The white cabinets heave with Transyl-

O+4 ▮▮▮▮▮ 652

* * * * *

A LARGE ROOM IS
AVAILABLE IN EAST
STREET. ONLY FOR EUROPEANS
HINDUS & SIKH
MONTHLY RENT £400
BILLS EXCLUSIVE.
CONTACT. 079▮▮▮▮794

vanian beers. Behind the checkout a depressive with strained hazel eyes and a huge florid face spends the day fiddling with her phone until it runs out of battery, and then starts again. She is about thirty-five. Her head slumps into pink-fingered hands as we talk, and then she begins to mutter, then curse everything about this lane.

'This place is horrible. I hate the fights. The moment Friday night starts . . . Romanians start beating Poles who start beating Irish . . . and they don't stop until Sunday. It's frightening some-times.'

There are two straight-up Polish mini-markets on Neasden Lane. I find the same stories there. Nervously a big-breasted twenty-year-old cashier, with a chewed lip and a locket round her neck, uncomfortable in a pink crop top, fidgets and mumbles – some Romanians raped a Polish girl.

'The Romanians and the Poles . . . nobody drinks like us . . .'

She draws breath tensely in the yellowy gloom: they say, these Romanian bad men were here before they were supposed to be. When they got deported, Poles snaffled up their jobs, and squatted their park-bench hangout. But the Romanians returned: they wanted both the bench and the building work back. The rape was their revenge. The fidgeting cashier wants out of Neasden.

I record her stutter.

'They are not fighting ethnic battles, y'see . . . they just drink themselves into a stupor and then fights kick off between them and the Irish. Every weekend . . . the same thing happens.'

Along mangled Neasden Lane, the Irish pubs still fly sun-faded green-white-orange tricolours. Council posters call to study for the citizenship test. Ghanaian women inspect fruit and veg piled high outside the Kashmiri butchers. Pakistani, African and Eastern European lives float past each other. Barely touching. Men brush up in the festering pub. Women occasionally talk in the Turkish mini-market.

Imagine Neasden as a shop, it would come out like that mini-market: Way2Save. Polish rock music blasts out. The shop smells of flour: fresh Anatolian pide bread is being made round the back. There are sacks of African powders. Pakistani confectioneries and

WĘDLINKA

PUSSY energy drinks. Here the obese Polish stacker, packing up the flatbreads, laughs off the fights with her throaty chortle.

'Oh . . . Neasden! My little Eastern European village. They are fighting yes . . . but it's not serious. Men will be men. This is perfectly normal . . . You know our kind. We can get angry at everyone.'

Charlie's dirty-faced Irish pub is for the all-day drinkers. Beery gloom over heavy wooden furnishing. This is a fight pub, where a pissed Romanian at the bar sits staring at a jovial Nigerian waving a pint of Stella. The unshaven Romanian labourer with a maudlin, furrowed face gestures me, to talk about fights.

'The fight . . . I fight not only Polish . . . not only Irish . . . I fight . . . people not my friend . . . I fight Romanian . . . I fight Polish . . . I fight Irish . . . I fight the black. But my friend I not fight . . . My friend Polish . . . my friend Romania . . . look even he my friend . . . !'

The builder points at the elated Nigerian dancing slightly to Rihanna on the pub stereo. But he is so drunk he has forgotten what we are talking about.

'Fight . . . ? Why you wanna know fight? Romanian fight?'

I step outside.

There is a tension between Eastern European men and women on Neasden Lane. The women are exasperated with insecure building-site boys. Men who think it's completely normal to come home seven hours late pissed out of your mind. Boys who are making less money than them at the till.

Eastern European men tend only to meet others at work in hard hats. But the women are in the shop fronts. They find the Muslims flirtatious and sober. The threatened Polish and Romanian males in tracksuits and gold-spray chains know this, of course. Making them more violent, more macho – and more anguished.

This is London: advertising is never far away. These men are being bombarded with powerful sexual imagery. Hoardings for techno-objects. Their electrical screens shimmer with glimpses of consumerist paradise. This is what lures them here. But Neasden has brought technological happiness no closer. They rarely feel prosperous: only when they take the bus to Westfield mall glinting into the motorway and spend time in its white echoing vacuum. Resentment fuses with boredom and emasculation in alcohol.

Hurtling commotion is at the end of the lane.

Neasden is dissected by a geometric carriageway in the North Circular. The inner London orbital tremors with heavy lorries and coaches, hissing a white noise. Hateful underpasses are the only crossing, into ready-made urban rape scenes. This dim tunnel below the North Circular is decorated as if for children. Walls are lined with large wipe-easy coloured tiles shaped into big red buses and little blue boats. There are pools of urine where a white tramp strums a guitar singing his own version of 'Wish You Were Here'. I stop.

'So, so you think you can tell . . . is this your Heaven or Hell?'

A black teenager runs gasping past me through the underpass. I shudder. Is he being followed? But I am being racist. Not too long ago two teenagers were shot in Neasden for their iPods. They were Eastern European – aged eighteen and nineteen – and were left screaming on the pavement outside McDonald's. The boys that shot them were not men. They were fourteen and fifteen years old.

The tramp is still singing, a bit louder now.

'We're just two lost souls swimming round this bowl.'

Neasden Lane over the North Circular is quieter, more isolated. There is an abandoned estate agent, which homeless Romanian migrants keep breaking into. There is a Romanian bakery selling its loaves through a rustic plastic hatch. The smell of flour and dough wafts into the drizzle. But I walk into the Afghan butchers.

This gabled parade has been pulled violently down the social scale. The Afghan, Romanian and Somali shops are grinning like they are wearing someone else's clothes. But the block is a pyramid of immigrants. The freeholder is an old Jewish geezer from Golders Green who gets the bus down to talk to the Afghans once or twice a year.

'It was a London surprise for us . . . a Jewish.'

I sit on a crate of baked beans, talking, chatting with the butchers.

The Jew has a soft spot for them, he is a cockney feller, and he calls them the lads. They tell me the Jew cracks his knuckles when he talks and laughs infectiously that the way to get rich in this country was buying up what the English think is trash.

Lads, the Jew tells the Afghan butchers, I have my hands on a hundred and twenty corner shops across north-west London and my English neighbours up and down my old terrace looked at me like I was collecting freeholds to a hundred and twenty garden sheds. The boys who have taken on the butcher's shop laughed confusedly with him. They had never met a Jew before. But they like him.

'The Jewish told us the upstairs, there is a spare room and we can rent it out, as a secret, to whoever we want. He is a clever . . . this Jewish. So we found some Chinese people and they live . . . I think four, or five of them, in the room upstairs and we keep it a secret. And they pay us some rent. The Jewish, he comes to us and he tells us when we see him, "Lads . . . the only way to survive in London is to buy property . . . and then to never let it go. Otherwise," he says . . . "you're fucked."'

There are two of them who run this place.

They are so bored: we sit talking for four hours.

Sabir is the boss and a hair-gel addict. He smiles easily under a charcoal moustache like any man who knows he is good looking. He has pale pink skin and black freshly gelled hair. He slices and rants about Neasden: hacking and mincing the halal mutton he orders in weekly from an Indian Muslim abattoir in Birmingham.

Sabir is pissed off. Yesterday he came to work and found a Romanian with a brick on his head. The man was unconscious and bleeding outside his shop. There was blood in a trail coming out of the subway. There were fingermarks of red smeared over the coloured tiles.

'There was two Romanian and one Irish I think . . . and the fight happened at six in the morning. And the Irish won with the brick. Now the Romanians are too much. There are a lot. And they are all troublemakers . . . because they don't have house. Look at that windows over the road . . . the Romanians break in three times to go in those closed-down flats. They are mostly drunks. Majority of them are now in this area . . . Bringing the violence.'

He chucks the knife so it slaps raw mutton.

'The Poles were not really bringing the violence . . . Romanians are bringing the violence. Romanians are too much here. We are really fed up of the drunks. Especially these Irish people coming in here wanting Red Bull for no money. If you don't give them the Red Bull then they break things.'

Then throws up his hands.

'But the black teenagers they are the worst. They think . . . They are the one. They are very dangerous. Black teenager in Harlesden they see only all back people around them . . . That's where they are. They are not scared of prison . . . They are not scared of being inside. They are happier in the prison than outside as they can get free burgers in prison. They won't be able to get free burgers outside . . . !'

Sabir knows he is not supposed to say this. He has recently become a British citizen and on the unforgettable day when he first received his own maroon passport he opened it up and read the first lines – *Her Britannic Majesty's Secretary of State Requests and Requires.* The Queen, he explains, has given him his rights. But in exchange, he elaborates, the Queen requests her subjects to speak kindly of all her children.

'This is why you must not say about the black person the truth. The Queen she wants there to be peace in London and this the only way. I think this is a very good idea . . . from the Queen.'

Sabir gestures to Shafiullah to back him up here. This is his sideman. But Shafiullah is still not listening. He is dark-skinned, with thick, bouncy black hair, and a mouthy grin that painfully turns into a smile. He seems much older than twenty-five, his face drained with late nights.

Sabir kisses his teeth and flicks his wrist at him.

'Shafiullah is only miserable because he becomes like an English . . . He forgets why he walk five thousand miles to Neasden. Because when he looked out his shop in Afghanistan there was not Polish fighting with bricks . . : But Americans and Russians fighting with machine guns . . . ba-ba-bam . . . Shafiullah he was walking over many dead Afghans every day on his way to school. This is never going to happen to Neasden. This is place that is so beautiful . . . because it is so boring. Only some drunks fighting and that's it. The Neasden it's a rubbish in the London . . . But it's like a peace beauty in this world . . .'

He grips the counter and laughs.

Shafiullah is not listening. He mumbles to himself, trying to wipe clean the grease-encrusted meat fridges nobody seems to have scrubbed in weeks, that he thinks the shop is dirty. As the light fades he stands, harangued by Sabir, behind the till, behind the chocolates and in front of the cigarettes.

He thinks these customers are strange.

Shafiullah takes their loose change and peers into them: one drunk after another, squiffy old Irish, bloodshot Africans, and Poles or Romanians, with that overpowering breath. Shafiullah shakes his head and ask himself why they don't realize the alcohol is killing them. There are crack-heads in Neasden who come in too. There is even one black man, so thin the bones in his legs are showing, who comes sometimes and shouts outside for Pepsi in the middle of the night.

'There are not many English . . . in the Neasden.'

Shafiullah tells me he wants to make English friends. But he hasn't managed. There have only been a few times when he really spoke to some of the English. He says he used to work as a cabbie, before Sabir took him on, and sometimes they would drunkenly open up to him.

'You know a real Englishman, when he is so drunk, he vomits over the car and the first thing he says, even when he is this drunk . . . is sorry. I was amazed.'

Shafiullah is writing little poems under the counter in a kiddie notebook. They are love poems. The gloom seeps into the shop. He looks at me: sometimes he wakes up on grey mornings before coming to the shop and asks himself the same question over and over again. Am I depressed?

Then he waits in the drizzle for the bus to Neasden.

But he is already thinking about her.

'The worst day in Neasden was when they tell me she marries.'

The villagers back home told him over Skype.

He felt a cold flush, then a hot one. Then he sobbed.

Now his days come and go. The bus journey comes and goes a hundred times. He wakes up asking himself the same question. It comes and goes. But he keeps on seeing her. The moment he lets his mind wander – at the till, in bed, on the top deck of the bus, staring out into the itchy, sooty, particle-dust haze over the North Circular – he keeps imagining her face flickering in and out of the static in his head.

'I came all the way here . . . But I can't feel happy.'

Shafiullah crossed thousands of miles for Neasden.

The knife slices with a thud onto the board as bloody mutton hunks become tiny cubes between his fingers. Evening begins to swallow outside into a soupy blue. The parade is closing up. It is getting cold again. I look behind me. The North Circular overhead begins to glow: hundreds of twin yellow lights coming closer – hundreds and hundreds of twin red lights moving away.

Shafiullah is beginning to talk.

PESHAWAR – LONDON

Shafiullah woke up. Somebody was coming back in and he was very excited. The lights were switched off now. But the boys kept whispering. They kept passing the rollup around, laughing, muffling it, catching each other's eyes, all collapsed in each other's laps. He had never felt more alive.

Outside, they were kissing everywhere, they were kissing on the benches, they were kissing in the parks, they were kissing at the bus stops, they were kissing in the stairwells. One brother had seen two kissers with hands slipping into blue jeans. One brother had even seen two men kissing. Outside, everywhere, they were kissing – kissing wherever they wanted.

'And then she put her hand . . . like this.'

That night they kept on talking in that basement flat. The refrigerator hummed and groaned. But they had never been so happy. All of them were teenagers and twentysomethings. All Afghan, all men. And they had never been so excited. Because Athens was halfway to London.

One brother was lit up from his smile to his eyes. He was one of the boys. He had shaved his beard and there was creamy gel in his hair. This was what he had come here to do. And he was going to tell them everything. This night he had been with another one. Now he was back, bragging to the brothers: how she was curly and generous, and sucked, and what's more, she was his third.

Shafiullah had never been so happy. He smoked and swapped stories. These were the brothers he had met on the road. Some had stolen cars to get across Iran. Others had jumped out of speeding night trains to tumble into Bulgaria. There were some who the

Turks had shot whole rounds at, who had scars from the mountains. But now they were seeing results: this was amazing, this was so amazing.

Afghans, the ones who were on this road, how they loved it in Athens. They loved that polluted evening blue and those smells of roasting meat. This was the other world they had always wanted: the legs, the hair – there were women everywhere. The boys went every night to the squares. They trembled as they tried to take it all in: the tight tops, the short pants, the flick of skirts.

There were brothers who were appalled, they had never wanted to see this. Those were the ones on the run. The older ones who didn't want to shave. Because you met a lot of people on the way: you bundled into a car, you crossed a border, you traipsed through a mountain pass – and then you never saw them again.

And they were all different. When Shafiullah was thrown in prison in Turkey he got to know this. Thug-faced Turks had locked him and Tariq up for trying to swim across the river into Greece. Their wallets, they had grabbed them – confiscated them – and hurled them yelling into that damp and clammy cell.

They grew fidgety and weak as they heard their guards laughing – and the slap, slap of them playing cards. They had learnt how to sleep crouching up. Because that cell was filled with so many Afghans this was all the space they had. They were there for a month and they were always hungry, along with a kid from some-where in Bangladesh.

And they made friends, of a sort. There were the big brothers like Sumaray who were always joking and breaking up fights and teasing the youngins about things they knew about only in the abstract, like condoms. And there were the old beards like Majid. They never really told you why they were on the way to London. Old beards were always elusive. But you could always tell. Because they were either on the run from the men with guns, or they were on the quest for sex.

Shafiullah didn't want to think about prison in Athens. These were the most beautiful days of his life. Come dusk he and Tariq had gone to dance in that Afghan shop in the Muslim people's quarter. There were maybe sixty people then: all of them adventurers, and on their way to London. And that night they danced, and spun Pashtun CDs and grabbed each other by the shoulders. And as the singing got louder and louder, and as the excitement rose, they felt themselves coming alive.

Shafiullah kept repeating – Am I dreaming, am I really here? Has this really happened? Am I really halfway to London? That day the brothers had walked everywhere; they had wanted to see everything. Tariq, what a man, had even bought a throwaway camera. He was a rich guy back in Afghanistan. Shafiullah had gone up with Tariq to the ruins on the outcrop to take thirty photos of them throwing out their arms out and shouting, 'I'm alive,' over the whole concrete jumble of Athens.

That night in the basement flat he kept thinking, Has this really happened – is there really going to be no more mud, no more ripping vegetable roots, no more village, no more being who you are born to be? That night the boys kept talking. They were teenagers mostly. A few still had fathers. The boys kept on bragging, and laughing: we are the rebels, we are the ones who don't care, we are the ones who want to be rich, who want to ride their women – we are the only ones who are ever going to feel alive.

It all seemed so far away. But there had been a boy in his village who had flown to London: in this village, where they were all farmers and where they worked all day but somehow there was never enough of anything, the family of that boy became rich. They told everyone in the market that he was becoming wealthy, becoming fatter – that he was a chauffeur, and making so much money he could send them a Western Union once a month. And they invited everyone in the village to see his sticky printed pictures of brown towers and a huge wheel with that boy, who used to be here, who used to be us, throwing his arms out into the air, and smiling in every one of them.

Shafiullah was not like them, he was not the same, he was not like the rest. Shafiullah wanted to talk and talk and talk, and stay up

talking girls and poetry and fucking for three nights straight: until he felt that tingling presence. He wanted to slip off into the desert, assume new identities, sever his friendships, burn his clothes, speak seven languages, sleep late, speak verse, see Paris, and drive fast on empty streets with nothing in mind except falling in love and not getting arrested.

They mocked him for that. But he didn't care. He was sixteen and he wanted to slip into those sticky pictures. There was a country where a poor man could become a rich man, where a peasant could become a professor, where there was so much work, and so much money, you could own a car, eat only meat, wear only jackets, and help the people stuck back here. This was why he wanted to open his eyes in London.

There were villages where they talked about Berlin and there were villages were they talked about Vienna. But this was the village where they talked about London. There was not one boy here who did not know about Neasden. They talked about it when they played catch in the dust. That was his village in London. They talked about it when they hoisted up the water. And tried to imagine what that was.

And every year they knew more about it. First came the phone line. That hero, that prince, out there in Neasden, would call maybe once a month and tell his mother about his success. Everyone was dazzled by what she said: his glossy-haired daughter was at school for free, when he was sick the doctor checked him for free, and when he had a problem the government spoke to him for free and told him everything he needed to know. Oh, how was the life in London!

Then, from China, his uncle brought a television to the village in his pick-up truck and they knew even more. There were some days when all the boys they would all sit and watch the video cassettes he brought. Their screen light would dance on the whites of their eyes and the Bollywood singing would rise, louder, and louder, until they were all silent and too excited to even blink.

He knew he was not like the other boys. They were donkeys, really. They would never think for themselves. They would never really realize there was more than the village. This happened slowly. Perhaps it was the night they watched the Hindi film where outside the big house they refuse the poor boy in rags to ask for his love, and he leaves for London and becomes so rich that he wears only suits and lives at the very top of the tallest glass tower, until he returns for her. Perhaps it was the night that he realized there was only one thing he could be here on the edge of these folding blue mountains: and that was poor.

There was a stretch of mud they called a street and he lived at the top and she lived at the bottom. There was no way he could ever forget her. Her face had become an interminable loop. Her eyes were there when he closed his own. Her brown pool eyes that were the shape of almonds. He wanted to touch her lips and see her hair and run a finger, as she shivered, down her spine.

There were boys in the village that had told her how he felt. There were people who had seen him hammer that long poem of Rahman Baba to her courtyard door. He had read it out softly and hoped. But why would she ever come out? He was what he was: not rich, not holy – nothing, nothing, nothing at all.

There was no way he could ever fuck her. None. There was no way he could ever fuck anyone here: or anyone he wanted, at least. Here farm girls fucked farm boys. And you fucked one person, otherwise they shot you in the back. The daughter of the village policeman: forget it. The more he wanted her, the more he saw the back of her blue hijab, the more angry, the more spiteful, the more unhinged he began to sound in his head.

What could anyone do here apart from fuck around with the sheep or go into the mountains and get your head blown fucking off by the Americans? These were the blue mountains of his ancestors but to live here would be to live slowly turning brown and withered like a dying plant. The life here was the life of a man always asleep.

There is no way you can live calmly when you know there is something better. There is no way you can live calmly when you keep on glimpsing the other world. Those were the American years, and traders were flooding the village with mobiles and televisions on their little pick-ups from China.

Now there was nobody in the village who had not seen the better life, or those dancing American women. Nobody who did not know what a living room could look like, with space, and three sofas and a garden, or how really a kitchen should gleam. Those televisions flickered and told them night by night how wretched their lives had always been. But Shafiullah kept on repeating: this was all in Neasden, all in London – his if he could get there.

Peshawar was not far away and all Afghans knew it really belonged to them. That was where his uncle was taking him. They sat on the bus: it shivered, and snaked, as the electricals importer from China tried to talk to him about risk – and minimizing it. He ignored him. Was it years or was it months he had been begging – in meals, in fields – to send him to London to make so much money he could support every one of them. Was it years or was it months – every harvest, every milking – he had been saving everything to prove to his uncle to lend him the rest.

The old man knew Shafiullah, he was his responsibility. There was no father since a mujahideen had taken his revenge one summer for what happened in war. He knew Shafiullah was the one. There was no risk of him not paying him back. And after a few years having him in London, he would start to make him money: with two real earners supporting his mother and sisters – and you never know, maybe even getting the other boy over when he was man enough to risk that long way there.

Shafiullah was not planning. His heart was beating. His eyes were staring into the mountains but he was seeing other things – seeing convertibles, blonde hair, cities of glass – a mash up of every village rumour he had ever heard and every Bollywood movie he had ever seen. His uncle kept repeating: you have to be careful, you must be careful – there are thieves, there are guards and there are tricksters on the way to London. His uncle repeated many times on that bus journey that the smugglers would get him as far as Great

Britain and that villager, the chauffeur – whom he should call uncle – would drive out to fetch him.

The journey is not difficult. The journey is easy. The journey is often exaggerated by the teenagers who tend to take it. The agent is talking. They have tried to make the office in Peshawar as nice as they can. There are plant pots and computers and a rather fetching globe. They negotiate to the sound of air-conditioning: there are some immigrant agencies that can smuggle someone all the way to Britain, this one works only into Europe. Their prices vary depending on the level of service. This one is all inclusive: food, shelter, transport – not to mention the crossing of the borders themselves. They negotiate $10,000 and a passage into Greece.

Shafiullah was not thinking of his mother, and his sister, and his other sister, and his brother crying as the bus left that wretched place – because there is no happier place in Pakistan than the tea houses of Peshawar where the boys gather, the nights before they leave for London. Shafiullah was happier than he had ever been. Forget those vegetables. These were the people he had always wanted to know: brothers like Tariq, who loved rock music and wanted to be famous, brothers like Salar, who wanted to have a girl in every land on the way. They couldn't stop talking, and rushed to look at the photos of these places – Rome, Athens – in the all-night computer cafes.

He first saw them glinting in the sun: the six motorbikes rolling in to ride them across the desert. These would sneak them over the border. And, he could only think one thing: Fuck Yes. Behind the Afghan bikers rose up columns of dust like the trails of a hundred Djinns. The sun bounced from their mirrors as Shafiullah saw they were wearing the sickest sunglasses you could find in Peshawar. The agents were whistling and waving – quiet, come to this point – as the agents' buses rattled on stones and rolled the adventurers in. There were a few who were suddenly becoming very religious, cupping their hands a bit, holding, or sharing their pocket prayers. But the rest rolled a few cigarettes and were too excited to think about God, or even to talk.

God is Great. This was it. There was nothing better than this.

There he was clinging onto the Afghan biker with Tariq and Salar. Holding on to the bike was to hear the screeching and the racketing thunder of the wheels flipping off hundreds of stones and thousands of pebbles. The agents had been very strict. You had to be very quiet. And no matter how much you wanted to for fuck's sake don't stretch out your hands or start shouting wooo. They had a deal with the border guards. But there should be no taking the piss.

Shafiullah gripped tight as the biker accelerated into speed. And there was that voice: goodbye Pakistan, goodbye Afghanistan, goodbye no running water, goodbye no kissing girls, goodbye annoying turbans, goodbye primitive, restrictive village. He clung on – and he could tell with his twitches Tariq was frightened.

Come on, quickly now. The agents on the other side were whistling. Come on, get a fucking move on. The agents piled them, all thirty of them, onto the back of the pick-up truck. Crushed, and cold, the immigrants tried to share some water and biscuits. The bikes had been too much for some people. They had fallen asleep. But Shafiullah was too excited to even imagine what it felt like to ever want to sleep again.

That night on the floor of some hut they talked amongst themselves. Tomorrow was Tehran. They were getting a bus to Tehran. They liked rolling that word over and over again. There were some who were too excited to even sleep on the bus that came in the morning. Everything, all the little things, and all these huge things – motorways, petrol stations – were in all these different shapes. And they wanted to see it all: not miss the glimpse of one mosque, one tower, one railway, one roundabout.

But Tehran, it was more beautiful than it had been in their dreams. The government here had done much for its people. Shafiullah pointed to Tariq, who seemed quiet and hungry, this incredible sight. The roads of Tehran were huge, double, dual carriageways, and in the middle – wide enough for a football game – were flower beds that proper officers, in proper uniforms, were watering for the delights of the people. What an amazing sight.

They came in with heartbeats into the amber lights merging on the freeway. But the agent got up and walked adamantly up and down the walkway of their secret immigrant bus. 'The rules are the rules. You cannot go out. You cannot wander. Iran is a strong country and if Iran's police find you they will throw you in jail and out into Pakistan. Have I been understood? You must stay in our rooms at all times. There it is safe. Have I been understood?'

Everyone nodded. But there was happiness in the group. This was their dream. And it was coming true. There was too much adrenaline for Shafiullah and Tariq to sleep. The immigrants were all there in a heap, rolled out on little mats on the floor. Here everything was exciting: the sound of the city outside, the car lights on the ceiling – it pushed them into a state of excitement which they had seldom felt. There was so much happiness amongst them. And on the third night Shafiullah and Tariq slipped out and walked into Tehran. They saw huge shops and lit windows crammed with food: and what was rising, as they shot looks at each other, was something close to joy, or something maybe even stronger and unknown.

After the third night the agent hurried them into a bus. They slept more easily but they tussled to sit by the windows: to watch the towns and villages passing, one by one, the minarets rising like triumphant spears, entrenched in the green hills and those tumbling mountain faces. They were coming close to the Kurdish villages. What came next, the agents had warned them, was the most dangerous part of the golden trail to London.

Shafiullah stumbled and fell – and thwack – he tasted blood on his lip. They were maybe a hundred, a hundred trudging Afghans, slipping, and scrabbling down that mountain stream. The agents had been adamant: you must not make a sound. But that was too difficult. Their hearts were beating. Their hands and faces were scratched by a thousand branches. Then the dogs went off: calling and jumping and yelping on the ridge. The searchlights swirled: once, twice. And the Turks' border guards fired.

They shared these stories in that room in Istanbul. Shafiullah took turns with Tariq to move his hands to show how they had cowered and gripped until the border guards had moved on. They tried – but it seems you couldn't – to give a sense of all those hours, that whole night, those half-seen fragments, where they lost their toenails and ruined their shoes, scrabbling on foot over the Kurdish mountains. They tried – but they couldn't, even with their hands – to explain the rush, the cold-water relief, the hardening of the world, which they had felt seeing the glinting outline of the agents' pickup truck over the Kurdish mountain at dawn.

They opened another packet, lit up, and talked. Others were not so lucky. Some had picked pockets to get across Iran. Some had been deported back. Others had to go north into Russia. Some had got into drugs. Others had simply disappeared. A few had fallen in love and stayed shacked up in Tehran for months. They smoked and talked it all over. But mostly they came back to the last border. They shot people there. There were people dying. There were people starving. And there – they threw you in jail.

They warned them. But the worst thing happened. There was a real army on this border. Their boots were clean and they kicked him three times in the chest and cursed him in their language that he did not understand. Their knuckles met his face when he tried to pounce and resist. This was the border of Europe. The country of Greece. Those wanting to enter, they imprisoned them for it. And as the storytellers all say, the frontiers of any paradise are as gated and unreachable as his kingdom.

That month – or was it six weeks – crouching, sweating, hungry, was the month that he learnt that prison is about patience. There is a way, but it's not that easy, where you can slow your heartbeat, and bring that glaze down over your eyes. There is a way, but it took quite some time, where you can stop thinking about food, about London, about Neasden, a way where you can stop thinking entirely, and only breathe, in and out, so softly, and feel over and over, alone the air sucking in over your teeth.

Majid and the old beards, the men, the runaways told the boys firmly, whenever they heard them fear-whispering – no, they don't deport, this a temporary detention. But they only believed him when the Turks came into the cell with a dozen more people from Bangladesh, or maybe India, and threw them out to make room. They stood there blinking in the sun before phoning the agent. The voice down the phone was flat and apathetic. They would send a car and bring them back to the safe room.

Lying inside the lorry he felt the wheels grind to a halt. This was the border. Again. Shafiullah in that moment was all things – explorer, animal, stowaway, king – between the cardboard of eight huge boxes. Bright white light came through the cracks. He tried not to breathe. There was rapping and a thud along the cargo frame. The engine roared. And when the dark shapes of the agents unbolted them, he was so giddy, so flushed, that he almost slipped – the ground under his feet was Europe.

Athens, so much happened in Athens. Happiness, from the moment the agents unlocked that lorry and hurried them onto a train – a real, elegant, comfortable train – to the moment the agents slammed down the hatches of the shipping container outbound for Italy. Happiness, they were free to walk around. Locked into that container, with the faint rocking from movement, they talked about girls, about the gleam of the sea, about what they wanted in London. The container was warm and calm and Shafiullah slept deeply. Tomorrow another beautiful country.

The first three days in Italy were close to desperate. He had lost Tariq. His container had never arrived. And well that was that. Everything here was wet from rain. That first night was so wet, Shafiullah and those boys from the container turned frantic. They began rummaging in the bins and pulled out the crinkly black lining to cover themselves with, and huddled in arches of stations, under the pigeons, trembling, feeling the cold numb whole sections inside their heads.

The agents can never guarantee you will reach your destination. This is why the money is always held by a broker in the market. This is a man who cannot just run away – trust is what a money trader depends on – and when you leave down the golden trail you leave him that $10,000. Whenever you cross a border you have to get the message back to him. And he will then release the cash bit by bit to the agents after each frontier.

Those agents mostly cover getting into Europe. You usually need to find another agent to reach Britain once you are smuggled into the other life. They usually ask for $5,000 and this usually has to be up front. These guys are lorry guys. They have to know everything about lorries: which fleet pays the worst, what country has low fines, which types will cut a deal to smuggle a couple of dozen people in.

They threw him out in Calais and told him to wait. This was the last border. This would take time and they would have to be patient. But there were thousands of lorries thundering onto the ferries and the protected trains every day. And the agents said there was only a matter of time before one wheeler-dealer took the $1,000 a head. Then the agents left them: they would call when it happened.

There were so many immigrants in Calais that the Afghans would walk freely. They were everywhere: on the benches, in the boarding houses, sleeping rough or meandering aimlessly along the crash and wave of the sea front between the gulls. He had never seen so many immigrants: hundreds, it seemed thousands of Afghans, if not more. And there were the Pakistanis and Bangladeshis, the Syrians and the Iraqis, the Albanians and Africans and so many people from places he had never even heard of.

Albanian agents prowled certain streets. They would punch and kick the Afghan dealers who tried to approach any of the Albanians wanting over. These men were violent, there was no messing about, so even the Afghans stayed to their own. Besides, there was more than enough work for everyone. There were more and more of them. There were some that came organized, there were some that came on their own. There were the ones he saw in the park with brown bruises and broken legs who had tried to leap onto the trains and failed. And there were the ones nervously smoking in hotels with a man looking for a lorry.

There were two classes of travel. There were what the agents called the coffins: these were cheaper and were metal cases the size of two men, strapped under a lorry's suspension, where its middle set of wheels would normally be. There was no room even to wriggle in those. These slipped through quite easily. But they were dangerous: one skid, one crash, and like too many Afghans you would be crushed and mangled on the motorway.

You would see the limbless, the cripples, sometimes waiting, sometimes begging on the streets of Calais. This was a damp country, he thought. And there were so many immigrants here they could no longer frighten them: there were no longer enough police to arrest them all. Their shrivelled arms and ripped faces made Shafiullah choose the more comfortable class of travel: the one inside the container itself. This was much less frequent than it had been, and needed special deals.

There were some people who waited weeks. There were some people who waited months. But he was lucky. The mobile rang. Hurry. The agent had found space for three of them in a lorry heading over. Shafiullah barely had time to greet the other Afghan, around his age, and an Iraqi who seemed considerably older, before they pushed them in – slam, creak – and the container was locked.

He could see the other boy's eyes in the dark. They had nothing to worry about. London was the country of rights. London was the country of humanitarians. They couldn't touch you there. The agents were clear. All you had to do was tell them you were running from a war country and came from danger. That way they would never send you home. This was a just country. This was the most just country in the world.

He was trembling as the lorry bleeped and heaved onto the train. This was the country they had always talked about. The country of Neasden. The country of London. The city where everyone is rich. The city where you can become rich.

They panicked with a sudden thud and voices. Then nothing, and the lorry rocked gently. He could not count the time that passed. It ended with the crackle of the wheels scraping into concrete and gravel. The huge machine cleared its throat and groaned as it gathered speed. His heart had never beat faster. He started to talk to the other boy and then to laugh. That was the crackle of small rocks on the road into the golden city: where they were so good, and so rich, and so wise, they took anyone from any war country and made them a son of their own.

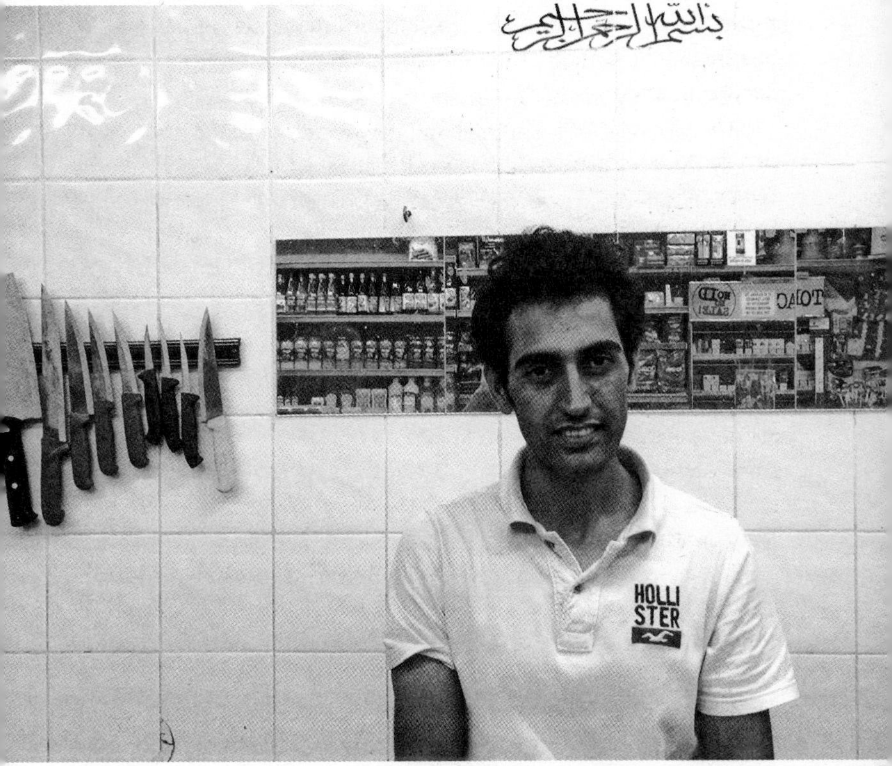
بسم الله الرحمن الرحيم
HOLLI
STER

They were both laughing now. They didn't care. They knocked over the boxes. They started trying to open a crack in the huge back flaps to see London and its lights, all bright and blue, flooding in for the first time. Then the lorry started to slow down and pulled up on the hard shoulder. There was the sound of a door slamming. The driver was staring right at them.

'Hello, officer. I'm a truck driver just coming in from Calais. I was driving and I heard some scrabbling round the back. And now I've checked . . . I've got some migrants in me back. Nothing do with me, officer. They must have broke in or something.'

They came quickly. But the boys: they were so excited and joyful to be at the end of the golden road that they began shouting out – *Hello, Hello* – and waving out at the policemen. Shivering with happiness.

ELEPHANT AND CASTLE

The bus up from Peckham shudders to a stop on the New Kent Road.

A wrecking claw works. My eyes blink with dust. I am recording the machine tear down partition walls and floors. The beast bleeps back, it bleeps forwards, its metal muscles, painted yellow, chewing into the concrete.

This is the frontline of new London.

The estate rises up six storeys, ugly like a decked paper tray. Elephant and Castle is where Tony Blair came in 1997 to give his first speech as Prime Minister. People cheered. He called them 'the people forgotten by government'.

Now, one by one, their homes are being knocked down.

At the bus stop I watch the wrecking claw chew into a corridor balcony. Behind me I hear the lilt they call Street: the London voice, almost Jamaican. There are two teenagers, flirting and unaware, involved in their own conversation. He is brown, a stocky Punjabi, with a ball head, perfect teeth, and thick beard, under a slightly tipped Chicago Bulls baseball cap, in a grey hoodie. She is slight, long headed, and white, in black leggings and sleeveless blue puffa, and pressing her upper lip down, suppressing a smile, she pretends to disagree, and twirls herself round to please him, lifting herself off the heels of her feet, knowing where his eyes will fall.

This was the Heygate Estate. The three thousand people who lived here have gone, pushed out of booming inner London to the fraying suburbs. Placards promising future penthouses ring the site: glass towers, exposed brickwork and fruit trees. Less than 2 per cent of the new flats will be rented out by the state to the poor. This land is now too valuable for concrete sink estates. Louder than the wrecking ball is the rumour. That the government wants to socially cleanse the inner city. Thirty times all over South London I have written down in street interviews that someone thinks the government wants to push poor black people out of the centre.

This is how poverty is being redistributed. All over the administrative patchwork of the city there are estates being cleared. There are demolitions, and there are sales, but they add up to the same thing. The quarter of London that rents from the state is being slowly displaced: into the outer ring where they can afford the bill. Old immigrant London is being pushed out of the inner city, to what was once its poor white fringe.

I stand in front of the sixties shopping centre under an office block of Soviet dilapidation; they call this grey and smudged box of glass and steel Hannibal House. The flagpoles stick up, forgotten, over the shopping mall beneath; the scuffed blue plastic rimming the long glass windows is streaked with odd white smears and cheap plastic stick-on numbers for a SUPERBOWL. Racks in front of me are stacked with migrant newspapers in Russian, Lithuanian, Spanish, Arabic and Brazilian Portuguese.

This will all be demolished soon. Inside the mall a yellow light glints in streaks over beige quartz tiling. Day-off builders in white trainers, crew cuts and white-lined sportswear drift in two-man crews into the Polish bar. Bolivian men, with dark, reddish skin, haggle for matching blue umbrellas from a surly Afghan, who mostly seems to sell trinket jewellery in a glass box near the tired escalator.

I brush past two ageing Somali men, beards greying, in flat caps and long coats, hanging around dejected outside the orange-covered doors of RIA Money Transfers. A frumpy Colombian woman in a green raincoat sits chewing from a can of sweetcorn, with a look of pure satisfaction, in a defunct leather massage chair. This was where I meet Akwese.

He is Ghanaian, a squat man, and complains he is cold as we traipse into the street market ringing the mall. But when we sit for coffee he suddenly jitters. In the rain the pavement glistens. The clouds are cracking open. The wind is making everyone in the market bristle: the African women with head wraps and hoop earrings, piled down with plastic bags, rushing with intent for the bus, and the clear-eyed Roma beggar girls in their swirling green skirts, moving furtively between the metal-pole market stalls, and the dishevelled Afghan hawkers, flogging unlocked phones, phone cards and bundles of fake white phone chargers.

'Do you want anything.'

Akwese is so tense he will have to pay for this he shakes his head adamantly. But he is dressed for the occasion: a mustard shirt, green trousers, Louis Vuitton brown loafers that are clearly fake and sunglasses, even though there is no sun, which he never once takes off, the whole time we talk inside. This is because Akwese wants to impress in his clubbing best: and shades is the P. Diddy look to the press.

'No . . . I'm fine for coffee . . . Fine, really. Let's go.'

Akwese realized he was fucked in the kitchen.

The sweaty faced Australian chef was barking at him to hurry the fuck up. Akwese was dripping sweat in the back of the boutique Knightsbridge brasserie. He had lied to them that he had done this kind of work before.

Of course he hadn't.

He pulled his hands out of the sink. He had torn his yellow gloves on the tips of his fingers and his hands were red, boiled and bleeding. They had lied to him back in Ghana.

Migrants had come into his little timber shop on that red dust road, and told him London was easy. That in the rich man's city the kitchen boys were relaxing because they had a big machine to wash their pots and pans for them. That there in the kitchen all the boys needed to do was stack up them plates and switch the machine off and on.

But there was no machine in the French restaurant.

The Australian was swearing at him now. Threatening to call in the South African manager. He was a white guy, and well vicious.

'Give me some fucking pick up.'

Akwese was frightened. He couldn't afford to lose this job on the first day. The meat-smeared Australian was coming towards him. Akwese grabbed the stacked frying pans next to him without thinking.

It took a second to feel the pain. The gloves melted into the pan side and mixed with frying fats and five seared fingertips. He screamed. So did the Australian.

'You fucking idiot . . . !'

This is the first thing he tells me.

He fidgets nervously, unused to telling his life story.

Akwese is clutching onto his black shoulder bag, filled with sweat-reeking work garments, and of course, the fluorescent uniform of the menial underclass. These are the clothes he wears every day, but the clothes he will never put on Facebook. They are worn, from scrubbing, from work. He puts his hands in his lap, and slouches back in the seat. And he begins to talk, his voice slow, and slurry, about everything that happened to him.

'They had lied to me back in Africa.'

They had lied through their teeth. That smug cousin, who came back with wristwatches for all the elders and trainers for all the youngers, was lying to him. You could not earn £3,000 a month as a cleaner and send bare money back to Africa. That slick schooldays brother who got up and made testimony in front of the whole church was lying to him. You could not set yourself up as an international businessman in six months in London.

'They was all lying.'

This is a deep voice.

And he twitches, as he begins to share things with me.

'I worked for my father . . . We had a little timber shop. We were selling woods, many kinds of woods for the home, for the fire . . . Y'know, lots of very good woods. And I was often stopping the mens who had been to London and asking them to tell me what it was like.

'There was one friend who used to come and buy some woods when he was visiting us in Ghana . . . He was looking fresh . . . He was really inspiring me about London. When he came to buy the woods he was saying us that London is second to heaven . . . a city where every man is rich.

'That the black guys are having fun in London.'

Akwese regretted making the journey the moment he walked into that kitchen. It had all gone horribly wrong. His back hurt: he was sleeping on the floor in Peckham. His wallet was empty: those five years of savings lasted barely three weeks. His whole plan of setting up an international business: now he knew that was peasant fantasy. He hadn't come here to wash dishes. But here he was.

'When I entered into the kitchen . . . I was horrified. Honestly, I don't want to lie to you . . . I wanted to go back to Africa. It was too hot, too stuffy, too cramped. I wanted to cry. What, this is my London? But there was nothing I could do . . . I was stuck now.'

Akwese had not thought any of this through. Nobody had warned him about the papers. Nobody had explained to him about the legalities regarding the right to work. Nobody had made it clear the system was different here.

'To be honest with you . . . When I was on the plane coming into Heathrow, I was shaking with happiness . . . I had this plan to start importing and exporting fresh clothes from London to Accra. But nobody had explained to me about the papers. Like most Africans I did not even know I needed the work papers.'

Akwese lets out a sad chuckle as I rip open a sugar tube. But I begin to notice a distant note in his voice. At the next table, Chinese students nervously flirt over a marshmallow soup of hot chocolate. But here, Akwese talks to me about the past five years as if they had happened to somebody else, or were a bad dream he barely remembers.

'I thought this was the way to come and make money . . .

'I had got a student visa for me and a student visa for de wife . . . So we just overstayed and started working. We had to work to survive. We had no other choice . . . We had to survive. We had to pay off our debts to my family who lent me the money to come. But we had not understood . . . now we were illegals. That we could be arrested. When we realized my wife began to crying on the spot: we had left our children behind. We had told them we would be coming in a few months for them.

'Now we were stuck.'

Akwese hated being a beggar. But someone without the right papers has to learn how to beg from his friends. He begged them to spend a week here and a week there. He begged to unfurl his foam mat on their kitchen floors. He begged them for thirty quid here and forty quid there.

'The disappointment . . . It was bitter, so bitter.'

Akwese learnt to slip out of sight, to scarper and to disappear. He would see policemen and run sometimes. He would see policemen and just dash. Akwese knew what happened if you got caught and it was too terrible to even think about. They told him they were beating the black people in those camps. They told him they might not even send you back to your home country but to anywhere in Africa – like Somalia – and Akwese shuddered to even think of it.

'The humiliation . . . It was painful, so painful. I had wanted to come here . . . to become a businessman . . . a respectable man . . . and I was living like I was a criminal . . . always running, always frightened, always paranoid . . . when I saw dem officers.'

His eyes keep flicking down to the recorder.

'It was bitter . . . so bitter . . . To be honest with you I imagined that London was second to heaven. That there was streets with glass on them and some kind of electronic buildings and houses with huge spaces for you to relax. Honestly . . . I was imagining London more beautiful than it is . . . like a second paradise . . . Y'know with more marble, more glass, more gold homes . . . and all that.'

The Knightsbridge brasserie he found work in mainly served Gulf Arabs. They never bothered to read the menu carefully and kept sending food back, hyperventilating when they found unexpected little pieces of bacon between the salad leaves. They were always hollering: 'How could you do this to me? Why you try to insult me?'

The chefs terrorized the kitchen boys. The chefs had power. They were foul-mouthed bastards who could sack a man on the spot. The moment they began sweating, they started swearing. And would take it out on the Nigerian and Ghanaian kitchen boys.

'I worked in the French restaurant for two month. They paid me every month, at the end of the four weeks, and then at the end of the third month they went to me, "Where is your papers? We need to see them to pay you." So there was no choice for me. I had to leave . . . without wages to live for a month.

'I wanted to start crying.'

Akwese squirms as we talk.

I can tell how unusual, odd, exciting, it is for him to share.

'When I was leaving I looked at the peoples who was eating . . . They were having like big steaks and big wines on every table. Laughing and everything . . . I picked up the menu list, and every-thing they was eating was like £40 or £50. That was the cash for my whole shift. I looked down the menu list and thought, I cannot afford to have even one dish here . . . And I thought, The barrier, the gap, between me and them . . . That's impassable.'

He slipped out into the drizzle. The street lamps were on. Tree skeletons leered over the wet tarmac shimmering with light. The double-deckers glowed out against the night, their upper windows all steamed up with the cold.

'Bruva, I cannot tell you how much I hate begging.'

There is a whole illegal city in London. This is where 70 per cent of Britain's illegal immigrants are hiding. This is a city of more than 600,000 people, making it larger than Glasgow or Edinburgh. There are more illegals in London than Indians. Almost 40 per cent of them arrived after 2001. Roughly a third are from Africa. This is the hidden city: hidden from the statistics, hidden from the poverty rates, hidden from the hunger rates. They all discount them: a minimum 5 per cent of the population.

But this London is not hidden from the employers.

Akwese faced the worst that winter. The other kitchen boys had given him the low-down. The trick illegal Africans were pulling was working through the agencies. You just went there and signed on.

They didn't ask you for anything. Then the agency paid you, not the company. That way nobody was going to get into trouble with the police.

'The worst moment came when I was working in a big supermarket warehouse out in south-east London . . . It was huge, it was dark, it was damp inside that warehouse. Everyone working there was the black people, of course . . .'

He had never felt the river cold. That damp kind of cold that hardens your jeans, has a sting to your eyes, and gets in under your fleece. His father had died in Ghana. His mother and sisters were crying to him over the telephone. The brothers were arguing about inheritance and property. There was no way he could get there.

'The warehouse gave me a picking and parking job . . . That's what they call it. They give you this little small truck with a forklift, and then you have to drive around picking and parking the crates of veg, the crates of breads, whole crates of potatoes, in their bays.'

The warehouse was not insulated. The wind crept in during the winter. The wind made hissing and mewling sounds like a cat. Akwese was thinking about the rent. He could barely cover it. He was seeing his wife only in snatches of a few hours here and there. She was scrubbing on the night shift.

'We were crying together and praying together for the papers. Because that was the only way we could see our children again.'

The forklift was pulling up twenty crates of wine when it really hit. He was stuck here. Possibly for ever. Angry. Frustrated. Exhausted. This was when Akwese realized he had ruined his life.

'That was when I heard my thinking. What am I doing here? When I could go back to Africa where there is sun . . . where there is my baby boy and my baby girl and my happiness . . . But I can't . . . I'm locked, in London . . . coz I'm an idiot . . . Now the only thing I can do is keep my head up. Things will get better eventually. Maybe if I pray I will get the papers somehow . . . Maybe . . . Maybe.'

Two months later, the warehouse sacked him for negligence.

'The next job I got was in the area of the white community in south-east London. The place is called Bromley. There are many whites there . . . not like the rest of the south and east in London.

I found some work as a car-washer there. The owner was a Kenyan guy. He had one employee. He was a Zimbabwean. He was hating me from the moment I arrived. Swearing at me. Shouting at me. Throwing foam at me. He was scared I would take his washing job from him.

'He was a media-studies graduate.

'But after a while he stopped throwing the spray in my eyes . . . He was very inexperienced with women, this bruva. He was having lots of fighting with the missus. He was asking me for advices and I was giving them. We were scrubbing windows, bonnets, wing mirrors, talking about his missus problem and I was helping him. We cleaned so many boots and back seats we became . . . sort of friends . . .'

This went on for five years.

The Zimbabwean was the one who first cottoned on to the new car wash over the road. They peered across as they hosed and wiped down the Fords and the Nissans. Then the cars started thinning.

'The man who opened the wash was a member of the white community. And the cars . . . Y'see . . . they started going to him. And not the African wash.'

Six months on – the Kenyan was out of business.

Akwese was desperate. He had been lying to his family back in Africa. Saying he was very close to the breakthrough moment. That his international business was almost ready to launch. Akwese was still in debt.

'Y'see, with no papers . . . this is how you think.'

Falling through the cracks forces you to lie: it forces you to lie for your money, it forces you to lie for your family, it forces you to lie on your Facebook, when you post shaky phone shots of Tower Bridge, and the flowers of Hyde Park, but above all falling through the cracks forces you to lie to yourself – that all of this is gonna work out somehow.

Ghanaians tipped him off there was good work underground. That down in the Tube they needed thousands more cleaners to pick up all the shit that millions of passengers dropped, puked or forgot every day.

Akwese says he knows all jobs in London follow the hierarchy. That there is such a thing as African work and Polish work. This is second nature to anyone living on low pay. They know which employers take on people like them. The same goes for the Tube. More than 95 per cent of London's thousands of Underground cleaners are immigrants, and more than three-quarters of them come from black Africa.

'They said, the bruvas . . . they like taking us down there.'

The first thing that hit him was the smell. That smell you catch sometimes on the platforms, of metal on metal, from the heat and the friction of the wheels pounding the tracks. The rusty smell, that mixes with sweat, that mixes with soot; the smell that can make you dizzy sometimes.

He was nervous. He heard this was a dangerous job. He heard last summer that a Ghanaian cleaner had been shuffling along the platform with his litter-picker and fainted onto the rails. They said he was electrocuted. Then hit by the train.

Akwese was told to wear a fluorescent yellow waistcoat and was stationed at Edgware Road. He found the crowds difficult at first. There was something unnerving cleaning against the swaying flow: thousands, tens of thousands of faces, coming the other way. Some people can't cope with it and leave.

Akwese settled in at Edgware Road. There are platforms outside here. Like a real railway, he thought. This was where he learnt to fear the station master calling out, 'Code Three, Code Three,' over the sound system. This is the code for vomit, faeces or other human fluid. The cleaners have to rush to the broom cupboard and grab the red gloves, the red mop and the red bucket. The danger kit.

Akwese works the late shift. The drunk shift. The whole of working London merry and buzzing, shouting and kissing, clambering unsteady onto those last trains out of Edgware Road. Every day, there is someone having a bit of trouble. Yesterday Akwese saw a woman so drunk, she slipped on the stairs leading down to the District Line. Her dress was half undone and he wanted to help her. But regulations say help cannot be administered by the cleaners unless requested.

Akwese thinks he has the easiest cleaning job in Edgware Road. He says there are four kinds of cleaners working on the branch line. The easiest is being a train picker. That is his line of work. You have a little rubbish sack and with one other picker you jump on every passing train when they stop at Edgware Road. You have three minutes to pick it clean: out with the *Evening Standards* and the *Metros*, out with the sandwich boxes, the Coke cans and the Twix wrappers.

'Sometimes we pick knickers . . . We go in and we pick them. Three seats away there is a used condom. We know they are doing it on the Tube only minutes before. But we do not understand how they can have the time to finish so quickly.'

Code Three on the train and the picker has no choice but to run to the driver and tell him to hold the train for a few more minutes. The pickers at Edgware Road used to get a special voucher for mopping up a vomit. But this was over now, because the Nigerian boys working King's Cross were busted, in hock with the train drivers. They were upping claims there were more vomits than there really were to land themselves even more sandwich tokens.

'But we clean a lot of vomits. Lots of strange vomits.'

He pauses.

'And lots of blood vomits.'

The platform pickers have a tougher time. They have none of that bounce on, bounce off. But they have to deal with more piss. There are lots of guys who just whip it out in the tunnel. This enrages them. They will see men doing it on the wall and want to beat them with the picking sticks: but according to regulations the only thing they can do is call the station master. And by that time the pisser has always hopped on and gone.

'They are white guys mostly.

'They smile at us when they are pissing.'

The platform pickers have to deal with the criers. They come up three or four times a week in the busiest stations like Edgware Road. They are almost always women. The station pickers will be humming, something sweet from back home, picking up wrappers and the papers, when they hear suddenly: blubbing, moaning, echoing down the tunnels.

'They are ladies mostly . . .

'They sometimes go, "Go away we are OK." But usually they come with us to the staffroom and finish up their cry there. They are usually crying womens. We think they have been let go . . . We sometimes see the ladies looking at the rails, crying . . . And we go, "Come with us and finish up your cry in our room. You are beautiful lady. No need to cry." But they are not only ladies . . . Sometimes the mens cry too.'

The boys who have it really tough are the accommodation cleaners. They are cleaning the stations. This is tough. Because usually when somebody wants to Code Three he does it carefully before entering the system. They are the ones who wince coming into work. Nobody knows why, but every day somebody left his mess on the floor of the public toilets at Paddington station. Always in the men's.

The boys in accommodation would watch the girls coming in off the streets every summer. They would see their hair waving on the warm gusts, which sometimes blow out of the lift shafts, or the tunnels, and pine for them. The most beautiful ladies in London, the pickers knew, are the mixed. That frizzy hair and the thinness and the golden-brown skin. They would turn away and think, How beautiful London is becoming. That one day we will all be beautiful like Brazil.

'But the boys are sometimes shocked . . . There are men, sometimes, holding hands and kissing . . . with their fingers even going down to the waist. We never saw this in Africa. We know this thing existed. But seeing it always in the tunnels in the last minutes of the late shift . . . this makes us very shocked.

'But the worst job, that is depot.

'I have a friend, he works depot . . . The boys there they have to scrub it down clean. They have to make it shine. We are only picking. But they have to do the deep clean. My friend, he told that depot it's the worst, because when somebody jumps they have to pick bits of the body and the bloods off the train.'

The pickers all know it happens. The pickers all know when it happens – it happens quickly. There was a Ghanaian at Earl's Court

who was picking up some *Metros* one morning shift when he started having casual conversation with a man in a green jumper. This was a nice surprise.

'He was a white guy . . . He was saying, "Yeah it's so hard to make money in this country . . ." He was saying, "Yeah it's tough you know even when you make money in this country . . . you gotta pay it back in debt and everything . . ." And the next thing . . .

'The man, he jumped . . .'

The pickers all have their stories. The girl with the blue dress who jumped and made no sound at all. The old man in glasses who fainted and was fried on the track in front of the Ghanaian picker who works lates at Oxford Street. There are some uneducated pickers, who said they saw them waiting on the platform, when the station was locked up and closed, waiting for the train that killed them to come back in the morning.

There were 643 suicide attempts on the Underground between 2000 and 2010. And the pickers have seen a good many of them. This happened to Akwese, too. He knew it had happened when he heard the train toot over the sound of the bones snapping on the rails. Akwese ran to the platform. The white women were screaming, the black women were screaming, and the driver, a white guy, he was standing there on the platform, red, and blubbing.

'That day I was working with the Bulgarian picker, and they went to us, "Go and get some water for the teams who have come to take away her body." And that was when I saw her . . . I came to the platform, and the body was there, under a plastic sheet . . . and then the wind blew, and I saw it . . . There were huge tears in the body and you could see the bone. She was a Portuguese . . . she looked like a mixed race.'

Akwese shuffles, wrapping his thumb in his fist.

'Afterwards they took the body to the staff room and left it there . . . and I was talking to the station cleaner. She was an old Ghanaian, and she told me, ten years ago or something, it happened before like this. And the next day, there was a woman, the same woman she said, standing by the staff room, with this funny smell. All the day she was standing there . . . until the pickers came to her and she ran, and nobody saw where she went, or on which platform . . .'

Every station has its stories.

Akwese knows there are two Ghanaians working at Paddington. When there is a Code Three, he will often not have enough time to jump off the train before finishing, as the doors lock him through to the next station, where he will cross them boys and make some casual conversation.

The two pickers are Big Yaw and Baby Yaw.

Big Yaw is very uneducated. He can barely even read. He hates everything about London. Nobody knows why, but he has ended up marrying a frumpy Jamaican mama in White City, and never gone back to finish the house he claims to have been building all these years in Accra, thanks to all this picking. Those are his savings, which he's barely seen. But to anyone who will give him two minutes he will show the same grainy phone clip of the concrete walls of the unfinished Ghanaian dream home.

'London. It's a mistake. I'm stuck picking down here . . . till I die.'

Big Yaw and Baby Yaw spend all day finding things they could never afford. They will be picking a tunnel and then: a new iPad. They will be picking a train and then out of nowhere: a wide-angle lens camera. They will be picking the lift, then suddenly: a Louis Vuitton bag filled with neatly folded clothes.

Big Yaw and Baby Yaw hear the stories. They know there was a Ghanaian at Bayswater who found a bag with crunchy white powder, £75,000 in cash and a French pistol inside it. They know there was one picker from Cameroon who returned two Chinese ladies their purses and they invited him out for dinner at Claridge's.

But they know, better than anyone else, everything in the Underground flickers on CCTV. This is why they are always too scared to touch whatever they find, beyond quickly handing it over to the station master.

They see weird things down there. There was the time Baby Yaw saw a woman with two heads getting off the Bakerloo Line. He was horrified. He couldn't look. Everyone around him was screaming and running. But Big Yaw, he had seen darker things.

Big Yaw has the respect of the community, because he lived through the bomb blasts that ripped through the station. Big Yaw had been sitting in that claustrophobic white-tiled staff room, listening to the old boys talk about their half-finished gazebos back home, when he felt shaking and heard the shrieks and screams.

'The English . . . They call it the 7/7.

'I heard the shaking and I thought, "It's gonna be injuries." So I ran downstairs. There was black and smoke and glass all broked, and everybody crying and screaming . . . My uniform . . . It was covered in black and bloods and everything.

'The body of the bomber was there . . . He looked like Asian.

'He was wearing shorts. When we knew it was him . . . We just threw him. I went in to carry the ladies. I saw I think . . . Maybe four bodies. But they did not scare me. When I saw the black people bodies in Africa . . . They scared me. But dead white people. They did not scare me. Why . . . ?

'I dunno why.'

Big Yaw wants to show no emotion and he manages. He only glares at me as I ask him these questions he finds strange and irrelevant, in the white-tiled cramp of the staffroom, which now and always smells of nose-stinging cleaning fluids. The trains are rumbling, somewhere. But Baby Yaw has had enough. He shakes his fine bracelets and tries to laugh it off. Five years of Big Yaw is more than enough. He is the RMT Union rep here and keeps trying to get Big Yaw to part with a few pounds of his money.

'But he's too uneducated to understand the concept of a subscription.'

Baby Yaw is almost half his age: a fresh thing of twenty-six. He has a Microsoft computing certificate and managed to fix his overstay into a permanent leave to remain just before the Home Office slammed that loophole shut. He is good-looking, Baby Yaw. But I can tell in those eyes, he is tired.

'Y'know what, man?

'These old guys they are down here picking . . . and for them that's it. They are picking until the end. But me the only way I can go is up. I began at the bottom picking the rubbish. I can only break out into the streets and see the sun . . . Maybe even I can get as far as the Customer Service . . . one day. I know a lot about the Underground.'

Baby Yaw is a clever picker. He hangs around by the framed station maps, hoping to see the tourist girls getting confused by the coloured squiggles, before leaving his picker a few metres back, and strutting up. Beaming, Baby Yaw comes up and explains that the Circle Line had once been a circle and that the best clubs are in Piccadilly Circus.

'Sometimes I even got a few numbers, bruva.'

For the pickers the worst day is always Wednesday. That is the day the *Evening Standard* publishes its property supplement. There are whole Tube Lines of prices and colours and splashes of smiling blondes caressing silvery fridges. Big Yaw shoves the thousands of supplements into his bag snarling. Big Yaw refuses to look at them ever again: that is because someone had told him he would have to be picking down here for forty years to buy his muffy flat in crappy White City estate.

Baby Yaw always takes a peek. He thinks differently. Baby Yaw looks into the *Evening Standard* and sees, between the adverts and the pictures, hints of what he and his children might become.

HAMMERSMITH AND CITY

Big Yaw rides home on the pink line curling west into White City.

I write down what he sees. These are the modernized carriages, the big ones, where a hundred thousand humans have not worn in the seats. These are gleaming plastic spaces: fitted with bright, electric-yellow hand poles, the ones I see gripped tightly by the muttering old white woman, her hair a purple wash, in a fluffy green coat with an emerald brooch, her face pinched in irritation. This same hand pole leant on by the limp, weakly muscled Indian teen boy in a black blazer, his blue sports bag at his feet. His eyelids are closed and his mouth curls into sadness. I watch the old picker ignore these people. The litterers do not interest him. Big Yaw gazes blankly. He doesn't read the newspaper. He doesn't listen to music. He stares out the window. I stalk him with my notebook.

Any day he finishes morning shift, he hands over at three, swipes himself into the system, enters the tremoring carriage, and stares out the windows. After Paddington the tracks roar above ground. I watch his veined eyes stare out; he barely registers the white lacy backs of flamboyant villas, with their endless pointless chimneys, lined up in military symmetry, over the tracks from huge, tagged-up raw-concrete walls, where the train rumbles under the ramparts of the Westway, a huge pillared flyover, thundering with its chromium traffic. He stares blankly; the whooshing line passes can-littered thickets, ferns and myrtle shoots, growing under the barbed wire lining the rails.

I watch his blank stare until the train is running level with the Westway, rushing in moments over the frilly stucco market street at Portobello Road, then flashes into a Legoland of grey brick estates,

towers shaped like cheese graters and switchboards, each balcony topped with black satellites, for Arabsat, SAT-7, or NC+ Poland. He stares every day into this fifteen-minute landscape, through five Tube stops, over which the life expectancy of an average Londoner falls by eleven years.

The picker stares at the jumble of iron-roofed storage yards, into corrugated warehouses and huge pickup depots, hiding behind the silvery cladding of the enormous Westfield mall, nestling like a spaceship between the expressways, then out into a disused multi-storey car park, the concrete skeleton of a dead space, before the line skirts the huge white dirty satellites of the British state, pointing up from the now empty BBC Television Centre. The doors preep and shudder. And this is where Big Yaw huffs and shoulders up his rucksack and hops through the carriage doors to trudge home into the White City estate.

I watch him round the Day-Glo workmen, like him, ripping out miles of old carpeting from inside the BBC. This serious beige building – they once called it the factory for television – has been sold to make way for penthouses. He ignores them. Big Yaw turns the corner on South Africa Road and enters White City. The precise geometry creates a force field of silence and intimidation. There are no shops and no pubs. There are only reddish blocks rounded with narrow balconies built for the poor in the 1930s with all the affection of a stiff kiss. These surly matrons are cramped and to the point – shorn of all Victorian fantasia and ornamentation. The bare brickwork emphasizes the point: these are charity blockhouses, with a 40 per cent child-poverty rate.

I follow Big Yaw down Commonwealth Avenue until he reaches his block near the sleazy red front of an old boozer. The General Smuts is now a mosque. The old pub sign now reads: Egyptian House. Draped and creased plastic hoardings call out for Arabic lessons and the Koran, over furled-up blue blinds, where the cracked plastic lettering still reads SMUTS BAR. This was a football hooligans' hangout regularly outed by online threads as the roughest pub in London.

Today knife fights have gone. But non-believers are not made welcome where the beer garden now serves shisha. Paranoia lurks on the estate: the Muslims are taking over. The white British are leaving: their share of residents fell 35 per cent between 2001 and 2011. Along from the dead pub an unmarked beauty salon, behind frosted-glass windows, says: WOMEN ONLY.

A week later I take the same train as Big Yaw: 3 pm.

The carriage jolts then whirs, drowning out everything but shouts and the recorded female voice calling out the stations' names. I let my eyes fall on the man opposite me. He is looking for something. He is black with a huge spoon-shaped face and the grey whiffs of an ageing beard. Fumbling a bit with some papers, he takes out a little prayer book. Between the thuds and the roars he begins to sing – half under his breath – the lilting of the Koran.

The clattering dims, the tunnel is gone. I look around me. But the faces of those beside me hardly change as the station gives way into the amber light of the afternoon. Everyone is either phone staring or unfocused, elsewhere. Because there is something intensely private about the Tube. Everyone surrounded, but alone, cramped, fixed in spot, but loose, in thought, between things: these are the faces of people worrying and dreaming.

I count the stations: eight to go. The jolts now sound with a low rocking thud. A black man in buttoned-up crinkly grey shirt and a blue raincoat sits with his hands locked over his grey rucksack on his lap, his eyes closed, with his face pulled into an expression, mixing exhaustion, enforcement and release, that I cannot figure out. A Filipina with heavy eyeliner, her black glossy hair pulled back very tightly, cradles a brown leather handbag with fake bronze straps, and pulls a squinting look of confusion into a pink-cased iPhone.

There is a spotty white boy, with a thick fringe of caramel hair, his skin in places translucent, in blue corduroys and a two-button-open lumberjack shirt, listening to the tiny, preening, near-black-skinned Asian girl, with pouty cheeks, red tights and liquorice wellingtons talk about meteorites. He seems in love. Three seats along, an Eastern European girl in grey leggings and a black-and-white-striped Puma hoodie rubs her eyes and sighs, craning her neck to the window, then breathes, peering out.

I count the stations: seven to go. A fine-featured Spanish man with pinched, worried eyes is eating pistachios. Two Somali girls in matching purple hijabs are hurriedly removing make-up after school: lipstick, gloss, eyeliner, mouths slightly open in inspection as they pass their clutch mirror back and forth. A slender Chinese man is reading from a flimsy pamphlet, given to him by the Jehovah's Witnesses. Through the clunking doors at the station I can hear him muttering the names of strange countries: 'Mad-a-gascar. Afghan-i-stan. Hun-gar-y.'

And next to him, but at an unbridgeable distance, sits a Vietnamese woman, in an undone black puffa jacket, with a simple blue shirt underneath, both ears riddled with little goldish bands, who squints with devoted seriousness at a printout Word document, which to her satisfaction she meticulously highlights green.

I get off at Shepherd's Bush Market. This is where the gang leader has promised to meet. The old train bridge gives on to the Uxbridge Road, its long stretches of gammy clay brick parades know their place, winking and dealing, with Jamaican patty shops, corporate pawnbrokers and Afghan pound stores. We are two terraces off White City estate.

This is where two BBC comedians used to linger in the caffs and eavesdrop on the cockney rag-and-bone men gobbling their fry-ups. They found them so funny they inspired *Steptoe and Son*, a comedy of two Shepherd's Bush junk-peddlers stuck together in their scrapyard, as the inner cities are going to pieces, squabbling, and stringing each other along, unable to escape poverty, or each other. This Shepherd's Bush is now gone. The last pie-and-mash shop is condemned. The dingy Irish pubs that used to get tagged up – *Support The Real IRA* – have closed. The greasy spoons have turned into Lebanese and Syrian bakeries. The wreckers' yards have locked up.

The Steptoes and Sons today are the Arabs and Afghans in the pound shops. For a moment I watch them: the squabbling kebab men and the second-rate spivs peddling fake resinous Qatari perfumes, rushing in and out of the market, in puffas and keffiyeh, to escape it for moment or two in the wail of the dingy basement mosque. And then my eyes linger over the road, next to the betting shop, on the Polish builders always hanging around the dishevelled Bartek delicatessen, touting for cheap tools, eyeballing the black girls, with figures they can only dream of. These guys call the Uxbridge Road the street of the Muslims.

I wait under the train bridge as an Eritrean beggar, his face sucked of colour, pleads in Arabic, and watch the Ghanaian Jehovah's Witness hand out her pamphlets in Amharic as the Somali mummies float past, in black fabric swirls from head to toe, drifting in and out in friendship crews from the I Love Hijab shop, cooing into their prams, at their shrieking happy babies, in the mellow sun.

They trundle on to the playground swings on Shepherd's Bush common, where heavy traffic spins round a dystopian mockery of an English country green. Flanked on one side by a bad-breath Edwardian parade of craggy roofs and sooty gothic lintels, where over the grass and the gigantic plane trees – the place country shepherds once rested their flocks the night before the London slaughter – four enormous council estates sulk like milk cartons, with some of the poorest 10 per cent of kids in England, built over an asylum for Jewish prostitutes and the old rag-and-bone yards. Three minutes further on, over the hurtling roundabout, revelling in their stucco lingerie, are the vamped-up mansions of Holland Park Avenue, running all the way to Notting Hill.

'Welcome to the Bush favelas.'

The gang leader does not like this name. He thinks gangs are for little boys. He likes to call the operation his business, and himself a boss. He is Caribbean but looks pure African, flabby more than muscled, with a fold of skin at the back of his melon head. He is short. The first thing I notice is his lips: they are chapped, peeling, burnt black, from non-stop skunk smoking, and his skin is coarse and dry. I already know his street name: Moses X.

'Bush ain't one place. Y'get me?'

I know this. I grew up here too. But we grew up in different worlds – black, white; middle class, underclass. I grew up always knowing but never feeling the gang battles going on around. Apart

from once. The boy who lived next door to me was Jamaican. We would play football, sometimes. But when we were around eleven his mother sent him away to live with his sister in Hackney. Somali gangs were beating up young Caribbeans outside the Tube station. They were knifing them. And she thought they were going to come after him.

'London's raw like dat, man.'

The gang leader speaks Street: the accent the authorities call Multicultural London English. This is the new cockney. That old accent is set to vanish from London in fifteen years. Anyone young now speaks Street: a flattened tone, that no longer drops the [h], inflects a little like Jamaican, with hints of Urdu, which crushes the grammar round the edges, the way a second language speaker might – until *them* becomes *dem*, and *this* becomes *dis*.

The gang leader hates tracksuits. Moses thinks these are for little hood rats. He wears the mature style: an unzipped blue hoodie, blue denim jeans, and a low-cut white T-shirt opening onto his chest tattoo. He walks slowly, like a foreman round a site, and every few minutes throws a glance to the sideman he has brought along for reassurance. We enter Shepherd's Bush Market.

There is only one white British fruit-and-veg seller left, along this meandering stretch of wistful railway arches, under which runs a hubbub of scruffy, cheeky, street stalls. 'Boss' has almost replaced 'mate' as the universal Street greeting here. But the new Steptoes and Sons are still failing. I have asked them one by one. The Sudanese falafel man is struggling. The Jamaican CD stand is pinching it. The Afghan bric-a-brac is not doing so well. Sections have closed already: and where the Sikh clothes racks and the Pakistani crockery shacks were the speculators are drilling the foundations of more bankers' flats.

Moses squints at the hoodie coming towards us.

'Y'see man, we all see the streets differently. You'll be here and you are seeing white guys crossing for a shortcut. Maybe some light-skinned girls you fancy. But basically you see out of this mess people like you. Me, I'm seeing that fucker in the corner . . . ravaged by the road, smoking bare crack for months, hanging there for his shot

. . . I'm seeing that spindly fucker, the one in the Nike High Tops there . . . who I know delivers . . . pacing this way to meet some fucker who's gonna pick up.'

Sideman laughs on cue. He's a giggly guy, a caramel-skinned Jamaican, a beautiful man, with round big eyes that light and sour as he speaks, with a centimetre of tattoo under each of them: a teardrop under one, and the map of Africa on the other. His voice careers up and down in an affected black American accent that you often hear in Shepherd's Bush. He dresses old Yardie style: and that requires a denim jacket. Quickly after meeting he cracks his first gambit – about being arrested on this corner for rushing to back up his brother with a small Samurai sword. But he quickly shuts up. Sideman may be taller but is inferior. His job here is flattery and support. And that means fawning to the boss at every moment.

'Gotta keep the man alive . . .'

Juddering power drills pucker concrete under Shepherd's Bush Market. The work has begun: whole sections have been warded off. Stalls are being packed up. Spaces are being cleared. This yearning curve under the rhythmic beat of the Hammersmith and City Line is now being socially sanitized. The plan is simple: the new owner wants coffee, boutiques and cheese for the French bankers in Holland Park. Hiked rents will drive out the pots, yams and plantains for White City.

Both are only fifteen minutes' walk.

Moses talks sociology as we walk further along under the arches. 'They want dem poor blacks and Muslim riff-raff out.'

I try and get the market into my notebook: the sullen Afghan man in see-through plastic glasses and a red hoodie slumped over his market stall of fake watches and trinket jewellery, with creepy plastic heads exhibiting his hijabs. The white-bearded Sikh standing under the arch of the train bridge impatient over an array of teapots printed with the faces of Princess Diana and the Queen, behind two stacks of gaudy prints of a superstar Jesus and flash-font Koran calligraphy. The stall piled high with rolls of blue foam and bubble wrap, and the squabbling father and son under the dripping halal meats hanging taut in the butcher's.

'This is London bruv, they kick niggas out if you can't keep up.'

The Sideman laughs on cue, eyes down, clapping slightly.

I listen as Moses holds court. He talks with abandon, he falls for every flattery, letting himself tumble into my recorder, his voice full of release.

We sit in the strip-lit backroom of an odorous Somali caff concealed behind the stalls flogging hundreds of tracksuits and hijabs hanging from their poles. This is one of his command centres. He eats with his fingers. His hands pick into the stringy white flesh of this fish. The Sideman has been joined by a younger. He is seventeen, tops. Face crunched under a blue waterproof hood. He sits waiting for his orders for the afternoon. I look at this fresh-faced little boy in the hood, whose eyes shoot straight to the floor. He looks like yet another black Oliver Twist.

'The thing about dis work is good help is so hard to find.'

Moses is unable to keep off his throwaway phone for long. Calls are incoming every twenty minutes. There is a bruva in the lock who wants money transferred into an account. There is a carrier he shrieks at when she dials in, blubbing she has gone down in Ashford. And one after another, each stuttering, almost panting, call the impeccably elocuted public school boys – almost begging.

He puts them on loudspeaker.

'Listen to him, fam . . . listen to that voice . . .'

His crew cracks up at the accent. Sideman sparks up some skunk. Moses keeps on sniffing and touching his nose. The more he talks the more he gets lost into tangents and the more his rants edge into megalomania before he finds himself totally lost, and asks me what the question is again. There is a trembling vulnerability behind this that Sideman keeps butting in to lick and caress. The trains rumble on, minute by minute, outside. As we talk the market shutters are already clattering shut.

But Moses doesn't give a fucking shit.

WHITE CITY

Lucifer taught him how to stab people.

You never whip it out from the hilt. That way you're gonna sever some major artery or something and boom you'll be in prison. You gotta grip it by the blade. And then boom – punch him in the face – get a fingergrip round that neck and bam-bam-bam, thwack it like this, right in his back shoulder. That way it's more like a punch – a humiliation – and he'll freak at the first trickle and pussy the fuck out.

Moses had been rolling with Lucifer for around six weeks when they burgled their first money house in Holland Park. It was a right beautiful money house. The walls were white. The front was stucco. And as Moses creaked open sash windows the night-time living room glinted with silver and screens. That was rule number one: second-floor windows are never alarmed. Lucifer was precious about rule number two: grab that jewellery box first. Always. If you're lucky they'll be some antique diamonds or something to sell to the Indians. And rule number three was make for the car keys: because if it's a money car with some electric bleeping your getaway vehicle is sitting pretty.

'Mum, I'm smoking.'

Moses never forgot his first day in London. Everything was big. Everywhere he was looking at big things. A train. I've never been on one of those. A bus. A big red bus. I've never seen anything like that. Everything was like Gun Battle shanty back in Grenada. But bigger. With none of that wooden shit or chicken wire holding everything together. But none of this fazed Moses age twelve. Only that vapour. The moment he stepped off the plane: haaaah – what the fuck was that coming out of my mouth – unbelievable.

Please pass along→
the platform

SHEPHERD'S BUSH

'Mum, look, I'm smoking . . . Look, I'm smoking.'

Moses knew his mum was a strong woman. But she was scared as shit those first weeks in White City estate. There were only a few things she knew about London. She knew the place was crawling with paedophiles. Everyone back in Gun Battle knew this about the English. There was so many paedophiles in London they were arresting them every other week. Everyone in England could be a paedophile: the comedians, the policemen, the headmasters, even the preachers. All through that first year – it was the year 2000 – she was chattering scared for Moses.

'You know what's funny, bruv? The white people are always thinking, "Yeah, those immigrants, dem frightening niggas bringing in dat crime." But the immigrants, they are the ones who are scared shitless . . . "Fuck, I'm in London, he might rob me, is he gonna rob me, why is he looking at me?" Everyone back in Grenada knows it's live here . . . Especially for niggas.'

Moses was not even allowed out at first.

'Mum was so frightened of paedophiles she wouldn't let us play outside. She was locking us indoors, begging me to watch the younger brother . . . But what she definitely wasn't frightened of was gangs. And we had pitched up for a better life right in the middle of a war zone . . .'

Moses worked this out as soon as she opened the door.

'Let me tell you what White City estate was like back then . . . Irish lot over there, new Somalian lot over here, Jamaican drug dealers over there, English pub-heads over here, crack-heads over there. Everywhere guns . . . And every day we had a new stolen car . . .

'But you know what the funny shit was? Here we were in the White City favelas. Little niggas in the ghetto . . . and we had all the new shit, all the Gameboy Advances, all the PlayStations. Coz dem crack-heads would be breaking in everywhere . . . and bringing it back to the block and selling it for dirt cheap.'

London was like someone had turned off the lights. Everything in White City was grey: the clouds, the concrete, the motorway, the estates.

'You didn't even need to tell me, I knew . . . That growing up here was rank. When I arrived at twelve years old, that smacked me right in the fucking face. I knew dat White City estate was way more corrupt . . . way more dangerous, more full of disillusion than anywhere in fucking Grenada . . . I swear within six months of being here I had lost 75 per cent of my morals. And I was ready to jack kids . . . and send anyone to sleep with dis fist.'

The first thing you steal is always bikes. You would be hanging out playing football and skipping class with the kids from your block. And the older brothers would always be there. Hanging around. Rolling. Looking fresh. And they would always pass money to the youngers. They would toss the little bikers ten quid to keep a lookout for police. And they would start giving them little lessons: always keep your hood up for the cameras – and pull that string tight around your neck.

Moses hugged the block. That's what everyone does when you got no dad and your mum is working night shifts scrubbing the toilets in BBC Television Centre – the other place they call White City. So, you get tight with the boys on the block. First it's only football. Then it's everyone jumping on their bikes to beef some estate that dared beat up some bruva for his fiver. You gotta keep up the respect. Otherwise those fuckers will be here spliffing on your lawn.

'You never even notice it when it begins . . . You'll be rolling, little posses of five, ten after class . . . and bam . . . Did someone just grab that phone? Bare jokes. You'll be chilling and some bruvas will roll up with new bikes. Nice innit? Wanna come grab some for you and your bro?'

You get tight with the boys on the block. You know everyone: before you're thirteen you know who smokes and who shots. You know that those old Rasta stubble heads who slaved on the Hammersmith and City Line their whole lives ain't got no pennies to rub together; and you know that bleach-teeth gangsta in Becklow Gardens got so much money he's paying fifty quid a head to little bikers to deliver his shit to white boys down Fulham way.

'But you also get to know the borders. Black boys can see the borders in London. This area is Bush territory . . . Don't cross here,

that's Grove boys. Right up to the McDonald's, that's ours . . . Over there, that's Grove territory . . . and they'll smack you coz one of our boys got beef.

'You know the borders before you know how to roll . . . Don't cross over to that estate because that lot will fuck you up . . . We got beef . . . Don't cross into that estate, they've got beef with our block. But you can go there coz dis one's brother chats to that one's brother . . .'

There are some things everyone knows. That sugarmen are like footballers. They don't last long. Thirty, forty – and you're burnt out. Everyone knows it only looks like the easy way when you're bloody seventeen. But everyone in White City also knows the only people who make as much as sugarmen in London are the bankers.

'It's about who you are . . . Are you some sucker who's gonna do three GCSEs and go join dem other niggas in Tesco bleeping that shit and get replaced in six months by a machine? Are you gonna be like your sad old pops slaving away on the Central Line and who can't afford two fucking pairs of trainers? Or are you someone who's gonna take that risk? Are you gonna shot white? Because unless you magically become a lawyer . . . gang-banging is your only go on the big-money roulette.'

It's all about personality, really. The older guys are always keeping a lookout on the kids. Who's not focusing at school? Who's looking for excitement? Who wants thirty quid to take some bags to Camberwell Green? The older guys know the kids. They've got extensive information on them. And they know how to reel them in.

'That's how I met Lucifer. That old smoke was a right bastard . . . some fat piece of shit . . . And I'm sixteen, I'm hungry, I'm in London . . . and I want London . . . I want to look fresh, I want to dizzle dem bitches, I want fine wines in Kensington Roof Gardens . . . not hanging out with a Pepsi down KFC.'

Moses was watching TV. They loved period dramas in London. They loved people dressing up and living like it was the old days. And Moses would be thinking, Shit. That's how I was living four years ago. He would blink: and remember Gun Battle. His grandfather's shack. Even them oil lamps they had when he was really small. Back when the only TV was the one up in the corner in the local wooden store.

'Back in Grenada, we was living 1,000 per cent in the same ways as when they freed the slaves . . . The same shacks, the same everything. Let me tell you it was the slum of the slums . . . I saw people get knifed before I could even walk, get their guts cut out and everything. But I always, always had work ethic . . . Come seven years old I was working . . . picking up nutmeg on this plantation kind of thing. And now I'm in London. And I've got a choice: do I make bare money fast . . . or go to college?'

Lucifer was cool at first. Hey, bruva, have a toke. Hey, bruva, let me tell you a secret: that shithead you think is your friend – he's not your friend. That guy got a plot to jack you. That's my information. I got my sources.

Moses would roll with Lucifer up and down the Uxbridge Road. You see that Somali cafe? That place ain't real. You see that launderette? That's not real. Think that place made a profit since 1997? You're having a laugh. Just look at that place. Bruv: they're all fronts. Now you see those Pakistanis, all proud and everything?

'Look bruv. Get real . . . Everyone knows how it rolls round here. Those Somalis . . . They're not broke. They're rolling in it . . . rolling in white. Those Pakistanis and Indian bruvas . . . Think they made all that money from corner shops and halal chicken? Course they didn't. Those shitheads flew in from India with suitcases of heroin . . . bought one house, bought another house, then they bought the whole fucking parade. And now their children are pharmacists and going to uni or whatever . . . Chatting fucking bare shit about their work ethic. You having a laugh?'

Lucifer seemed wise. Lucifer seemed hard. Because those were live days round Shepherd's Bush. Ninja was running his crew up. Brutus Maximus was about to go down. Prince was about to pull out. This was when Lucifer passed Moses his first eight ball of coke. Take this, my man. Take this and shot it to your mates. And pay me back on a nice rate. It's good shit.

'I fucked up . . . Of course I fucked up. Anyone sixteen was gonna blow that whole grand on clothes and bitches . . . And I came back to Lucifer with nothing. I was terrified. I thought he was gonna bust my balls. But that fat fucker knew what he was doing . . . That was his plan. "No worries," he said . . . "fuck dat money. We'll make it back together . . . Now just roll with me for a while bruv . . . and I'll take you down the road, and show you certain things."'

Before you've committed a few crimes you have no idea how easy they are. You don't know that if you punch someone and swoop for his phone the chance of them catching you is next to nothing. You don't know until you roll around the hood selling little pouches of white that everyone seems to be sniffing. You don't know till you hand over £50 to a policeman that these guys are as hungry as the rest of us.

'That time . . . everyone was trying to make it . . . and I'm not trying to be funny but everyone seemed to be doing worse stuff than me. Some right nasty shit innit . . . like robbing old ladies, breaking into old people's homes, it's jokes, there are bare jewellery boxes in there . . . Y'know, breaking in whilst people was sleeping . . . calling for a car . . . and making off with the TV. Raw kinda shit.

'I swore to myself . . . I'm gonna do this for one year . . . I'm gonna roll with Lucifer and get money. Biggest mistake I ever made . . . Turned me into a demon. Because I was rolling with a lowdown motherfucker . . . heartless monster. I tell ya . . . He's the kinda bruva who'd sell your little sister's pussy for a tenner.'

Moses knew the real gangstas aren't on the streets, of course. The real gangstas never look like they do in the rap videos. They keep as low profile as they can, or they've already gone legit, creating them property empires out of thin air. The police estimate there are around two thousand of them in London. And these guys are not hanging around looking for kids.

'But at that time I didn't realize that . . . I was psyched . . . I was rolling with someone I thought was hard. I was making a thousand pounds a night in money houses. I was making like five hundred a week on dem phones. I was getting a name, becoming a bad bwoy . . . and you know what? Bitches they always get wet for violence . . .'

Lucifer was a good teacher. There was bare rich territory next to White City. You only have to cross the motorway – the one always droning – and bam there was Holland Park. Those were them money houses: those big white pimp villas.

Those fuckers were always on holiday. There was nothing easier than scoping those sleeping beauties out on Christmas Eve: the streets were iced, the Range Rovers were in the country, and the only sounds were the click-click of those useless alarms. Lucifer had a good eye. He always had a knack for knowing when someone was away for a long weekend. Lucifer could read that stucco cold.

'Fill up that bastard.'

Moses would climb over the alarm onto the ledge. This was always easy. These fools loved covering their houses in columns and creepers. But climbing was why the prime professional rule was always do this sober: when money-housing, adrenaline is the only white you need. These idiots also loved them vintage Victorian windows: it was as if they wanted him to get in. And then with a dash he'd rush to the hallway and flick open the door: and Lucifer would be smiling in the orange-dark. Holding out that sack.

'Let's fill up this bad bwoy.'

There was much to learn. Lucifer would spark up and explain: always watch out for them crack-heads. They may look fucked and gaga, but they are dangerous. Dangerous for everyone. They'll be there, all skinny boned, begging with their crazy little stories, those bits of froth around dem lips, and all it will take is the police to roll up, lower that window and bark – 'Mate, we'll give you a pinkie if you tell us who gives you your shit.' And that crack-head will start shaking side to side, going, 'I ain't no snitch, I ain't no snitch,' but the moment the window goes up and the car begins to vroom, the crack-head always comes running. 'I'm not a snitch but there's this guy . . .'

Lucifer would exhale and explain: that's why you never shot to crack-heads. No matter how easy it looks. Because that guy, that poor fucker they fed to the feds for fifty quid, he won't be some main man, some pimping Turkish import–export, but a little guy, just like you, shotting on street level. And never forget the crack-heads: they

don't care about respect. And they are too far gone to understand logic. They ain't scared of busting you and getting the whole block after them. That fucker's sleeping on a cardboard box. He ain't scared of nothing.

'Bruva, dis became clear to me pretty quickly. There are two kinds fellas you meet on the road. There are the money-motivated guys. That's the bruva who thinks to himself, "I've got to get my face off the street. I've gotta go discreet. I've got to take no part in any of this batshit teenager beef between blocks, punching W6 for W12 . . ." Because those quiet guys are always . . . the guys aiming high.

'And then there are the fuckers feeding a habit. Those fools . . . They might even stab you in a frenzy, coz it's a physical addiction, y'know . . . Coz in that crazy moment they've got to have it . . . Those fools rush into corner shops and take out a blade for a can of Coke. But you know the irony? Those fuckers shotting something to buy some more, fuck they can last time, coz they never get beyond da petty crime . . . And those fuckers sometimes last longer than the rest of us.'

Lucifer was a good teacher. But he was not the right man to educate Moses about how much shit to consume. The money-motivated should never snort more than three times a week. The money-motivated need to be clean like nurses. But Moses was getting involved. Three, maybe four days a week, he'd wake up still fizzing from the night before.

Moses was seventeen. He kept on forgetting where he'd left his wallet, or his knife. He was losing weight. Five, maybe six days a week he'd wake up craving, and keep on trying to suppress it with skunk, sparking up and sparking up, until he became paranoid, and sometimes even cried. He was getting the shakes, spending faster and faster, always needing more.

'The first time I stabbed someone . . . It was only coz a guy wouldn't give over his shit . . . I went, "Give me your phone," and I saw him looking at me . . . his eyes narrowing. He was trying to bluff me, he was trying to gauge whether or not he could have me. Only coz that fucker was a bit broader, a bit taller than me . . .

'And I thought, "Shit this could turn into a fight . . . and that would make me tired." Y'know when you've got the tired antelope . . . And I thought if I get tired . . . I'll be sweating, I'll be wet. And I've got so much on me . . . that the police will catch me in seconds. They'll smell me. So I thought, "What the fuck have I got this on me for . . ." and wa-ch-iing I gave him my blade.'

They always ask a gangsta the same questions. Bruva, do you have a gun. And the bad boys are always quick to say yes. What they don't brag to their crew is that for business gangsters, metal is only show. You want people to know you have it. You never want to use it. Maximum amount must see it: minimum must ever hear it. And then they ask – Bruva, have you ever been popped? And Moses would tell those fuckers a statistic: a gun is fired in London on average every six hours.

'The first time I ran for my life it was in South, one a dem money safe houses, where gangstas keep dat paper . . . We was getting greedy, or maybe desperate. And I remember our foolery like crisp. Like in a fucking movie or something . . . bam . . . Run, get the fuck out . . . bam . . . Start the car, start the fucking car . . . bam . . . You know what's running through your mind at these moments? Not your fucking life . . . Nothing but . . . start the car, why the fuck won't the car start . . . bam . . . Hit the accelerator.'

Lucifer was fucking up. They had been rolling now for a year and Moses could see it in his face: he was shaving less regularly, was sweating more, his pupils seemed to be growing. They would be bopping down Uxbridge Road when suddenly he'd switch and lose his temper. Lucifer needed more. That's why he was ready to big up the risks. Fuck breaking into sleeping terraces for plasma TVs. They were going to raid.

Lucifer knew where the cash was. He knew cocaine was booming. White was going crazy in London. Everyone was doing it now: the investors were sniffing, the solicitors were sniffing, the students were sniffing, fuck, even the builders were sniffing now. Lucifer knew some gangsta was setting up every week and raking it in. And he was ready to pay cash for the address of every single Fresh Prince.

Moses woke up shaking after the first raid. This was stupid. Raiding money safe houses was insane. This was gonna get him popped in the head. Moses knew what was going on. Scientists had tested the water, and found this city had the highest concentration in Europe, higher than Berlin, higher even than Amsterdam. London was crazy for white: nothing, not even property, was booming faster – and this meant war in the East, and war in the South.

'Dis boom went crazy. Property boomed. Banks boomed. White boomed. Gangs boomed. So little niggas went to war and died.'

Ever since they had killed Popcorn a few years back the postcode beef had gone crazy between Hackney and Tottenham. Kids were even getting postcodes tattooed onto their fists: to fight for respect. Well, that was what those scumbags claimed, to reel the blocks in. Moses was certain there was only one reason they kept triggering each other in front of the ladies at the Pavilion out in E5: there were more and more rich kids snaffling up Hackney houses, and they all wanted one thing – white.

'That was when I realized. I was going to die.'

The whole thing felt weird. Filling in the forms. Talking to the smiling people. Going to an interview – yes sir, no sir – and wearing some plasticy green tie. But he was going to work as a social worker. Getting away from Lucifer had not been easy. Getting the course done had not been easy. This was going to work, he kept telling himself. This was about staying alive,

'I was eighteen when I finally left that fat fuck. The job I got was in a drugs rehabilitation centre. And the job they gave me was that of, like, an inspector . . . So I was rolling from one site to another in the borough checking the situation . . . What is their hygiene? What meds do they need? Do they need cleaning up?'

The homes were more like care homes, full of clueless Africans doing the work nobody else wanted to do: the excrement work. Moses never lost sight of this: I don't come from this country, the things that faze them don't faze me. He would move from bunk to bunk just waiting for that smell. And then he would grit his teeth

when one of the wreckheads failed their inspection. Moses kept repeating to himself as he put his yellow gloves on, 'I'm a humble man. I'm from a humble family. I can wipe this motherfucker up, and whatever.'

'Y'see, I would oversee them taking their drugs. I would have access to the controlled medication. I would be the one assessing whether or not you can come live in dis centre or whatever . . . And the whole time I'm thinking of dem kids I'd started shotting white to way back when I was rolling with Lucifer. And that's when I realized. In that centre stinking of tramps and cleaning fluids . . . That I was the one with the addiction. I was addicted to their money. I had to start shotting on the side.'

Moses hated everyone in the project except Lucy. She was a right fit Irish minx from head office who loved hanging out with black people. Moses took her into the grime scene. There was so much music round Bush back then. There were rappers coming out of every block. There was not a Friday without an urban rave. Everyone knew a sound engineer. And nothing made Moses happier than coking up with Lucy at the weekend and watching her smile so wide, as he showed her all these talented people in his world – all these beat masters, and storytellers of the street – who would never get their chance.

'You know what fucked everything up?

'Something happened at work, would you believe. I was twenty and I'd been there some time. And I was being picked up by my friends in really expensive cars . . . I didn't see nothing of it coz I'd been used to doing this . . . But to my colleagues you see, fucking Nigerian, fucking Ugandan, old school Africans . . . They kept asking, "Why does he have so much money? What does he do? He must be selling drugs." They hit the nail on the fucking head, bruv.

'They wouldn't get off my back . . .

'Those were computer-illiterate fools . . . But they kept putting the heat on me. They were fucking vicious and disrespectful to me. "Do you go to church? Do you pay your tithe?" I was like, "Who the fuck are these people." And they'd be like, "I'm noticing you are always coming in cabs. Mister, why are you not taking a bus?" And

I was like, "I don't want to take the fucking bus innit . . . " But they'd keep with the heat. "Why you are not bringing lunch . . . ? You are ordering pizza, now you are ordering chicken . . . You are always ordering things, ordering things . . . You must have a lot of money . . . Where is it coming from, mister?"'

But for Moses things were going downhill. There was more and more music, every night there was some bruva holding the mic, and there was more and more white. The beats were dropping, and he was getting twitches, whilst shotting wraps at night, or having a corner in the toilet to keep it awake, everyone was getting wavy, but he felt spasms, clacking through his jaw, right when he was trying to grin that baby grin, trying to be that partyboy nigga that white kids wanted him to be, because he needed those numbers, more and more numbers, always for white.

Moses woke up. His mother was screaming. She had found his gun in the fridge and bullets on the couch. She screamed louder. His nose was covered in coke. He had passed out from the high. She was crying, 'Please, please, the police will kill you, the gangstas will kill you, please, please, stop. My baby, why, why did I ever bring you to this country.'

'I was unravelling. My double life was killing me. I was taking so much white that I kept making mistakes, and I don't make mistakes. I control my world . . . I'd be going into work, surrounded by dem addicts crying out for dem meds . . . And I can't focus, I can't focus. I'm trying to stand and I'm feeling dizzy . . . And the moment work's out, I can't stop because my phone keeps ringing, because everyone needs their white right now . . . and I can't keep a handle on it . . . And bam . . . I'm losing money, I'm losing money, one weekend I lose seven grand . . . And I'm just unravelling, bruv.'

Moses was shaking at work when he took the decision. He was tremoring. There was spasm after spasm going through his jaw. He was still high and buzzy from the night before. He was shuddering. Flickerings of childhood went through him: the green, the blue, the kids laughing through the streets of Gun Battle. He emailed for help.

'I checked into the psychologist . . .

'So, I'm there, and I'm looking at this woman . . . and I can't tell her and I start mumbling. "Miss, I'm coming under work stress, I'm from a distressed home, I can't balance two professions, I feel I'm two different people, this social Moses, and this professional Moses, whose trying so hard to keep the care project going here . . . And miss, the most important thing, is . . . Y'know, I'm not meeting my financial targets."'

Moses listened to the psychologist talking in that white-tiled room. And he recognized something: the bullshit. This was exactly what he did with the addicts every day. Knowing it was a pile of shit. The key words. Talking about life goals. Moses put his hand on the back of the chair and creaked it back. He was listening to someone rattling off a memory script, in exactly the same vacant couldn't give a shit tone he talked to his very own incontinent junkies. 'Thank you, miss. I'll take that on board.'

Moses couldn't believe it was happening. Julius that African cunt had reported him to head office. They were sitting round that round table in the meeting room. Lucy was looking at the floor. He couldn't believe his ears. After everything he'd done for him on the computers Julius was telling project management he suspected Moses was dealing drugs.

'I was shaking . . . The meeting was going on and I was getting really fucking mad . . . I got really fucking mad like I was gonna break his fucking jaw. You know what I'm saying? I was breathing . . . I was breathing it in . . . Trying to control my world. In front of all my colleagues I was breathing in like a psycho not to fuck his fucking face up. And then Julius started going, "I have sons your age."

'And I switched. I got up. Locked the fucking door. And started screaming at those shitheads. "That's it, I quit my fucking job . . . I don't care what you fucking say any more . . . And what happens now I don't give a fuck . . . You can call the police. I don't give a fuck . . ." And that fucking African went, "Calm down . . ." I switched and I went, "Stand up. Come on, stand up. You wanna speak like a man sitting down, stand up and say that standing up . . . Otherwise I'm gonna fucking take you off your feet . . ." I was fucking screaming at him: "I'm not dealing drugs. You've got no fucking proof."

'So when I switched it up on that fucker, when I turned it up on him, I switched gears on him, you know what I'm saying . . . He calmed down. And that's when I had to fucking educate him. I said, "Let me explain something to you now . . ." I had to explain to that fucking African what he had done wrong. And why it was his responsibility as an older black man to fucking try and make life easier for me fam. And not try and make it worse for me when I was trying to get off the road . . .

'And then I slammed the fucking door, and fucked off.'

Moses closed his eyes as they dyed his chest tattoo: the eye of Horus, flanked by Horus and Anubis, because we both have good and evil inside us, and most black people have no fucking appreciation, and no fucking pride of the world culture they created in Africa. Moses was twenty-one. He was committed now. *This is what they made me. And I will be this man.*

He left his shirt unzipped when he went to the source. These guys were never black: they were always Irish, or Indian, and real Albanian fuckers. Those were the ones you never fucked with. There were a lot of bruvas who tried something funny. And they didn't even get a chance to laugh. These guys were making the real money. And Moses knew he may have a few bitches smuggling in a few grams stuffed up in condoms up their pussies. But that was never enough. Only small change. The source always gave him that grin: they didn't expect him to last the winter at first.

'This was when I realized I had to become a real fucking businessman.'

It took about a year, for Moses to cut down and get strategic. That's why he wanted in on the warehouse parties. Everybody knew what was happening. The white kids were getting wavier than ever. 'And dem pretty boys wanted to come down and blast out fake nigga tunes down in the nigga ass of London.' Moses wanted their money: and the first step – as always – was research.

'First I went online and I found all the parties in the area, yeah . . . And then I'd get a box of dizzle, chop it up . . . get my niggas together and go to all these parties. Talking to the bouncers, the security . . . using my personality . . . Heeey . . . Doing it ourselves and giving it to people for free . . . Heeey . . . Just to see what the security are like around people and drugs. This club's popping . . . This club's popping . . . Dat club's dead . . . And then I'd write down the list . . . and send in ma boys.'

Moses breathed out in the cold, like smoke.

He was talking with his block. He had been professional for two years now. White City was fucked. Everyone was going crazy. 'There was civil war: niggas were dying, bruvas were coming in and out the lock, and niggas were not even twenty and getting teardrop tattoos.' Moses was vexed at what he saw. These idiots were making a thousand pounds in a night and spending it in a day. Using his name from here to Peckham to get into clubs. Fools.

'Y'see, that's when I realized . . . I can capitalize on this. Coz y'know what my biggest problem has always been? It's good help. Good help is so hard to find . . . That's why I need dem bling-bling idiots. These guys . . . I send them in as my two-man crews. One bruva, one bitch. And I send dem into da fucking club or warehouse or whatever that I know is popping . . . The bruva gets wavy, goes around chatting everyone up . . . Heeey . . . And the bitch, she holds the food.

'But you know what I fucking love? It's single mums . . . Because a good business needs good mules. And a good business needs good safe houses . . . And dem bitches they are always hungry . . . They got responsibilities. So they can never dizzle me and fuck off. And they always need more money. And do they know anyone else? Course they fucking do . . . because dem slags' friends are all single mums. And I'm laughing . . . Because I got fucking safe carrier bitches.'

Moses was learning. Moses was taking it all in. He was laughing in the shower. What was becoming clear as a white high was that the quality of your business was the quality of your contacts. The richer your contacts, the richer your business. And that was when he realized that this business was the same as all other businesses – and that's all about showmanship.

'This, bruv, is what it's all about.'

Moses needed to be on the ground every fucking night. Looking for fools. Moses would spot them across a crowded room. Little fuckers who kept on touching their noses, sniffing with that permanent cold. Fools. Moses would dance up to them and throw that personality into action: heey, make them laugh, make them happy – and reel them in.

'I'll just see you . . . and know right then I want you in my phone. You know what I realized . . . a lot of dem rich white folk they are kinda nostalgic for the old ways. They want you to be respectful, talk nicely to them, they want a big black gentleman . . . Especially the ladies, they go crazy for nigga gallantry . . . But you gotta work carefully to get a client in your phone. It's like flirting, like nailing a babe – but you gotta bite you lip and do it with dem dudes too.

'This is what a good business needs . . . You need to aim, always, for the highest-quality client . . . and then know your niche. That's thirty to fifty prime fuckers . . . who are spending 10 to 20k a year on their nose. And when you got one, you got ten more. Because all their mates are crazy for white too . . . And we're talking profits: 600k.'

Moses had worked it out by now. He was twenty-five. The clients that mattered: they want to think they are party people, not fuckheads. And that means you have to play along. It's not just: 'Hey, how's it going?' It's feign an interest in all things: whatever they talk about when it hits – girls, boys, bosses – you want to talk about too. Easy.

Moses knew the better his game, the better the client. You need to eat with them, chomp pizza with them, snort with them, and, even if you have pushed all this cash into three flats already, crash on their couch like some little black boy who doesn't want to go back to White City. Smile at them like you love them. Smile at them with all that line. Because once they fall for it: you can do anything to them. You can make them wait. You can blow them off. And you can even shrink the wrap.

'I got no regrets, bruv.'

Moses was winning. He was cutting down for sure. And becoming more recreational. Moses was making an effort: and his phone was filling up with Kensington – baby bankers, fresh lawyers, Arab princesses, Russian types, Soho types and TV boys. Moses was grinning. This was London, and everyone was crazy for white. This was so easy. There was no way he could leave a club without money numbers.

'You've got to take advantage of the egos . . . I know exactly what they think of me. They think I'm a little black drug dealer. They think I'm broke. But I got more money than most of them. But I don't say anything about it to them . . . Y'know what I'm saying? When they go to me, "Yeah mate I just got my bonus and spent three grand going to San Tropez . . ." I'm just standing there and gritting my fucking teeth. I just went to the strip club and spent three grand . . . And you, you went on holiday and took your family away . . . They all gonna remember that shit . . . I don't even remember what I did at that fucking strip club . . . You piece of shit. But I don't say nuffink, man.

'When I see dem fuckers . . . Coming out of dem money houses, dem bankers and lawyers, from dem families that made dat cash from empire slave trade for sure . . . I just think, "You fucking piece of shit . . . You think you're the legit one . . . But you bastard piece of shit cunts . . . You think you're better than me. But I know . . . We're all trapped in the same fucking thing . . . I'm the criminal, but who created me?"

'Because this is London: and if you're not doing drugs you're fucking sex workers . . . if you're not fucking whores you're fucking gambling. And if you think you're so clean you're addicted to fucking champagne. Because this is London . . . Everybody wants white . . . And everybody wants to sell it. So who's fucking addicted to who?

'And I'm thinking as that shithead gives me a fucking tip, and smiles at me like I'm a little black boy, "You fucking cunt. I'm looking at you," and I'm thinking, "My watch is worth more than your car. And you know what, I'm no fucking fool . . ." I'm looking at that white Chelsea boy and I'm thinking, "You fucking smug cunt . . . I can read . . ." And I know that behind every rich family in London is a drug dealer . . . What was the British Empire fucking based on? Drugs: sugar, slaves and fucking opium . . . So don't you ever, ever . . .

'Give me any of dat moralizing shit.'

FORD FOCUS

I need to live in the new London.

This is why we have been looking for a doss house for days, first scrolling through the Romanian web listings, then calling up, one by one, the mobile numbers they post there. Now we are driving from one to another in a Ford Focus. Trying to get in. Earlier we were almost robbed.

I came up with this ruse a week ago, because you can't call up in English and get an answer. You can't call up in accented Romanian and get an answer either. They hang up immediately: police. This is why I have been driving around with the Interpreter, a Romanian friend, from Enfield Chase.

He is making the calls.

His lie: he's looking for work. My lie: I'm Russian.

We find the doss house the way everyone else does: online.

Romanians, Poles, Lithuanians – every mass migration has huge web portals where the migrant can find all the numbers he needs. These are some of the busiest classified sites in London. There are mobiles for forklift-truck lessons. There are mobiles for bosses after tilers. And there are numbers for shared rooms.

These are almost all in the decaying working-class suburbs: and in the East this means Newham, then out into Ilford, Beckton and Barking.

This is our third night out in the car.

The Interpreter is a recovering conspiracy theorist, who once went to find enlightenment in the Shaolin Temple in Tufnell Park. The Interpreter sometimes works for the police. He has no contract.

House

3 bedroom дом, East Ham, ная, мебель, рядом парк, нед.
079████828, 078████436

The officers call him up. Then he drives up to the station in this beat-up Ford Focus and charges them by the hour.

Sometimes, he is actually only an Interpreter. But normally the police don't give a shit, and leave him to take the witness statement. Often, they just bugger off, leaving the Interpreter with the Roma thieves, the wife-beaters and the prostitutes.

He looks at me at red traffic lights.

'The thing about Gypsies . . . It's just the lie, it's the way they always lie. They have this energy . . . it just sucks it out of me. It leaves me dry. And with the whores . . . it's the same, the lies are always the same . . . I'm drained with them, drained.'

He purses his lips.

'I'm sitting asking questions – why did you do this, why did you do that – and I'm watching every night for the moment, the lie cracks . . . and collapses, all over their face. Y'know . . . I like watching for this moment.'

We have been in the Ford Focus for three hours.

'I know what you want.' He grins at me. 'You want the same fucking Mo Farah wonder story. You want to make your readers happy. You want to make them comfortable with all this. I know your type. Well, let me tell you what . . . you're ain't gonna find it, bro.'

He almost shouts. 'Don't question me. I've spoken to more Romanians than you ever will. Thousands. And I don't see it. I see anxiety. I see exhaustion. I see powerlessness. I don't get no British dream bullshit. I see people very happy about the money, about having work. But I don't see people all starry-eyed. Now don't you pull your Jew grandparents on me . . . and be like, "Oh but it's the same," coz it's not. Your lot came over, whoever the fuck they were, and worked their way into a London with a big fat booming middle class . . . where you could buy a house for shit . . . And simples, be Mr Respectable.' He eyes me, like a man in judo. 'You can't do that now. Never. The Romanians, the Nigerians, the Poles and the rest of the rubbish came too late. The middle class is being squeezed to

shit in London. And all these Romanians coming in, they know they're never gonna be in it. So they ain't starry-eyed about this city. Sorry. They're as starry-eyed as any cleaner.'

He swerves, violently.

'I just don't get the happy story when I ask people. But maybe that's just the nature of stories. You ask someone to tell you a fucking story: they're never gonna go, "I've had a great meal and I'm full. Thank you very much."'

We have been driving in zigzags up and down the tight narrow terraces of Newham. We stop and take notes: the doors have metal grilles, and there is a lot, a lot, of rubbish. The Interpreter tells me this is how you know there is overcrowding. That the councils count the amount of crap they pick up and estimate the numbers. Not far from here we were almost robbed. The Romanian voice yapped at us down the phone: 'Yeah, yeah, come 27 R— Terrace. I'll be there at seven.'

This is what happens.

We knock at the door. A squinting Somali opens in his pyjamas: no, no, there are no Romanians here. There is heavy, heavy air. We turn around. Walking up to us is a huge decked man in a blue hoodie talking on his phone. That's his voice. The guy with the doss house. The moment he sees the two of us – he turns on his heel. He only expected one. And we are both wearing padded hoodies for effect.

We hear later that night there is a thief operating in Newham. He pretends to run a doss house for Romanians. Tells them to come with a month's rent. And then beats the shit out of them. And walks off with the cash.

'That cunt was gonna deck us . . . The cunt. Then he saw we were two.'

We are driving to the next doss house as the Interpreter talks at the wheel. Orange nightlights playing on his face. That morning he interpreted for social services. Two Romanians, with a baby. Those dumpy women from Child Protection wanted him to translate taking the baby away.

'When they got it, that I was gonna take their baby away . . . They went kinda white . . . The baby had a club foot and when the district nurse did an inspection on it . . . They found the club foot had been damaged. It'd been cut. The parents, they had no explanation for it. Like, y'know . . . I think maybe they'd cut the club foot . . . Or something, out of desperation, like they do in villages in Romania. But those bitches, they were having none of it. "Tell 'em, tell 'em, we're gonna take the baby away."' The Interpreter has a gravelly voice. 'The moment they realized. The parents . . . they both just curled up into each other and cried . . . they cried identically. She was on his lap. The women, they didn't give a shit. They went: "Take the baby." They gave it up so limply in the end.'

We stop. The next doss house we have a number for is in Barking. I feel an itch, a creeping itch, for drink as we walk through Forest Gate. We can't find a pub. The Interpreter keeps pointing out the odd shop with a dirty England flag.

'This is Muslim land, man, there are no pubs here because there are no English. But if you wanna go into one of those gross last of the English pubs we can.'

We can't even find one of them. We find a Chinese restaurant. A cheap and dim place. A maroon gloom. The tablecloths have cigarette burns. There is only one man in the back. One of the last of the English. Drinking pints alone. We ignore him and open up the notebook to work on the map. The Interpreter draws concentric circles.

'Look, what's happening in London, mate . . . Here's Tube Zone 1. Used to belong to the rich English. And then there was Tube Zone 2, Whitechapel, Notting Hill, and all the rest of it, that was the old immigrant land. Then there was Tube Zone 3, 4, 5 and whatever. That used to be posh or working-class suburbs. But what's happening now is Zone 1's being sold to the Russians, and Zone 2's being bought by the poshos . . . pushing the migrants into white land. That's why there's beef.'

We eat sticky meat cubes and noodles.

'Don't believe me? Let me tell you . . . Never, or basically never, do we get Romanians or Gypsies in the dock living in Zone 2. They've all been pushed out to Zone 3 and beyond. And it's the

same for all those doss houses listed on the migrant sites. They ain't there . . . They are all out here and much further out.'

The bald pink man stands up, holding his pint.

'Are you Je-w-ish?'

I blink. I can't believe it.

'Are you Je-w-ish . . . coz ya both bloody look it.'

I shrink into cowardice. The Interpreter does not.

'Yes . . . mate.'

He is coming up to us, the pub bore, now publess with the Chinese.

'What'cha doin' down 'ere, then . . . Why you not up Norf with yer lot?'

We stick our forks into the food and stare at it to make a point.

'Used ta be loads of ya down 'ere in East but you all fucked off up Norf.'

The drunk stands there. Pint in hand.

'What? I'm not gonna kill ya' or nuffink. Jus' sayin' ya bloody look it.'

NORTH CIRCULAR

I wake up in the doss house, with everyone else, at 5 am.

There is a groaning, and a coughing, and the heaving of four-teen men trying to make it to the bathroom. There is only one of these of course. How they swear, the lodgers, and rap on the door, grunting, in foul-breathed peasant Romanian, mumbling their morning curses, because we are way over an hour from the building sites out here, in this manky estate, at the ass end of Barking.

This is how I got here.

The thing about lying is that it drains. It sucks the energy out of you. It electrifies your shoulders and your spine, and it pulls you down under its load. But the thing about lying well is knowing this is only the birth of your lie. The longer a lie lives the easier, and the lighter, it becomes.

I turn off the motorway and loop round the roundabout into the worn low rise of Barking. The estate I am looking for curls into a winding close. My heart pumps. I am beginning my lie: I am a Russian illegal immigrant. I speak English – *very bad*.

I wear the lie: my clothes are a tatty blue puffa with a fake fur rim, smelling strongly of detergent, a grey hoodie with a chewed sleeve and a hood too tight on my head, black scuffed Puma track-suit bottoms and water-stained brown shoes. I repeat my lie time and time again in the car: I am here to work; but when they grow suspicious, I will take them into a bigger lie, that I am really a uni-versity educated asylum-seeker who is fleeing conscription for the frontlines in Ukraine. I bite my lip.

'My name . . . Alexey.'

Londoners think they can pick out European migrants by their faces. This is rubbish. The moment someone is not English they can sense it. But not identify what. And so they make their judgements based on clothes. These are very powerful things. Someone who looks a little darker than the English, with features a little more rounded, or angular, at a glance, the Londoner will think is French or Italian. But put on a hoodie, a puffa jacket and a tracksuit, the Londoner will see a Romanian, a Bulgarian or an Albanian.

On the night I arrive with my bags, eight hoods on mountain bikes are smoking skunk and cussing each other in front of the stumpy red-brick blocks ending the close. They glare at me, and fall silent. Behind them night windows glint and the purple sky is filled with the enormous skeletal black rings of the gasworks.

Over a barbed-wire fence behind the rubbish bins the wail of the rails never stops. As I try to remember the address I look around. There are clothes drying on string lines between the spindly trees over a scruffy lawn. This is littered with cigarette butts and beer cans up to spiked metal railings. There are marshy waters, there, under the concrete immensity of the motorway. Raised on stilts, it glows like frenetic copper circuitry from blazing headlamps under endless geometrically spaced lamps. This is the belt rounding the inner city. The North Circular: our unwalkable city wall.

The block door is broken, its key code bust, and the anti-burglary grille of the apartment is flung open. African men in body warmers slink in and out of the apartment opposite, avoiding eye contact. I knock.

This is when I meet the Matron.

She seldom ventures out and her face is blotchy and grey. Her liquorice hair is streaked with silvery grey and her eyes and mouth are numbed into a permanent squinty glare of refusal, indignation and hate. Even if she smiles or laughs her mouth never quite leaves this upturned angry pout. The Matron takes no excuses and brooks no late payments. And when she walks her bulk up and down the tight corridor, in her black nightgown embroidered with white patterns, the boys shush and wrap it up.

This is how she runs the doss house. There are supposed to be two bedrooms and a living room in this low-ceilinged old council

block. But there are fifteen people here. Seven in bunks, shared mattresses and camp beds in the sitting room. Four sharing two single beds in the bedroom and three in the cramped room she shares with her husband and son. And there is one night-worker, who I never meet, who sleeps in one of the beds we use in the day.

The Matron's arms ripple with wobbling fat as she shows me into the cramped kitchen. The trains fling themselves past the rattling windows every few minutes as she distractedly explains what I need to know about Barking.

'All the English have gone. There are very few left here. There are only Indians, Romanians and Africans. The English, they don't care about this place. They are all living in Spain getting tanned and fat off the benefits this country gives them for free. You'll be dealing with Lithuanians and Poles, if you stay, on site.'

There is no way she will go back to Romania. Her daughter followed a man in construction here six years ago and told her there was money to be made. There is none in the Black Sea port they come from. And she needs to make money for herself.

The Matron is married to the Corpse. His eyes are no longer living. His mouth never closes. He dribbles, and he either lies collapsed in bed vaguely listening to warbling Romanian television tittle-tattle, or hobbles into the stairwell to phlegm and smoke. His hair is white and he is most likely cancerous, and from his breath, certainly an alcoholic.

'You do understand? This country is not easy.'

The Matron looks at me with teacherly concern. Though she never tells me, her crinkling hair and byzantine eyes give away she is not a pure Romanian, but with the blood of a Roma, or a Jew. She moves to the cupboard and offers me a shot of brandy. She blinks at me, in a pitying way, then grunts.

'Welcome to London. The work is hard. The salaries look big but what you save is small. There are not as many scams as you think.'

Sleep is only ever shallow in the halfway house. This is normal for the poorest migrant builders. In my room, we share beds, and only one is remotely double. The prices are so high in London: for rent, for travel, for food, for alcohol, bunking up is the only way many survive. As much as 40 per cent of new immigrants in this city have been accommodated with an increase of persons per room. This is what that statistic means.

'London is a fucking bitch.'

The first builder I meet they call the Joker. He speaks with smirks and hops up and down on his heels as he belittles me. This is the way he likes to dress down the new boys. He is balding with an aubergine-shaped head.

'Why is your English so bad?'

The Joker has worked as a plasterer all over Europe. He speaks some French, and quite a lot of Italian, and considers himself quite the linguist.

'You don't need to speak it. You just need to understand what the foreman is saying. The rest is easy.'

Like all linguists, he is a natural mimic, and amuses himself in the mirror imitating the foremen and the white English he very occasionally meets. 'Aright, mate . . .' But tonight he is pacing round the tiny kitchen, lit with a naked low-energy bulb, gripping his hands into fists, and not drinking a milky cup of tea he poured sometime back. 'This is London . . . There are niggers everywhere, the Indians and the Muslims control all the shops, and the English hate us, the people who build this fucking city. Have fun.'

I get to know the bedmates, of course.

To my right there is Sliceface, who has a huge scar curling up the right side of his face like the half-grin of *Batman*'s Joker. His chin is also scarred and he has around his huge muscular arms two black-ink tattoos, like a pattern in marble or neo-fascist code. He is so concerned about missing Romania he has brought his own digi-box with him. This is what he spends most of the evenings toying with.

Sliceface is fifty-one and his face is knobbly and nodular. His forehead is sloping and lined. His is a jutting jaw. He wears thick plastic-framed black glasses, under his three-week-old crew cut, giving him a kindlier appearance than I think he merits. He is a window-fitter. But like everyone in the halfway house Sliceface says he's not like the others. His nephew is coming over – for real – and they are going to set up their own company, sometime very soon.

Most evenings he wears a blue T-shirt shouting: KYLIE SAYS RELAX. Sliceface knows maybe forty words of English, and speaks with a terrible slur thanks to the old rips in the side of his face. He rambles on some evenings about how he was a national boxer back when Romania was Communist, how he punched national champions all over Eastern Europe, in Hungary, Poland and Bulgaria.

This seems to make him happy. But one evening, he comes back broken and withdrawn, mumbling that some inexperienced bastard had broken his tools. It is only then that I notice his hair is thinning and greying and his scrunched brown eyes are full of worry. He looks into me and says, 'You should go to Italy. It is much better. I've worked in Germany, I've worked in Spain and I've worked in France . . . And I tell you Italy is the best. At least the women are attractive. Unlike those here. And the food is good. And the weather is good. Not like this shit.'

He stops. Letting the swoosh and rattle of the lorries on the motorway come through the window into our silence.

Sliceface sleeps in the same bed as the Baby. He has protruding blood-red ears and his skin is pink and lardlike. The boys tease him for never needing to shave. His eyebrows are thin and unfinished, hardly filling the bones they are supposed to cover. He is frightened, I feel, here in the halfway house, of all these strange men with stories that don't quite make sense, and when I catch him peering at me, he rushes his tiny black peasant eyes into the corner of the room.

The Baby is twenty-one and when he heads to work in the morning he makes his bed, or the half he shares with Sliceface, like a good boy or a disciplined recruit from military service. Then he sits there on the springy bed, his can-shaped head before the window, black in a box of purple light, and for a few minutes he cups his head in his hands, and then with a shake like a wet dog leaves for work.

Baby wakes at 5 am to drill solar panels (illegally) into a concrete base somewhere over the M25 – cash in hand. He has no idea where it is, exactly, only the two-hour commute to get there on the buses out of Barking.

'You know what I'm worried about.'

We are talking one night.

'That when I want to fuck a girl . . . I need a car or to go back to hers. The English girls are drunk slags who are pissing in the streets they are so drunk . . . I saw them! It should be easy.'

Sliceface roars throaty laughter.

But I can tell from the way he grins that Baby is a virgin.

I wake up at 6 am.

My third morning here. Fog rises from the marsh waters and swallows the motorway so you can only see the sodium lamps hanging like lanterns in the dawn lilac haze. I pull myself up and do what the Matron bluffly says – if I want work, I will have to tout for it outside Wickes. This is the building suppliers' in a metallic hangar where the boys are lining up for jobs. Everybody in the halfway house tells me about Wickes. It's where you go, all over London: for cash in hand.

There are some days where eighty or ninety Romanians tout here. Here the white vans slow down, a beaten door is thrown open, and sometimes a ruddy, neck-tattooed English, with stickers for Help for Heroes on his van, will bark his price for some loading or plastering. Those are the good days. Because usually a Pakistani, a Turk or a Pole will pull up – and they make you name your wage. And this is when the striped joggers and the fleece hoodies and the fake Adidas puffas will push and jostle to grab it. This is where you get your workers for dirt.

These guys all say the same thing.

'They never pay minimum wage. They make us fight for it. And they know we have no choice. That we are hungry.'

The raised motorway yawns above us into a bruised grey sky that has swallowed its sunlight. There are forty puffa jackets touting here. These men in paint-flecked fleeces, joggers, combat pants and hoods will be pacing the kerb in their battered work boots for the next eleven hours: muttering, tensely waiting for a white van.

They have riven faces, reddened like drinkers, and move slowly back and forth, bent and gnawed by each passing hour as a white van fails to turn up. And here the builders, the plasterers, the tilers and the carpenters swap stories. There are those seven lads living like mice in a rickety garage nearby. They are plasterers roughing it. There are tilers who have been sleeping in their cars. Then the joiners butt in saying the minimum touting wage in London is one chicken and chips. They scoff, hunch their shoulders and point at the two hooded carpenters, stooped and dejected, with blank eyes wide from hunger, their hands trembling and jerking as they pinch together mean little rollups.

I look for work. But there are no vans. This is when I meet Hoodman. Like everyone touting he says he is not like the others. He is a professional. He wears a scuffed old jean jacket and never takes off his bright green hood. His eyes are amber and his face is wrinkled and wan. He is a jokey fellow. Everything is there to mock. He pulses off an exasperated, bored disgruntled energy. This feels different to be around from the walking defeat of the others. Hoodman communicates only in slang; to anyone who will listen he will witter on that he worked at the best vineyards in Moldova and is not one of these stooped, low-energy sullen vegetables.

'Some days you get a bunch of Pakis in a van who want you to shift their stuff for them. Some days nothing.'

There is no work. Another whole day wasted. We leave when the light has become a grey that hovers in a twilight haze. It hangs there and darkens as the street lamps begin to clack on along the motorway. Hoodman grunts and walks with me back to Barking along an A-road, and across a small park.

'Look at this park. You'd think you're in Pakistan. Just look at them everywhere. All these shops in Arabic. This was not what I expected.'

The trees are bare and lifeless and the grass is mostly mud. Two women, sheets of black cloth with only their painted lashes visible,

sit on a bench, their manicured figures over matching leather hand-bags with a bling-bling gold clutch.

'The English fucked off from this city. They didn't like all the languages they didn't understand around them. All of these people speaking Indian and Pakistani. Look at this . . . I'm a Romanian, you're a Russian, that guy there is black. They don't feel comfortable here any more.'

We walk past the dead pubs. The Bull is boarded up. The Ram is gone for good. On the scuffed-up street behind us men are packing up a hundred metal-pole market stalls for the night. The clanking of the metal on concrete clinks around us.

'You know these people, they are not like us in Romania, or in Russia . . . They truly believe in rights. Here we have rights . . . You probably don't understand that yet, but if you come and tell them you don't want to die for Putin in Ukraine, or you come from a war country in Africa, they are so moral they will make you one of their own. Amazing, no?'

We talk a bit more, as we drift past the RIA Money Transfer, the SAM 99p, and the 97p Knockout, the Cashino and the GLAMOUR Touch skin-whitening shop, the whole time the Hoodman smokes, and checks out the butts in clingy black dresses, that are supposed to be modest, of glossy-haired Indian girls, striding out of the Tube. We sit on a bench opposite the pawnbrokers with the WE BUY GOLD sign. The Hoodman smokes down to the line.

'Brother . . . You come from Russia. I'm telling you, go and apply for asylum here. Go to one of those Indians . . . They have these little law shops where they only make people asylum claims . . . You'll get it, I'm sure, this is the country of rights . . . They are so just and moral, if you tell them you are running from Putin they will make you British on the spot. This is how this country works. They believe in the rights . . . This how all these guys came here.'

Hoodman fucks off. But I hang around the station. The trains are emptying out Office London at the rate of one every two min-utes: carrying out the foremen and the drillers, the receptionists and the secretaries, the checkout girls and the newsagent boys, the office

managers and the team leaders, in their thousands, onto this concrete orange parade. I crave for Camel Lights, as I watch and linger.

A balding Asian man, in his fifties, in a cream flannel suit and a burgundy scarf round the flakey skin of a smoker paces up, round and past me, adjusting his black comb-over before rushing after a tiny woman, striding on ahead in a red-sequined headscarf, clutching four orange shopping bags, in a brown pleather coat rimmed with faux fur.

An unshaven African man in blue tiger-striped pyjama trousers and a thin black anorak shivers and flicks his shoulders back and forward from the cold; he stands reading the *Sun*, but every time a train empties, his pussy eyes scan the ticket lines.

A gangly Romanian guy with a rose tattoo on his neck, gesturing in a black college jacket, both sleeves kilted leather, is flirting with a teenage Roma girl, eyes bright, in skin-tight blue jeans and a tight motorcycle jacket, touching her raven hair, and pulling those exaggerated, wily faces men only do for a reason.

The air has grown sharp.

You never really get to know people in the doss house. They come, they go. They keep themselves to themselves in the stink of work boots and sour mood of poor sleep. But you get to know the personas they put on for the boys.

There is the President. He is stubbly and fleshy, with love handles he rests his hands on as he moans. He usually wears a crisp white hoodie with lighting strikes on it, and ends every statement with a snigger as he talks. His face holds many emotions: and they pass quickly over him as he speaks. He is tired. He has been hammering wooden garden fences for a bearded Pakistani foreman and gives me clear instructions for looking for work.

'You want to get an English boss on your shift. They are lazy and gentle. You don't want to get an Indian or a nigger or one of those crafty Pakis. They will work you like a slave. And they pay very little.'

He abounds in tips, especially concerning the Tube. It is too expensive: crazy expensive, two hours a day, in and out, for almost

all of his shifts. But he brags to us he has an answer. The President
boards the Hammersmith and City Line at Barking by pretending
to be a cripple. He hobbles up with a stick to the ticket barrier and
they let him off at the other end.

'It always works.'

The President hunches with resignation. He tells me there are
'niggers' everywhere in London who bike around stabbing people
in hoods, but not to be scared of them. He is a Roma. And he is
called the President in the halfway house because he says his life's
ambition is to become President of Romania just to sell it to Putin.

Nibbling on processed sausage, the President hangs around the
kitchen looking, sometimes surely, but usually resigned. He has a
slumped posture. And when he laughs it has a sad, throaty ring in
it somewhere. But the boys all pick up on his faintly feminine
manner and the way he lingers in the corridor telling the new-
comers what to expect as they build London.

'The English, they are very lazy. They are working so slowly.
They are working so gently. Like they have become slow-witted.
They pretend they can only lay seven bricks an hour. Can you
believe it.'

Baby bursts out laughing. But the President goes on, without
waiting for him, his voice, soft, sad and faintly lilting.

'Something has happened to the poor English. They look very
sick like they have become ill. Their skin looks like they are dead.
They look grey off their drinking.'

Sliceface takes his eyes off some celebrity TV scandal show with
salacious witterings about male escorts, and nods.

'This is their country so they take all the easiest jobs for themselves. The hard jobs, they go to us. But so many of them are not
working. They are so lazy . . . The English they think you deserve
£2,000 a month for driving the bus. Can you believe it.'

Both of them laugh.

'They have become lazy, I think . . . Because they get things for
free. They give you a free house. They give you a free operation.
They give you a free everything. This is a rich country, you know.
All of Africa, the diamonds, from the mines come here. All of India

too. And from Russia it is the same. They have colonies because all the rich live here. That's why they can afford to give all this stuff for free.'

There is a naked girlie on the TV screen and Baby and Sliceface forget about London for a few seconds in the soft-focus folds of her flesh. The President is not interested. He leans his forehead on the doorframe. It is unclear to me who he is talking to. Maybe himself.

'What do I like best about Britain? I hate the weather. I hate the damp. Everything is grey and ugly. I hate the women. They are so ugly. The work is hard. There are niggers everywhere. The prices are terrible. I hate the fact that I wanted to buy a jacket and the only one I liked was £300. To be honest the only thing I like is the money.'

The longer I spend in the doss house the more cockroaches I begin to see, scurrying behind the kitchen table as I eat, rushing ahead of me in the tight hallway as I come in, dashing along the crevices, between the bedding and the wall as I toss and turn, as the three others in these touching two beds, exhausted from construction and driving, snore like buffaloes.

The longer I spend in the halfway house the more I realize it is falling to pieces: the paint peels, black and white, from the rotten window frames, and shoved into the cracks are flimsy pieces of foam that make no difference to the whistling draughts that creep into the room, cracking the builders' voices, and coughing out in the night.

The sheets are not washed between lodgers, and the plywood furniture – camp beds, bunks and springy old mattresses – is disintegrating with each passing night.

Over our heads thick, scaly sheets of charcoal dirt cover the pipes and the water surfaces. The bathroom is a ceiling and four walls, covered in black cratered Martian moulds, growing like a leopard pattern, flowering and spreading as the fourteen shower each day.

There is never silence on the lines. The trains rumble steadily out of the distance like monstrous machinery; their carriages beaming with light rush past both windows at night. These are the evenings when I sit under the flickering naked bulb in the kitchen and talk with the Professor. The shoulders of this older man are pinched up, and fingering his cigarette packet he narrates the evening news with what he remembers from the programme last night.

The Professor corners anyone in the kitchen with his views, and begins, whether they wanted it or not, to tell them about the Eurozone crisis or the frontlines in Ukraine. His brown hair is streaked with silver and his face screws upwards with anxiety: gullied and canyoned with black lines. He is not a Professor, of course, they only call him that in the halfway house. He is in reality a welder who has run away from his wife in Romania at the last possible moment before infirmity and is now cracking up as he traipses up and down Barking looking for work. He wants to talk with the stammering loneliness of a man married for so many decades the silence scares him. One evening he turns to me.

'I'm working in the black . . . for a black. It's not serious work. I go in and screw a little bit here and a little bit there in his home and a few others and he pays me in cash. But he's a nigger, what do you expect. But you can't say that in the street here. Here amongst us we can speak the truth. But in the street say that and you'll get cut. You'll get stabbed. You can't say that as the English will get upset. They are very protective of their niggers.'

The following evening the Professor is close to tears. He is now unemployed. His brown eyes and upper lip are screwed up into a draining anguish that leaves him at times jittery, and others, listless, splayed on his camp bed. The trains thunder like approaching artillery as we talk in the kitchen. The Professor looks into the rumbling as in the window rushing lights flash, flicker, and past.

'I can't stay here . . . I can't stay here . . .

'This is not what I expected.

'They hate us, from Eastern Europe . . .'

He takes out his cigarette packet again, rubbing the plastic outer casing on, and off, on and off, with a crinkle-crackle.

'They are very tolerant here.

'They tolerate the Indians and the Africans and the Pakistanis. The Romanians . . . They tolerate us a little bit less. They only tolerate their colonials. The people they are used to ruling. But they hate us. They hate us because they don't know us. And because we arrived all at once.

'And it wasn't just us Romanians, but all these Polish, and Bulgarians, and Ukrainians. They tell us that on the sites the wages they used to be £12 or even £15 an hour. But now they are only £7. Minimum wage. It's not that we stole their jobs. But we out-competed them. You see we are here. And we are ready to work ten, fourteen hours. For them it's eight hours and finish. Not us.

'That's why they hate us.'

BECKTON ALPS

We are stuck in traffic.

Pawel does not look like a builder, with his thick black glasses and plush grey mane. Pawel doesn't sound like one either. Inside his overheated white van he talks about Communism, literature, politics, chess: everything he lost in 1981 when he became a dissident refugee. He misses those first buildings days.

'You know what it was like then? Back in the eighties, the nineties, when I was first building, your painter, he would've come from the Warsaw Academy of Fine Arts . . . You'd tell him to rip off the wallpaper and throw on three thick coats of paint and he would just begin telling you about Polish minimalism. Your bricklayer . . . He would be a sociologist, talking Hayek when it was tea break.'

His voice purrs.

'Those days . . . When we finished and the sun would come pouring in . . . Loft conversions were very popular then, that's what I remember . . . We would have all these nice chats as we cleaned up. The English . . . hah, they probably thought it was football we were always arguing about so passionately.'

The man driving the white van is an eighties political refugee. His very first job on site was wall painting, in a building trade then run by Irish wide boys. Pawel is one of the old Poles. Today he swerves the corners between his sites. Pawel is one of the winners: one of the make-it-up-as-you-go-along building bosses who enlisted the mass migration in 2000s.

Pawel knew London wanted those bathroom refits for cheap. And he has been rewarded for it. As we hit red lights, he reminisces:

how he walked this street when he owned nothing, only a small ripped suitcase, when he slept in that mite-infested bedsit. Today he owns a house in Balham, a chalet in France and an apartment in Warsaw. As the van whirs to leave I ask him to place his class.

'I'm not middle class . . . I'm an immigrant, I'm not part of that.'
He squints at me.

'I'm privileged . . . I got the chance to be both Polish . . . and a little English.'

Like any mansion builder he knows everything about the rich.

'These people . . . They like the Polish because they hate having the white English inside their house. Those boys, they are so rude. They come in and they go, "Put the kettle on love," then sit on the sofa. This make the rich very tense. They like my boys. They are silent . . . They can't speak English, so they're very polite.'

Pawel tells me he needs more labourers on site in Pimlico. But the first work he has for me is helping out in the white van. Like the boss of any building firm, Pawel spends eight hours of the day, or more, driving around. But he is not only picking up stacks of timber, buckets of paint, sacks of gypsum and crates of bathroom tiles. The Polish white van spends its days circling the sugar-icing streets from Westminster into Kensington. 'I need to inspect my sites . . . and talk plans with lonely wives.'

Pawel and I begin unloading at the first place we stop. 'You know where they come from now? The villages. The longer this goes on, the emptier Poland gets. First I had architects, sculptors, engineers. Now we have village people and peasants.'

The numbers confirm. More than 60 per cent of Polish migrants working in London today now come from troubled small towns and the countryside.

'Those coming are not the educated ones, like it used to be . . .'

Together we drive long afternoons around Pimlico. But these rows of white dolls' houses are not all the same. There are lines broken up into damp little flats, let out by the council, their paint faces all cracked, facing freshly veneered mansions, newly owned by the Russians. Pawel knows quite a few of them.

'You know what breaks my heart?'

He glances at me.

'That my job is to destroy London. They call me every week . . . and every time they want the same thing over the phone. White walls with chrome finish. Minimalist, modernist. That's what the Russians want. The lovely things I rip out . . . the mouldings, the wallpapers, the carved old basins . . . You wouldn't even believe.'

Anyone in Eastern Europe can recognize the secret police: those eyes, the tone of voice, the smile, that drinkers' skin. Pawel ran away from them when Moscow forced Poland into martial law. Now they have caught up with him. But he doesn't seem to care. He is more annoyed how rusty his Russian has become: but it is still good enough to have three Pimlico Ukrainians as his clients.

That said, he rarely sees them.

'They come quickly, when they want to buy . . . And the English, they rip them off every time. They lie to them. "Yes, Mr Boris, this place is so prestigious. Yes, Mr Boris, this place is so close to the Westminster palace." He imitates their fawning lisp. 'These guys were nervous . . . they were politicians in Kiev and they needed this money out very quickly. So they believed, the stupid fools, those English suits trying to pick their pocket. Nobody bothered to tell them that opposite is the council terrace, with a hoarder, with rats, with loads of mental-health issues. Never trust an Englishman in property . . .'

Two Chechen brothers with light green eyes look after these three empty mansions. They are both very fashionable: bearded, trim, with navy sweaters and boutique scooters.

'They look after empty homes for the owners. They are politicians . . . and in Ukraine those guys always need a safe place to run. The Chechens, they are like a brand . . . They are security, very good security. The other Russians recognize it. But they are always having parties I think . . . Then calling me. "Pawel, can you come and fix this in the bathroom, urgently please . . . Pawel, there is something that has gone wrong in the master bedroom, please, hurry." They always pay me in cash.'

———

I work for Pawel on a site nearby. My job consists exclusively of loading rubbish. There is more of this on a building site than you can possibly imagine: wood shavings and plaster drippings, untold chunks of MDF, boundless rubble, foam wrapping and glass shards.

Renovating a £2.5 million flat for £7 an hour are a bunch of dreamers. There is Stas, who in his ten years working in London has learned only twelve words of English, most of them swear-words. He is a living dictionary of farming obscenities that should be preserved by the Polish Academy for post-industrial generations. He likes nothing better than ripping out windows and spitting long distances.

For ten years he has sworn at co-worker Jacek, a spindly painter from Kraków who knows maybe twenty words of English, all of them paint-related. Pawel says they are both like sailors, renovating London for nine months and then back to Poland. Stas claims to have a wife but I find this difficult to believe. Like many a sailor, he doesn't know how to live another way.

Jacek has a colonel's moustache. This painter is here because his daughter has Down's syndrome. Every pound he can spare is sent back to pay for her care home in Germany. He wells up red, explaining there are no such institutions in Poland. Jacek's sacrifice means that at the age of fifty he has shared dank rooms his entire adult life.

Lunch breaks on the worktops around the pots and drills and coiled wires are like a property developers' convention. Plasterers keep interrupting each other: 'This flat is pathetic. Not even a key to the garden square.' The painters puff up to interject. 'We decorated a £3 million mansion in Wimbledon last week!'

Lunch brings Stas and Jacek out of their squabbling and into conflict with the youngest labourer in the team, a grumpy, heavyset joiner whom both inexplicably call Miner. He is a newcomer, in England only since 2009. The boy knows some English. Just about enough to read. But Miner was permanently alienated from his life in a cramped flat above a halal butcher in Wood Green when a plumber was called in an emergency three years ago. The Essex man left the *Sun* next to the radio and switched off the Polish pop music the boys played at every hour and in every house. Miner opened the paper. He was horrified.

'Why you English always saying things like, "We like Polish . . . The Polish so hardworking . . . The Polish so good." Why you say this to my face? When I open the paper, I see all lies about Polish. They say Polish stealing, Polish drinking, Polish taking the work . . . You English only pretend to like Polish . . . English must be lying when they talk to my face.'

Miner is, like almost all builders, an obsessive saver. But unlike the rest, he is neurotic about it. He is always on his mobile phone calculating the precise value of his savings. This is because like many of the young ones he thinks he is only here temporarily. He is saving to build a house, a dream mansion. Miner needs £30,000 but the exchange rate and the influx of Romanian labourers are working against him.

He rolls a cigarette.

'Those Romanian . . . They are like, how you say . . . like cowboy. They never have insurance paper. They never make, how you say, the health and the safeties . . . They working for nothing. Romanians making Polish wages go down . . . They working for £4 an hour. The Britain is mad to let them come . . . The Britain is mad.' He groans. 'The Romanian, he not the worst . . . The worst, he is the Albanian. They coming more and more to the London . . . They are thief. They like work building too. They come find Polish . . . Go, "Yes, we pay good, we have good work, one week, two week, easy cash, no problem, no contract . . . No worries, mate."'

He draws breath and begins looking for a framing square.

'Then they throw out Polish . . . He work maybe one month, but they change job, say, "You got no contract," and never give Polish money. The Polish, he gets beaten. My friend, the Albanian they beat him . . . hitting him, hitting him. He come to me . . . Teeth is gone. Albanian mans . . . They are only peoples in London who scares me. They look like white but they are really like Muslim . . .'

Miner, like everyone on site, knows that the artful dodgers of Eastern European London are the Albanians. They are the only people the Poles are frightened of. Builders talk about Albanian scaffolding teams and construction teams with a stutter. They tell stories of Poles who went to work for Albanians only to be beaten into a coma when they asked for their wages. They ask how Britain could ever have let such dangerous people in.

I tell Miner how I like drinking in the Albanian pub on Kilburn High Road. This looks like a normal pub. Your classic dark-wood faux-Tudor watering hole. But outside they charcoal-grill meat like in the Balkans. Guys in gold chains and blue fashion-striped jeans sit smoking with girls in polyester fluff collars. Inside the horrible, sticky pub the carpeting is English, but everybody drinking is Albanian.

I brag to Miner how I love boozing in this pub for its mafia stories. This is because the Kray Brothers of today's London are from Kosovo. The Balkan wars brought at least thirty thousand people from Kosovo and Albania to London. It brought with them a couple of hundred gangsters, hardened KLA veterans and sworn brothers from born criminal clans of the Albanian south. I tell Miner their story over cigarette breaks. The one Albanian-translators for the police let me record in that pub.

They found work as bouncers, at first. At the millennium those running the brothels of Soho were Maltese. An old-established mafia. The Albanians disdained them as weak Soho bisexuals in pink bow ties and floral shirts selling only ugly girls from Newcastle upon Tyne. Barely warm in their leather jackets, smoking cigarettes at four in the morning outside the Maltese brothels on Greek Street, they hatched a plan. They would conquer Soho.

The first Maltese to fall went on his knees when the bouncers pointed a gun at his head. Quivering and pathetic in his purple jacket he agreed to sell up. But now they needed girls. Girls who were better and cheaper. One Albanian got in a truck and drove to Moldova. They trundled around the peasant villages promising glittering careers in waitressing and modelling. Then they raped and trafficked them.

This is how the Albanians destroyed the Maltese. But this was not the biggest Albanian cash cow. That was Westminster parking meters. This borough used to have fixed coin-operated machines. The Albanians saw them and their eyes lit up. Hundreds of thousands of £1 and £2 coins could be harvested this way. At first they beheaded the meters and drilled them open to see how they worked. But an easier way became quickly obvious. They bribed a Ghanaian traffic warden for his uniform and the all-crucial key. And got to work.

Miner says he knows this story. Not what happened next.

The police translators explained: the Albanian mafia by 2005–2006 became dizzy with success. They had conquered the brothels and stolen the parking meters. But then they overreached. The 'harvesters' had divided up Westminster into two. But the deal did not hold. Meeting in a crusty basement bar in East Acton where they played cards and downed shots in the evening the meter bosses confronted each other. It ended in a shooting.

Too many girls were being trafficked into Britain. Brothels were multiplying, now mostly operating out of Bayswater and Kensington flats. The police swooped and arrested the Albanian dons. They were shocked. They had never expected fifty-year prison sentences. They needed a new business. Five in a car, they drove to Green Lanes to speak to the Kurds. They had a proposition to make.

Miner listens as we unpack a washing machine.

Kurdish London began as little fruit and veg and halva shops in Haringey in the 1980s. This was when every single word in Kurdish was illegal in Turkey. It was a time when affiliation to the rebels could see you strapped onto a metal surface in a dungeon as the Turkish police switched on the military junta's anthem. This dissecting table would heat up until screaming the cooking man would confess anything. The song playing on the radio was always the same. 'Turkey is my Paradise'.

The rebels would come along Green Lanes shaking cans and asking the shopkeepers to give money for the revolution. At first they gave them coins and notes from their child benefits. But it quickly became a protection racket. Still swaggering, and peppering their demands with Marxist mantras like before, the Kurdish resistance had tapped the forbidden business for funding. The heroin route passing through Turkey.

This is the London Miner knows: where the social clubs look dowdy. Bare. There never seem to be more than two leathery old men there playing chess. Sometimes the windows are whitewashed over. But this is misleading. These eerie gathering places covered in PVC tablecloths and framed prints of Anatolian Alpine peaks are really the headquarters of billion-dollar businesses. There are some that never shut. Brutal-looking heavies in brown leather jackets loiter at the door smoking all night. Hoodies drift in and out.

This is where the Albanians came. The place so many others have come at some time or another. And they began the offer with the usual platitudes, 'As fellow Muslims,' but cut straight to the chase. They would help the Kurds get the gear across the Balkans for a share of the profits. The alliance held up for a couple of years.

The Kurds themselves were snared in the early 2010s. The clans of Green Lanes fell upon themselves. Dons were gunned down whilst having their beards trimmed in criminal barbers. Kurds and Albanians decided it was time to make the big money. They went into property. The money was laundered through hand car washes in Tottenham and Kilburn. But the estate agents asked no questions.

Miner shakes his head.

'The Albanians . . . we are scared of them . . . We see they sit in Costa Coffee, on their phones making crime, and we stay away . . . They are violence, mans.'

Miner cracks his knuckles. He spends his days drilling and sawing, mentally sketching the mansion he will one day build. He wants it to look like a red-brick Edwardian vicarage. He will get a friendly metallurgist to erect a London post box as a souvenir outside. He will be happy there.

If Conservative MPs ever deigned to talk to Polish builders they might discover people near-identical to the Norman Tebbit fantasy of the working class. Industrious savers. Family people. Willing to work for nothing. Fans of Thatcher, the Soviet-fighter. Disgusted by trade unionists and completely depoliticized.

Polish churches are full every Sunday. London was long a city of empty Victorian chapels. These frumpy Gothic naves now echo to Polish mass or Nigerian choirs. Polish churches are full of toddlers and pushchairs. Teary tattooed plumbers cross themselves. Hard-up meat packers shove £20 into the collection boxes for the nuns needing furniture in eastern Poland. Masses are sung for the war in Ukraine.

'Polish people think English churches only very, very weak.'

I go drinking with Miner. The evening is colours: lilac, mauve, pink – a Monet of clouds. We begin in the newsagent, filling his blue plastic bag with a dozen cans of Lechs. It tears. Traipsing home, Miner shares his confusion about the English.

'Why do they give the benefits? Why £60 a week and a flat for free for the lazy pig . . . when he no work? Why this happen? Poland . . . no money for the pig . . . no nothing for the lazy pig.'

Polish builders have little time for the white working class. They think they do not know how to look after themselves. They think they talk like black people. They think they look sick. Like they are going through a very hard time. Some think they are stupid. Polish builders buy food in bulk to make the cheapest packed lunches.

'This, is the only way a poor man can eat . . .'

But why do the English wander into expensive sandwich bars and lose more than one hour's wage for just one meal deal? Polish builders think they are out of their minds to spend three hours' wages on three pints in the pub, when you can get eight tin cans for that, and even drink them in the park with roll ups and everything.

'The English no understand money, I think . . .'

Miner snatches the police notice in his letterbox. 'Fuck! Not again.' He quivers in rage. 'The black people . . . They are stealing again!' There has been a robbery in the area. Miner lives in the part of London rinsed as Poundland. Dirty parades of betting shops, twirling doner kebabs, payday lenders, unlicensed pawnbrokers and signs for WE BUY GOLD.

'The black people . . . They are crazy people.'

We crack open the cans. They froth up. Miner drinks, then grows flushed. There are six people living in two rooms. My friend, his girlfriend and his father in one room. In the other Margarita the cleaner, her boyfriend (who had just lost his job at a recycling dump) and her tired mother.

'The black people, they like to fight Polish . . . We have friend, he work with us, he's a old guy. He work with the woods. He was living Streatham. There the black people, they are very big . . . The night time he waiting for the bus. Then black mans they come to him. They have hood up . . . Like this.'

Miner's chaffed hands pull up his own.

'They seeing our friend with the smoking. They see he is old man, weak man . . . Blacks they attack . . . They beat him, they beat him . . . Because they want his lighter . . . They want it for their smoking. They always robbing Polish mans, and flats. They live like bush.'

Polish builders are a little bit racist. London is home to more than 150,000 Polish migrants, probably. So keen are they to save that little bit extra that many go under the radar to avoid tax. This is why every builder I get to know on site has been burgled. Their flats are always the cheapest, built with flimsy locks. The kind that can be undone in ten seconds. Sometimes landlords are in on the racket.

Burglars love Poles because they are paid in cash and hide it in shoeboxes. When they see builders and cleaners moving in over the road, they are already laughing. They can sometimes make £5,000 from one bedsit. And they know the Poles will never call the police.

Miner wants to relax by showing me pictures of £5 million townhouses he has renovated. I am saved from this melancholy slide show by the return of Margarita the cleaner. She is too attractive to ignore. Like all cleaners, this girl from Białystok likes to boast she knows everything about her homeowners.

'I could hold them . . . to a ransom.' She giggles, a little bitterly. 'I know everything about them. I know if they are drinking too much, because I throw out the rubbish. I know if they are smoking too much, because I throw out the ashtray. I know if they are smoking drugs, because I throw away and see the ends.'

She stands and I sit.

'I know a lot. I know that the woman I am cleaning in the Clapham, she cheats, because I clean the sheets. I know the banker who I clean in Clerkenwell, he is taking the cocaine, because I find the Oyster card with the powders on the table.'

Margarita usually cleans when the homeowners are busy at work. This is the way she likes it. This means she can clean with her headphones in and chat away to other cleaner friends, scrubbing and spraying right across stucco London. But there are times, in the gloom of an afternoon, when moving through the living rooms strewn with oriental rugs, there is silence and nobody to call.

'There is just one thing that makes me jealous . . . That they can go away . . . They can go on holidays, not once, but two times, three times. Go there where it is hot . . . They are calling me, every week, one of them is calling, "Don't come, we go France," "Don't come, we go Spain," "Don't come, we go to Greece." This the only thing that makes me jealous. There is nowhere I can go . . . only once a year bus to Poland.'

Margarita sucks her lips in. 'You know, we think the English womans . . .' She hesitates, breathes. 'We think they are very, very weak. They don't do nothing. But they saying, "We are very, very tired." There is a woman I am cleaning . . . she is in the Battersea, she has the three children, but she is sitting at home doing nothing.

'She has cleaner, she has a nanny, she has a man who come to make nice garden. Woman is sitting in the kitchen doing almost nothing. But at the end of the day she is saying to me always, "I tired, I am very, very tired." But why?'

Margarita bites her lip and wonders whether to go on.

'I think . . . we are much stronger than they are.'

My eyes invite her to continue.

'The English people, I think they are very lazy. They rich English cannot do anything for themselves. Every time they need like a hammer, or the water it is having a problem, they are calling, calling, people who must do it for them. The poor English, he is sitting at home, taking the benefits, he is no working . . .' Her voice becomes definite. 'They don't want to work . . . when it is difficult.'

But Margarita is like all cleaners. They never think of themselves as cleaners. They are always future professionals. They have big dreams about Britain, unlike their boyfriends, because they speak English.

'Few of the houses are really very, very dirty. Cleaning mostly about polishing and keeping company for the lonely house mother and the lonely old house lady.'

These hours of unsolicited advice are the free English lessons and British crash-courses of Polish London. English unlocks London. Before long, many start flirting with the charming boys behind the till at JD Sports. Those in love with Polish men start to tell them they want to have children here.

'There is times, when I take the vacuum over the big wooden floors in those white houses, when I think, "Why was I not born here? Then things would be better." Because I will never live like them. I have a lot of things, you know . . . I have television, I have laptop, I have mobile . . . But I will never have like them, have my own home.'

Miner's eyes revolve. He can't stand her saying this. This is how the Polish dream house slips out of sight. Just like Margarita, his girlfriend wants to stay. London has left its Polish builders feeling emasculated. A labourer earns £7 an hour but a cleaner makes £10 an hour. Workmen unable to speak English have little choice but to chase Polish girls they cannot afford the cocktails for.

In twenty years he will still be here, probably in Streatham. He will have a cocky son with literary or financial aspirations in a sixth-form college, flaunting a fashionable Polishness. He grunts at the thought. Children; this is something he really worries about.

'My friend, he has girl. Her mother is a Polish, she come from Białystok also . . . But the girl she becomes, like English. He tells me, that when you are working you never become like English. You come to work . . . You go home from work. But when you have the children, in the English schools, when they become like English, you have to become English too.' He mumbles. 'Otherwise, they become like strangers.'

I take the night bus home, and tired, I listen again to my tapes.

I can hear not everyone will be as lucky as Miner. The luckless in Polish London drink. Half-vagrants hang around outside Polish yards and churches looking for work. Every builder has a vodka horror story. Like the builder who tried to hide from his boss in a gutted house by lying under a plasterboard in the rubble.

I click play on a stammering, hoarse voice: too many Poles end up like Santa. This is what the English smack-heads call him, even though he does not know what it means. Santa is lucky. He tells me he sleeps in a German army-surplus parka he was given by some praying black people who walk around at night. Santa's head is round, studded with cyan eyes, and his thick grey beard has bristled out white on the streets. His street drinking began when he was swindled out of his wages by an Albanian.

Santa mumbles he spends the days wandering round Victoria Coach Station picking up cigarette butts, by their tens, and in their hundreds, and when the light begins to dim, blue turns grey, then night, he will forage for cardboard boxes and make a bed for himself on a marble floor under the columned portico of a locked office.

'The worst thing that happened . . . It was a few weeks ago. These men . . . They came and they started shaking me going, "Hey, what's up, mate . . . Hey, why are you sleeping, mate . . . Hey, do you want to dance, mate." They were drunk English.'

Drinking blights the Polish countryside. This has now come to the streets of London. The majority of tramps in the city are Polish and Romanian. There are at least five thousand of them. Over three thousand have been bussed home over the past five years.

There were Polish tramps in north London who were forced to work unloading trucks for Turkish shopkeepers. These villains paid them in the tramp's drink of choice – the cider White Ace. I cannot describe how bad it tastes. Others were found roasting rats in back alleys in Tottenham and Haringey.

These humiliated tramps are hiding. I found them hiding from their families. Unable to bear the shame that London turned out to be a soiled mattress under a flyover. They send emails from Kurdish internet cafes for one begged pound, saying they are better than ever. I found they sleep mostly by the river. It is calm there. Huddled up, they can sing romantic Lublin hobo ballads and roll cigarettes out of pavement butts in peace. They toast handwash cocktails and curse their naivety for thinking you could night-bus it to a better life. To mix these cocktails, tramps sneak into hospitals and surreptitiously squirt the alcoholic liquid from dispensers into Coke bottles. It really hits the back of the head.

Every year there is a service at St Martin-in-the-Fields for those who died on the streets of London. They are men who were run over by minicabs that never stopped. Men who fell asleep on the Thames shore at low tide but could not swim. Most of them were Eastern European tramps.

We all drink. Londoners navigate the city by way of pubs. Polish builders, not so much. They cannot afford it. This only isolates them further. At 6.30 pm, exhausted builders crack open cans of Żywiec on the Central Line. Everyone sneers at them. The Poles go east to Wood Green and Leyton. The Lithuanians take the DLR to Beckton.

I take the train home with Jurek.

He is one of the few Poles in a carriage of Lithuanians, Ghanaians and Nigerians. In the bluish gloom past illuminated Canary Wharf ride the bleary-eyed renovators and security guards of a city they barely understand. Jurek stares out into the drizzle. He is a phlegmatic labourer from Gdańsk. He commutes in every morning to Kensington. London construction is a game for the rich. There are no jobs building office blocks and data centres in the suburbs but they are three a penny digging basement ballrooms in the Royal Borough.

Back home, Jurek used to work at a sewage-treatment plant. All day he would stare at the shit daydreaming about EuroMillions. They sacked him. He had always loved gambling. So after three days' drinking he got on a night bus. There was no real plan.

He woke up at Victoria Coach Station, blinked, and looked for the Internet cafe. He found it upstairs. French, or maybe Spanish, girls with dreaded, unkempt hair slumped over the weakly cleaned tables. Their headphones crackled. The ageing Bangladeshi behind

the counter chewed gum and ignored the gurgling refrigerator. Jurek tried to inbox-fish the only London number he had. But he got lucky. Poles he met there told him their foreman needed extra labourers. The pay was only £5 an hour but it was in a pleasant area. They promised good tools. 'It's work for a few days, no insurance . . . OK?'

Jurek was gobsmacked by the white-icing mansions this Perivale Polish company was renovating. They had sculpted columns like ancient temples over the doors. Floral stucco mouldings rounded their ceilings. He was also surprised that everyone who lived in Arcadia appeared to be Filipino.

Every morning a busy little woman would unbolt the lower ground floor and dash out to stock up on brass polish. Jurek would make a point of greeting her: 'Good day, madam.' He imagined her to be the oligarch's wife. But she would giggle and rush inside. 'Thank you, mister.' He did this for about a month until one of the bricklayers took him aside. 'The owners are in Russia, shithead . . . KGB. These yellow people are the maids.'

Builders know clothes are very powerful things. Try sitting on the Tube covered in paint and dust and sweat after a day hammering and sawing and hauling. Commuters will make that one extra step away. Corner shopkeepers will sneer at you. You will become less visible.

The longer I spend with men like Jurek the more I realize how Eastern Europeans think of Britain as a 'mini-America'. But there is no British dream. They come to London inspired not by a dream of how great things could be, but by the knowledge of how much worse they can be. Talk of Britishness draws blank faces. Immigrants say, 'Britain is a land of opportunity.' But they do not feel particularly welcome. Like they are living in a spare room.

This is the way it is. There are roughly a hundred thousand people like Jurek in this city. Men drafted onto the building sites, into work that requires no English and no answering back. These migrants are almost all from Eastern Europe. They are the ones building the Prime Minister's dream city of two hundred new skyscrapers.

Margaret Thatcher loved the maquette of Canary Wharf. She listened enthralled as the architects explained how a light railway would extend through the razed old docks. There was a toy train running round the mock-up. The whole thing was over 10,000 square feet.

The little railway ended in acres of suburban housing. Little red-brick cottages arranged in geometrical closes and perpendiculars. The developers explained to the Prime Minister this was where commuters to the financial towers would live. Just twenty minutes away from work and on the water's edge. All of them property owners. How she adored the architects' model dream.

The Docklands Light Railway still has the feel of a scale model. The stations sound as if they were named after pubs: Royal Albert, Royal Victoria, Gallions Reach. But the high-rise housing over the easternmost spur of the DLR has seen happier days. Dirty England flags hang from balconies. Panoramic vistas over gargantuan retail parks. The Millennium Dome is filthy, begging to be torn down.

Beckton is the end of the line, rebuilt for a middle class that never arrived. Now superimpose a poverty map of London over a Tube map. Dark red runs along the line to Beckton. More than 30 per cent of the children here grow up in poverty. But there is worse data. London is statistically parcelled up into 628 wards. Beckton is the ninth most deprived. Twenty minutes from Canary Warf and its glinting headquarters of HSBC.

Beckton doesn't look foreign at first. The unkempt trees reaching over cracked pavements. The locals-only pubs. Grotty supersavers. Dreary car parks. Concrete on tarmac under steel pylons. Beckton looks like the abandoned set of *Brookside*. But when you listen, this Tube stop sounds like a foreign country. Everyone bleeping through the ticket barriers is speaking either in Polish or Bengali, Lithuanian or Romanian.

East London's Zone 3 is turning into a Parisian *banlieue* – poverty pushed to the edges. This has happened in Beckton. Here old whites sip Carling lager resentfully in the carpeted afternoon pubs. Escapees from the inner-city degeneration of the 1980s, they have been dealt a cruel turn of fate by the metropolis. The DLR dream brochure they bought into has turned into a place less than 25 per cent white British. Unable to afford a reverse white flight, back into Hackney, grittier types take to wearing England football shirts at every occasion. Eastern Europeans make up as much as 20 per cent of the Beckton population, Bangladeshis and Pakistanis a further 13 per cent.

The cloud light is bruised by the overcast.

I enter a hangar-sized Lithuanian supermarket. Lithuanian mothers push trolleys down pickle aisles of mindboggling size. There are tables of activists getting out the vote for a Lithuanian fracking referendum. Blue tracksuits lounge in the Lithuanian cafe-grill, talking about the creeps and the car thieves.

There is everything a Lithuanian might need.

Grotesque Russian paintings are being exhibited on the second floor, where there is a small bookshop stocked only with Lithuanian tomes and anti-Putin pamphlets. Three women are sitting at a purple kiddies' table in the middle, having tea. Chopin tinkles in the background. The owner is clinging on to prettiness with an appalling blonde rinse. It has given her hair the look of straw. Half-hearted attempts are made to sell me white chocolates. But I want to talk about Beckton.

She thinks for a moment, before being honest.

'I don't live in Britain . . . I live in Lithuania. I watch Lithuanian TV . . . I use Lithuanian internet . . . My friends they are all Lithuanian . . . This shop is Lithuanian . . . I only meet Lithuanians. The only thing I do in Britain is pay taxes to the British.'

Drinkers and stoners gather at dusk on Beckton's artificial hill above the retail park. Measures have been taken to keep people out. High metal fencing rings the perimeter. Inside, brambles and nettles have eaten up everything. The curve of the hill exhibits crushed beer cans and rusting trolleys. At the top there are twelve pieces of corrugated iron shoved into the earth, the size of shields.

There was a battle in Beckton. Lithuanians broke into this derelict site one night and painted the shields in the Lithuanian colours: yellow, green and red. This enraged the local whites. They gathered in a local pub and vowed to fight back against the immigrants. They stole in the same way and re-painted the shields as England flags.

I find where the fence had been sawn through. From the bottom of the hill I can see the paint is in good nick. It has happened only recently. A bunch of Bangladeshi teenage hoods stand laughing around the England shields, pointing at the view. I can smell the skunk.

These are the Beckton Alps. There was a gasworks here a few decades back that produced a lot of toxic waste. They didn't know what to do with it so they landscaped it into a hill in the 1980s. The planners were enthralled when they discovered the toxic dump had created a panoramic view over Canary Wharf and the City. It was decided to refashion the heap into an outdoor dry ski slope that the imaginary commuters from the maquette might enjoy.

Princess Diana opened the Beckton Alps. Photographs of her were taken at the summit gesturing at the view. She had a drink in the Swiss chalet-shaped bar at the bottom. But then it all went wrong. The slope collapsed in 1993, exposing the toxins and crushing the chalet.

Local authorities seemed to have realized by then that Beckton was not inhabited by the traders holidaying in Chamonix they had hoped for. The slope was sealed and left derelict. Metal hunks to keep the earth from collapsing were placed at the top where the viewing platform had once been. Chicken boxes littered the long grass. But, indifferent to this, people kept coming to roll joints or paint the hunks with national flags.

Two teenage Ukrainian girls from Dagenham in leggings and American baseball caps are taking pictures of themselves suggestively against the sunset. The Bangladeshi boys circle them making macho hoots. But they are too shy to speak to the hot girls. This only seems to make the Ukrainians more enraged. Their shoot is inching into the provocative.

This dance seems to have been going on for some time. I interrupt in the vague hope they might offer me some weed. 'What do we think of all these Eastern Europeans?' The boys look for words.

'We are all immigrant, innit? Our dads all immigrants . . . Your lot immigrants then?'

I nod.

The boys stare wistfully at the girls.

Dagenham has disappointed these teenagers. It was all pawn-brokers, fried-chicken places and betting shops. Dagenham is better than Ukraine. But they know it is not all that great.

The girls both wear very white trainers. The rushing-water sound of the motorway is not far away. The darker-haired one puts her hand on her hip.

'You know, there are no young British people round here . . . It's like this: Russian and Ukrainian people hate Polish and Lithuanian people. Eastern Europe peoples hate Indian people. Everybody hates the black people. Whites hate everyone . . . That's just the way it is.'

The weed smells good. Behind us and over the curving dual carriageway, those ridiculously named objects line up dark against a dim sunset: shards, gherkins and cheese-graters.

Like the City of Oz.

BERKELEY SQUARE

Engines roar and pop. And I watch the Arab supercars of Mayfair circle the darkness in the middle of Berkeley Square. The silvery commotion swirls. But the rows of neat black railings sculpted into little spears glint steadfast. They are dripping with rain, light-licked by the headlamps, as they ring the obscured lawns and fine park benches tightly locked away from the night. But the garden, the trees and the sculptures are all now lost inside a swallowing black gloom.

The space-age vehicles are heavy-breathing at the crossing as I rush under the thick warm summer rain. They roar as the lights turn green and the plane trees rustle gently in the shower. This is the square where Winston Churchill grew up. And this is the sound of the season. The sounds of the summer months, when the richest Arabs who now own these musty town houses of baronets come to London for their fun. They ship over their wives. They ship over their families. But above all they ship over their cars: to bolt and screech, around the fairground swirl of Mayfair, where they know they will be seen by the sheikhs.

The supercars are pulling onto a side street of soaring mahogany doors and glass fronts that open onto galleries and dealerships or sleazy theatrical restaurants with a whiff of a sickly perfume. This is where I need to be. The restaurant doorman greets me by the flame-flanked opening. Suggestively uniformed women escort me through the dim warrens of a clumsily faked Ming Dynasty wooden panelling, concealing the choicest tables.

This is where I meet Nahla. There have always been daughters like her in Mayfair: errant, raffish, refusing to marry to their fathers' wishes – their rebellion tolerated by Daddy, perhaps because he sees

in her eyes shards of his own repressed self. They have been here as long as the town houses. But the real princesses and heiresses here are no longer English. They are from Dubai and Qatar.

'I'm not like the others. I'm different.'

Nahla says this three or four times before I start recording her. And she immediately tells me she hates this restaurant because it reminds her of the others.

Nahla is bored. She is Egyptian and she lives like any child of enormous inheritance: attending parties, organizing nights – and as her elbow definitely plants on the table, dangling a diamond bracelet from her wrist, I listen to her rattle frustrations with her lilting fuzzy accent of international schools, secluded skiing and Mayfair's golden mile.

And she talks like someone who is used to being listened to.

'I'm not becoming English . . . There's a global culture. It's very hard to say what's making someone English. Like cricket and all that? That used to be English . . . But it's not any more. Y'know I feel in London there are so many people here from so many different places they've kinda created their own thing here. It's not like America, where they dismiss anywhere your family's from. London that allows to embrace where your families is from. But perhaps that's because English identity is very weak.'

I try and pin down her hissy voice in my notebook. Her grammar is lazy, her slurring indifferent to Received Pronunciation, the slang American not English. I sense her obsessions are indulged without challenge: she loves hip-hop, and she thinks it is fashionable, and she loves Notting Hill Gate, which she thinks is rather fashionable too.

Nahla ignores the waiter.

She is an Arab blonde and she pities the supercars. Nahla knows the season has started when their calls and texts start dropping. She ignores most of them. But then they become imploring, begging even. And the comedown emotions of the boy on the line always quiver the same way. Nahla, we can't go table-clubbing without any girls. Nahla, we can't come to London without going table-clubbing. Nahla, we can't cope with it back home, please come out.

'The super-super-rich boys . . .' Her voice is pitched to be dismissive. 'When they think of London they think of getting wasted, going to a club . . . They do it because they just feel more free . . . like in Dubai you're fine if you're drunk in the club, but the moment you leave . . . it's awful, you can get arrested. A lot of Arab men are very bottled up. They've got a lot of frustration. They've got a lot of things they gotta live up to like . . . like behaviour . . . like who they are as human beings. There are a lot of things they are expected to be . . . but London is so free. Arab men can do whatever they want in London.'

Nahla has a personal rule. More than three missed calls and it means you begged for something. But these boys break that on every occasion. They are Egyptians. They are Saudis. They are Qataris. And in a way, they are all the same. They are all waking up in their fathers' holiday mansions still buzzing. They are all dialling the same Moroccan brothers with sleek BMWs who deliver with discretion and Arabic to their bronze knocker doors.

Nahla sighs when they finally arrive. They are already stoned. They are chirping like birds about the order. They are little boys bragging they have 10 grams, and Valium and Xanax for the comedown. These painkillers, they grin, are essential to avoid any sketchy depressive episodes, come the pale blue morning.

Nahla says nothing. The playboys first check somewhere for dinner. But they sit there listless and miserable. The country is fucked. The other countries are even more fucked. And we're fucked. There's no future. They talk about nothing else – until they start to take turns to drift in and out of the toilet – and that's when the boys begin to slap their hands and start to smile like jackals.

'It's kinda like my good friends that basically all you talk about . . . oh, is how fucked being an Arab is, and we have nothing there . . . and how it's fucked for ever now.'

Nahla finds herself soothing the playboys. Don't worry, these wars can't go on for ever. Don't worry, they can't get any more extreme than they already are. Don't worry that your father wants you to marry that girl, there is always a way people can make things work out. But the boys will no longer be listening. Their pupils have swollen. They are forgetting. They are beginning to tingle.

'It's so, so, awful.'

Nahla loathes table-clubbing.

But for any heiress in Arab London table-clubbing is inescapable. This is what the season is all about. The black rooms dancing with bouncing sheens of light. The house music breathing and buzzing. The tables glinting with bottles and nervous grins. These are what the evenings are all about. Those without tables are nothing: senseless millers, fizzing nobodies, licked tourists – nothing.

Nahla watches the boys. They take their positions round the table. But these are almost preordained. Boys have their pecking order – Alpha Male, Beta Male. And they always come out in packs. Nahla watches them push and jostle and tease each other round with the first clinks. But she is never sure why they do this.

Nahla sometimes squints at the Alpha Male in the group. This is the big boy who is making the decisions. He decides when people are hungry. He decides when people are tired. He decides whether the Beta Males want Xanax or MDMA. But the Alpha always seems nervous and exhausted being boss man. The Beta Males make no decisions. But they always seem to be having a better time. They are free to have a shit time if things turn shit. They are losing themselves to the drugs and the music. They are assessing the situation. The Alpha can never. His reputation is on the block if the night fails: bad music, bad drugs, no girls – this is his rep on the line.

Nobody is as stressed as the Alpha Male in a table club.

Nahla looks around. The scene is almost always the same. There is always the Russian table. They always have the prettiest girls. But they seem to have this violent tic and are always telling them to shut the fuck up. The Russians never dance. They never seem to stop arguing about politics.

Ageing men with the piggy faces they deserve crane in and whisper their plots with arms round each other's shoulders. Their pale and bony playthings sit fingering the corners of their hair, or sometimes stare limpidly into the dance floor, with their enormous eyes.

The Gulfi tables are completely different. They are much younger for a start and these boys are never rounding off a negotiation in the table club. They are high, mostly, and as the beats begin to drop they will get up and thump their fists in the air and whistle and clap their hands over their heads with breathless escape.

But their faces are riven with panic about girls. There will sometimes be a few. But there are never enough and their dance moves are poor. This is where the fireworks come in. The Alpha scans the floor then flicks his wrist for the barmen: bring us the big bottles.

The Beta Males whoop. This is the big moment. The barmen bring out the huge curved bottles of champagne with fireworks fizzing on the trays around them and begin handing out sparklers, and the Betas Males begin waving, and whooping.

Nahla winces.

'They're whooping, "Money, money girls, look how much money I have girl, girls come jump on my dick . . . " Oh sorry . . . I just hate it.'

But it always ends the same way. This is always the moment when the Russians click their fingers and double the order. The Alpha's face crumbles as the Russians send the barmen around the dance floor distributing sparklers and glasses to the best girls jumping in their dresses to the beat.

This is when things get competitive. But there are patterns to these things. The Russians go more for the mixture of big bottles and small bottles. They pretend to prefer those old champagnes that are less bubbles and more wine in their flavour, but in reality they are craving the clear front-of-the-head high from clean straight vodka.

The Gulfi table goes only for the big bottles. That is because there are always guys nodding their heads to the beat, who are stoned and don't drink, and there is a limit to how thirsty people will get when they are that MDMA-fucked. The Gulfi table wants girls bad. They will try and approach them but often this doesn't work and they will creep back to the table with cracked grins and forced smiles. But deeper into the night more Gulfis will start paying and the barmen will bring them the best blondes with a wink, who charge boys by the hour.

There are other classic tables in the house. There is the Indian table. These guys never seem to get good seating and are often stuck in the back without easy access to the dance floor. They never dance and they never seem to have any girls. But they always stagger out like teenagers because they can't hold their drink.

And there is the Nigerian table. These guys are the only ones really dancing. They are not into drugs so much. They are mostly there for the cocktails and the whisky. But they can be very competitive, too. Once the sparklers get down they will get right in there. But their table only ever seems to have small bottles. This is why there are always rumours – once the sparklers go out, that those bottles parading about for the firework dazzles went straight back behind the bar – until the next round of whooping and sparkles hit the floor.

Nahla becomes exasperated. There is the boy who loses his jacket table-clubbing and begins shouting at her it is such a rare designer number that he needs three prostitutes to calm himself down. There is the boy whose morning flight back to Cairo is only hours away who rushes her into the toilets with him because he is spinning dizzy and does not know what to do about his wrap.

The boy stands there touching his temples with his delicate fingers mumbling, "Do I cut this into chunky beast lines for the table, or do I flush it down the gurgling water bowl?" And then there is that skinny boy, whose teeth are grinding so loudly it sounds like a small man in his mouth is trampling through sugar, who grabs her, as the house pounds and begins shouting. 'We're fucked. The country's fucked.'

Nahla sits with me in the restaurant and her tone begins to speed up. She ordered a salad. And she picks at it, as if calculating calories, and then leaves it soaking into the dressing. There is almost a speeded thrill in her voice now.

'I'm just disgusted when I see that in Knightsbridge. It stinks of

that perfume they spray. I hate the whole thing. I hate what they do. I hate that attitude. So judgemental. Very intense. And with the girls, they really struggle, like with life.'

The Princess is Nahla's best friend.

She is from the Gulf. Her hair is black and glossy and she wants so badly to be good. The Princess lies with her back on the fluffy floor of her bedroom stoned out of her mind contemplating the spot-lights in the ceiling. The Princess gets so stoned she contemplates the patterns in the mouldings until she slowly realizes she is hungry. Then she fumbles for her phone and calls her driver.

'Bring me McDonald's.'

The Princess then lies there for a little while longer.

Nahla has spent hours with her on this floor.

'There'll be clothes everywhere and sheets everywhere, and money lying there in cash in the drawers, and clothes thrown on the floor, as the maid's job is to pick up and put in the cupboard . . . But the smoke is the most big thing.'

The Princess has a lot of staff in this house. There are two drivers: one is Moroccan and the other is English. Their numbers are always in her contacts for when she needs them. Then there is a cook who comes in three times a week and leaves things for them in the fridge. Then there are whole loads of Filipina maids.

'She treats them like shit, you know.'

The Princess is not allowed a key to the house. Her mother is dead. She committed suicide a long time ago. She was on medications. Her father is needed in court in the Gulf. But the sheikh still has very strict ideas on how they should be raised. The Princess has a midnight curfew. Any later the Filipinas are under strict instructions to open the door and text her father in the Gulf the exact time of her return. That means it is never long before he begins calling in fury.

'Y'know it's always the same.'

The maid's rap on the door with the burger. The Princess pulls herself off the floor and opens it slightly ajar. The maid quickly sticks her hand through and then it gets slammed back shut. Then the Princess rearranges the rolled towel she always pads along the crack under the door and hungrily eats the grease.

Nahla looks at me for a second.

'That's the thing. I don't wanna be negative about Arabs. There are a lot of amazing things. But these are the things that stand out the most. Like even all the dealers in this area they will tell you all the best clients are Arabs and they will buy every drug under the sun in like mass quantities of it. And it really feels like . . . All these grams and grams and hundreds and hundreds . . . I think a massive part of it is they are so repressed.'

The Princess is always stoned. She smokes sometimes ten or twenty spliffs a day: not bush weed, but real London skunk. She begins skinning up in the morning. The white cloud light will be flooding into her bedroom overlooking the thousand treetops of Hyde Park when she first starts smoking.

'She's not happy, y'know.'

The Princess is not smoking for fun. She is smoking because she doesn't want to be here. She is smoking so she enjoys her movie. She is smoking so she enjoys her burger. She is smoking so she enjoys her bed. She is smoking because she is depressed. So, Nahla comes round and skins up and gets high and laughs and lies on the floor with the Princess. They talk about boys. Nahla tells her she has met a Ghanaian rapper in a club. The Princess reacts with shock.

'Do you know he's black?'

'Yeah, I'm kinda aware, you know . . .'

Nahla tells her she asked him to fetch her a black cab outside the club but he'd failed: no cab would stop for him in a baseball cap – unless she stood very close to him to ram home the point they were a couple that night.

'It's disgusting. But y'know . . . not a surprise, really.'

Nahla tells the Princess about her dreams: the Ghanaian rapper asked her in the club, 'What do you do, what do you love,' and she had gone, 'Umm . . . nothing.' She doesn't want to be like this. She doesn't want to be like the mothers who chill all day only to flit between Mayfair lunch and Knightsbridge gym. Maybe she wants more. To be someone. Maybe.

'Y'see my mum never worked . . .'

Nahla can't hold my eyes.

'I dunno what she did, she went for lunch went shopping went to the gym . . . I dunno what they do apart from play with their feet. But they don't aspire for more than that . . . But that's being Arab woman in London. A lot of that and a lot of them never got the chance . . . if they'd been men, they'd be banking, or whatever . . . So that's Arab lady London, a lot, a lot of, y'know . . . frustration.'

Nahla watches the Princess become more and more stoned.

She is not allowed boyfriends. She is not allowed boys in the house. She is not allowed to go drinking like Nahla. She is not allowed into London. The Princess is supposed to sit here in this plush fluffy bedroom in this huge rococo mansion in Mayfair with the Moroccan driver, the English driver and all the Filipinas until the sheikh phones her up announcing that her future husband will soon be on his way to meet her from Terminal 5.

Nahla watches me taking notes.

'I'm telling you these enslaved girls they are really unhappy . . . They are all bunning weed . . . But like for me it's difficult to put my head in other people's heads, and my mind in other people's minds, and know what they think . . . I find it difficult. But I know that what they are saying about the veil and God and all that shit, they believe Daddy . . . And they don't realize that the Koran, like yeah it's been interpreted . . . and everyone who ever interpreted it was men.'

The Princess keeps skinning up.

Nahla lies on the floor and they talk about girls.

They talk again and again about the princess who ran away.

'Like we had a friend and she wasn't allowed to speak to boys. And she did. And her parents didn't know . . . so she was lying, compulsively, constantly and now she's had an arranged marriage and she's over there. I think she's OK, y'know. She told us he's a bit more chilled about it . . . and so she's got more freedom now. And she knew her elder sister, she ran away from an arranged marriage, and they went and got her in Canada. And now she's married. Y'know, that's worse.'

Nahla and the Princess lie there stoned and they talk again and again about lying. They talk about the princess who lied to her dad about everything. They both know her: she is getting with horrible men with tattoos in the grimiest clubs, but lies to her parents she never ever touched a drink and still prays five times a day.

Nahla sighs.

'Y'know, it's really sad but I've noticed a correlation between the super-strict parents and the girls with low self-esteem and it's all about yeah like how religious they are . . . it's like about snapping the women so she's just there for feeding and fucking as you do politicking or whatever.'

They smoke more and giggle and text for McDonald's and then, it always comes up, they talk about marriage. The Princess sometimes chain-smokes. She smokes ten, fifteen, twenty spliffs one after the other until Nahla tells her to stop it – she can't keep up – and passes out on the fluffy floor. The Princess lives in an unhappy house. There are brothers who live there too. They are angry she is smoking so much. But they don't know how much. And they are all stoned in their rooms too.

The Moroccan dealers pull up outside, deliver more and the Princess comes back up to her room. The grey light pours in. There she seethes with resentment until she is stoned and sedate enough to relax. There is nothing she can change. There is nothing she can do. There is no way she can ever escape into London. Nahla also thinks there is no way out for her. She lies stoned with the Princess and thinks to herself, This girl is too lazy, too comfortable, too gone, to live another way.

Nahla is playing with her diamond bracelet.

'The main reason why I gotta get away from them is that's all they aspire to . . . is this, being a Mayfair housewife. Y'know, they are really lazy, they want to do the minimum they can do, they grew up with really pampered existences, their parents gave them whatever they want, and their parents were telling them all the time, "Don't worry about it you're just gonna marry some rich guy . . ."

So they think, "Fine, I can do nothing as long as I get an approved guy . . ." And then they'll do nothing . . . They'll chill, have tea, go to the gym, have nice bodies . . . but they'll just chill, and chill, and chill and their husbands will probably be having affairs. And the women . . . Oh they are not allowed . . . And I think they are quite content, until their husbands cheat and give them up for younger women, and they're like, "Why did I give up all of this . . ." The women, they don't really cheat. It'd be a massive scandal. No way could a woman cheat. But the men are saying, "Of course men cheat all the time."'

Nahla stops talking to me for a second.

Smiling, as if exhilarated she finally said it.

But the Princess did come out once. They began to go table-clubbing. But the Princess didn't know how to drink. Two hours gone and she would be collapsed on the toilet floor with Nahla heaving her to her feet to meet the midnight curfew before the Filipinas beamed that terrifying text to the sheikh.

The Moroccan driver would be outside waiting, and once he had whisked her home, the Princess would make him get her Mc-Donald's, and begin to feel guilty, and shaky, and grab her hijab, and put it on, and begin praying on the mat given to her by her father for forgiveness for having drunk the alcohol with Nahla the damned.

The Princess only once drank herself into a fury. Maybe she had not smoked enough skunk. Maybe we can all drink ourselves into a fury like this. Nahla wasn't sure. They went table-clubbing that night. But the Princess was angry: she drank and drank and drank, she mixed drinks, she took shots – and when Nahla came to tell her, 'You have to go now otherwise the Filipinas will text the sheikh,' she started shrieking, 'I'm not going, I'm not going, I'm staying.'

Nahla almost sing-songs.

'I can do whatever I want, I'm chilling, and she needs to go home and she comes, and I say you gotta come, but she got completely fucked off her face, and she's basically jumping on every single guy. I keep trying to get her out the club and she's flipping a shit. I'm not leaving. So the club closes and the lights come on. She's shouting, "I'm not going home . . . I wanna come to Mc-Donald's." And she's like come to all these guys and everyone we were with and the driver like flips.'

Nahla tried to talk to her on the street.

The Filipinas had texted the Gulf. But the Princess wasn't listening. 'I want to go to McDonald's,' she said. 'No, you have to go home. You've broken the curfew.' 'No I don't want to go home, I want to sleep at yours,' she said. 'No, you can't,' said Nahla. There was no negotiation. The Moroccan was taking her home.

Nahla's eyes narrow.

'Don't ask me that I mean how is she gonna come? Am I gonna come get murdered in my sleep by her dad! No! I thought, "He's gonna come kill us all." Because he can. He could.'

The Princess woke up with her head beating and shaking and remembered everything that had happened. Then she began to panic. And she began to smoke. The Filipinas had texted the Gulf. And there was not long now before he called.

The sheikh was crying on the telephone.

'Why did you do this? Why did you drink? You are going to hell now because you drank. Why did you do this to me?'

The sheikh was crying on the telephone and then the Princess began crying with hot tears. She promised him she would never drink and she would never go out into the night again.

We are waiting for the bus while the rain flickers like a thousand fireflies, through the electric haze of the street lamps. The night is never truly dark in London. This shower has come so very suddenly, and it is falling much harder now. We are all cold. The rain rattles and patters. These are some minutes before four: but there are already no seats at this tagged-up bus shelter in Peckham.

I have been here before.

Eighteen times I have walked up and down the Old Kent Road. Eighteen times I have country-coded the shop-fronts. Eighteen times I have filled notebooks with what people say: the cleaners, the mothers, the sisters. And they have all told me I will only understand their lives if I understand their shifts.

This is why I am standing here.

Mapping the hours of their commute.

Eighteen times I walked up and down the Old Kent Road. And I heard no cockney at all. I found the twelve pubs are down to one. The Duke of Kent has become a Nigerian mosque. The Canterbury Arms has become the Afrikiko nightclub. The Frog and Nightgown has been demolished. The Gin Palace, the Green Man, the Dun Cow and the World Turned Upside Down have all gone too.

I write what I see: the white British are almost gone on the Old Kent Road. Their population has fallen by 620,000 in London since the start of the century. They are overwhelmingly the old cockney working class. Between 1971 and 2011 the white British share of London's population slumped from 86 per cent to 45 per cent. This

is the new London: where 17 per cent of the white British have left the city in the first decade of this century.

I write down my emotions as it rains: ambiguity first, uncertainty second.

We need the N21 for the city. But the rain hardens, slows, then showers – until that sound seems to swallow everything. The night glows more intensely orange. We are becoming numb. And there is no place to stand either: because this shelter is crammed. There are ten, now twenty people, at this bus stop. And there is nothing special about them. This is just the night shift for the 250,000 migrant cleaners of London. The rush hour, before the rush hour, that makes sure all of our offices are clean.

I look around. This is a city where exhaustion is the face of the poor – and this is a face everyone wears differently. There is an old woman, shivering and scarfed, whose eyes have swelled and glazed. There is the thin boy who cups his nose in his hand, and a man, white stubble on his cheeks, who has buried his face into his rucksack and pulled up his blue hood. These are the night cleaners of the City of London, coming to clean a hundred toilets, and vacuum a thousand metres of grey open-plan carpets, between row after row of humming computer bays.

Five past four. You can hear snivels, and coughs, and sneezes. You look around. Everyone in the bus shelter is African: there is the squinting man in a cheap fleece and a little flat cap, clutching a little blue plastic bag, because it is useful. He is buttoned up, mumbling a bit, now shivering a little. There is a slender girl, a black kerchief over her braid, in a blue jacket, yawning with her hand over her mouth.

There is the built guy, somewhere in his twenties; his hair shaved, his trainers immaculate, playing quickly with his thumbs over his phone, before covering his face with his hands. And this man with a scarred face: jeans set apart, an authoritative stand, hands shoved into his pockets, who slowly bites his lip, and does not let it go. You can see it clearly now. Anyone can be a cleaner. Because there is a whole hidden city of migrant cleaners in London – with a population bigger than Portsmouth, bigger, if you count the illegals, even than Newcastle.

This is our night. And now the lorries are thundering past. They throw up water behind them, and with the nightlights, it looks something like sand. We blink and shiver. The bus must be coming – goes the wish, goes the whisper – as the cleaners become colder and colder; and I am watching, as the woman with the braid steps out from the shelter, into the rain. Can she even be twenty?

She looks at her feet, splashing in the water, and lets her eyes fall on the two red lines running through the gutter, and the pools of water there. And then her eyes turn back, over the pavement, over the hardened chewing gums, into the brown vomit the rain is rushing through into the drain, past the stamped coffee cup in the gutter, and the newspaper soaked grey, barely identifiable for what it was. And everywhere all these dozens, and dozens, of crunched Mayfair and Marlboro butts.

The newspaper-wrap fish and chips have gone. There are only chicken shops now on the Old Kent Road. And this batter and bone is what the night tastes like in London. There are a few still open, spilling out light, and a few staggering drunks, unsteady Romanians a few hours off site, stumble in and out, clutching their little boxes, singing something, wild and chanting.

Nine past four. And there is noise everywhere. The planes moan steadily overhead: and they blink steadily with bright red lights as they come to land. The white vans and the lorries growl and putter and roar as they rush, and stall at the lights. That sodium glint, the true colour of every city, bounces off the bonnets of a hundred roaring lorries on the stocking shift. The Old Kent Road is the way into London: and it always has been.

Ten past four. And there is not enough room under the shelter for all these cleaners, not enough room for the tiny woman with the two scarves and the brown hooded puffa that falls to her knees, clutching her rucksack, with a little fear of the dark. Like so many others, she is too old to be doing this: she will not last much longer on the four-to-six shift cleaning the City. You can always see it on their faces: that test of how a heart is beating, or nerves faring. It's in the eyes, how the body is coping with this bussing in, bussing out. When the pupils go beady, a little wild, and become a little glazed: that's when you know the shifts are breaking something.

You hear it first, and then come its lights, and with a tiny crackle of joy the cleaners move into the rain. The bus is coming. The double-decker – it squeals, it whooshes, and it bleeps open, its windows steamed and white, with nasty bright light. They clamber on and swipe: and it feels a little warmer. But there is nowhere to sit. The plastic aisle shining with the wet marks from boots are filled with hoodies and puffas, and the cleaners force themselves on, between a hundred others.

Fifteen past four. The bus is at its busiest now, with Ghanaian men coming in for the dirtiest, nastiest, cleaning in the Tube depots. These men, three workers on the upper deck, have already changed into the bright orange jump suit of the hidden classes. White music-cables dangle out of their ears, running over the firmly tied knots of their scarves.

London is so very cold. They call this spring here? These men are hunched slightly – and bloodshot. Looking out, away, from the bright stinging down-lighting of the night bus, through the smudgy circles they have made through the window steam. And I wonder what their music is that can take them so far away.

You can see it clearly now, how exhaustion is a very personal thing, how it takes us to our very edge. There are those who cover their faces, and those who bury them in their bags, and a few who chatter, and giggle strangely – in Romanian, or is it Yoruba – as the Middle Eastern growl of the driver calls to move down, move down, move the fuck down the aisle.

You can hear the roar of the engine and the screech-splash through the puddles. I can hear everything but see nothing, The windows are so steamed: the only thing you can make out is the endless lines – of those orange traffic lamps, one after the other, that give the night its colour, and those flashes, in and out as the bus screeches to a halt: of green, and red, bright deep light.

I will not find a seat. But those who have, snatch their shallowest sleep. Two Nigerian women are slumped at the front, bonnets pulled down, scarves tight, because this spring for them is very, very cold – and for a moment you catch a bloodshot gaze, as their eyes flutter to stay awake, and the bus drones, and moans, and they try and keep warm. And I crane around: am I the only London-born on the bus?

I push up to the window. Behind me, a Bolivian cleaner in leggings, one leg slung over her boyfriend, cradles his face in her hand, and whispers something in his ear. Her man is dead asleep, a South American, his mouth a little open, and she holds him, because his neck has given up. With the wrist of my hoodie, I wipe away the illuminated condensation, and look out.

We have left Peckham behind. And as we roar north into Walworth past drum-skeleton gasworks and wreckers' yards, I can make out the crusty shop fronts of the parade: the Pakistanis unpacking their crates at the cash and carry, the meat trucks pulling in from the abattoir outside Zam Zam Halal, the dark shapes of Afghans crossing their fingers for calls behind minicab windows.

But this parade only comes alive hours after the spring dawn, rattling up with a hundred shutters, as they unlock the betting shops, the switched-off Vietnamese nail parlours, the sleeping African praise shop, the Romanian grocers with the lights left on, and the South American greasy spoons, where they leave out Colombia flags even in the rain. I found only one English shopkeeper left on the Old Kent Road. The plumber's merchant between the shifty recruitment agencies where African women line up in the early morning to sign on for shifts, here and there, in the care homes, for the old people, where the English go to die.

Four twenty-seven. And clattering down the Walworth parades anyone can see the Old Kent Road is a street of hidden churches: Christ the Ladder, the Holy Ghost Zone, City Mount Zion. But these are African churches without spires, shoved into creaking old cinemas, dead bingo halls and musty old pubs. Their mission hoardings say it all, Raising Breakthrough Generation, the House of Refuge, the Church for Overcomers. I read the faces around me: the poor, the pushed around, the invisible.

Four thirty. We are almost north. The plastic floors of the bus

tremble with the growl of its enormous engine. And the driver shouts out in that strange accent again: there is no smoking, there is no smoking on the bus – and at the back, a Lithuanian, hood up, stubs out his light into his beer, and swears in a way nobody understands. And the bus groans on, with more and more Africans, Eastern Europeans and Latinos, pushing on at every stop along the Old Kent Road until suddenly, through the fingermarks I smear on the window, I can see it.

The river. And with steamed windows shining, our dark figures blurred, through panes of glittering condensation, the double-decker whooshes over London Bridge: and suddenly we have a sense of where we are: scale, even sky, electronic night lights – neons of red, orange, blue – rippling manically in the black violet waters of the Thames.

And now we are over the bridge, into the other London, and the scruffy parades, and the blockhouse estates, and the concrete junctions, are another world, as the bus wriggles through canyons of stone and monumental sculpture. It turns round these tall, unreal buildings, these granite colonnades of finance, and becomes small, tiny, and bleeps to a stop for the cleaners, under these glass pillars of wealth. And then it continues, empty into the night.

KNIGHTSBRIDGE

The Filipinas know everything about Knightsbridge.

The Filipinas are always watching. The Filipinas know everything about here. Today there are at least fifteen thousand servants here. The typical mansion will employ four housekeepers, two maids, a chef, a driver and, of course, a personal assistant – or butler. These castes have an ethnic tinge. The chefs are typically French or Moroccan. The drivers are mostly African or Eastern European. The butlers tend to be English. But the housekeepers are almost always Filipinas.

And they are always watching.

The Filipinas took weeks to persuade. The bosses are violent, they said. The bosses will fire us, they pleaded. But finally the Filipinas invited me for tea: on one condition. They must not have a single feature identified: no names, no haircuts, no eye colours, no heights or visible limps, or gaits, no addresses, no places of birth, no ages, no frowns, scars, or particular chuckles or grins. They could only be identified collectively as the Filipinas.

And once that was agreed, they promised me the secrets.

'Come on Sunday. Come for tea with us and Auntie Mia.'

As I come for tea the sky is muggy and grey.

Northbound carriages are sticky and humid. There is a clammy and heavy thickness to the summer air. The carriages are uncomfortable with sweat. Beads drip along the faces of the old men and damp patches grow under their arms. There are reddening faces and dehydrated eyes. There are sighs of relief each time the Jubilee Line scrapes and squeals to a halt. Thudding doors open with sudden gust of unbreathed, cooler, thinner air.

The station where I exit is twenty-five minutes north-west of Mayfair. Here the tracks run outside. The platform is a concrete slab between them, without pretensions. Blackbirds flick to and fro over the line, as if distressed by impending thunder. The tannoy is booming with a Ghanaian accent: announcing closures.

Auntie Mia's address is on a terrace backing onto the tracks. This is a shabby row of slate-roofed workmen's cottages. Their easy-to-crumble clay-brick facades each have a fooling-nobody bay window smacked to the left of their front door. The little romantic carvings in the corners of the windows are now creviced with a blackish muck. This is a row of people coming and going: another stopping-off point, of doss houses and damp rooms, in outer London, where transience, and uncertainty, is the rule not the exception. In a third of London's boroughs half the population churns every five years.

As I ring on the bell, I avert my eyes from little white boys in hoods, smoking skunk, coming and going out of the open door, two houses down, sweating a boredom that very quickly turns to menace. There is none in the Filipina house. Only commotion and cake smells. This is how the servants relax: with frenetic baking. The women sit me down. They are giggling and eating fried bananas and quickly stir mixtures as they snigger about their owners in a swirl of sugary fun. The oven slams open and shut with sudden syrupy wafts. This is their sacred time. The only hours when they are not invisible, silent, little women.

I start the recording.

And, with intensity, they begin to talk.

The Filipinas have seen it all: Doha, Abu Dhabi, Dubai. They have seen a thousand skyscrapers, a hundred gleaming airports, and a hundred days of smog. Every Filipina has felt like family; and every Filipina has been slapped like a slave. They have seen every side of them: the master's little smiles, madam when she cries. The Filipinas have seen what they wanted. They have shivered on rolled-out sleeping mats on the balconies of Beirut and sweated trembling on bunk beds in Bahrain.

They are enslaved by the Arabs before they realize what is happening, and they pray and cry and dream that the Arabs will take them to London. Because that's where you can run away. They pray and cry when master beats them, when madam bites them, when she slaps them, that one day, one summer, the Arabs who enslaved them as their servants, and locked away their passports, will want to visit London.

They dream always of London. They are dreaming of London as they are rushing up and down between the marble flights of stairs for their ladies; smoking, smoking, the ladies always smoking, dringing, dringing the bell to always, always, empty every one of the ladies' ashtrays. They are dreaming of London as they run from the dringing, to the dringing; the first wife she wants ironing, the second wife she wants cleaning, the third wife she wants smoking, and now master, he wants cooking.

They are ironing at midnight, those forty huge white robes that master in Doha sweats right through, and the forty polo shirts he bought in Dubai; and as they push down their thumb to spray, the crinkles and the pleats vanishing with the metal and the heat, they think about London. They never stop thinking about running away. And they never stop talking about running away; when they see each other in those silvery lifts, when they catch a glimpse of each other over those shiny tiles of the cool air-conditioned malls, when, every so often, the Arabs let them out. And always, every time, the servants talk about the runaway slaves of Hyde Park.

And then it happens.

The Filipinas arrive and in the plastic tunnels that lead them off the airliners they feel the cold, the cold they never knew, and they feel excitement and they feel alive – because the cold they feel is freedom. The Filipinas are trembling as baggage reclaim goes round and round – madam's Louis Vuitton, master's Dunhill leather – because they are feeling cold, and in that cold is everything the Filipinas in Abu Dhabi ever told them about London, the only Arab city where Filipinas can run away.

The Filipinas are always silent around their owners – and in the back of the car, those huge big black taxis, riding in a flotilla of three, one for the master, one for the madams, and one for the security and the servants, they are so, so silent, as always; but their eyes, they speak, huge, black, round, wide – as the headlamps rush past them, and the motorway gives way to hundreds, thousands, tens of thousands of little houses, with their little painted front doors. And they wonder where is the London Eye, how far are we from Buckingham Palace – as they keep on telling themselves, reassuring themselves, how often this happens, that this is not insane; how there are Arabs that come to London with three Filipinas and come back with one, how there are Arabs that come to London with ten Filipinas and come back with none.

The Arabs mostly live in tall white houses that look like sugary white cakes. They live in the Arab quarter that the English have called Knightsbridge. They are happy here. They are relaxed in this place, and when they are relaxed they become agitated, that something will happen that might unnerve them, aggravate them, and they become angrier, and snarlier, and curse at the Filipinas – get me this, get me that – they are princes, and princesses, and this is how princes and princess have always, always been. And the Filipinas become smaller, and hide faster, and spray quicker.

The masters, they are always worried in the season, flicking their wrists, and touching their watches, and going swipe, swipe, swipe at their phones. The masters, they are the ones that know what London is about – eyes, show, circus – and they are always worried that their five cars, their thirty suits, their forty watches will not arrive on time, for this is what the season is all about, walking, strutting, cruising up and down Knightsbridge and being seen by everyone that matters in Doha and Dubai. The masters, they live for the season, they live for the show – those eight long weeks of circus in August and September when Knightsbridge is where they must be.

The masters, they are the great-grandsons of warriors, the great-grandsons of men who could ride for sixty days through the empty quarter and slit the throat of an Ottoman spy with a piece of telegraph wire, but they are not like them, they are cowards; and the Filipinas know this, they know this only too well, they know it in snarls, and slaps and blows, because they know cowards are the ones who lash out at those that cannot bellow back at them – cowards, they always scream at their waiters, and they always roar at their staff.

Filipinas are running up and down, running up and down, those grand old houses built for servants, in the long, curved streets that run from Arab Knightsbridge right up to the grass, and the trees, over the traffic island at Hyde Park Corner. The Filipinas are always watching, the Filipinas never stop watching, because the Filipinas are always there – behind madam as she dresses, hiding from madam as she cries, waiting for the bell from madam, dringing, dringing, as she sits in the drawing room alone, all afternoon, waiting for someone, anyone, to come, or to call, or to invite her for lunch, to take her anywhere, even to Edgware Road.

But madam only ever goes to Harrods with the Filipinas, walking, her face covered, her eyes always somewhat dim, here, there and everywhere unable to know if the long black swirling cloaks and perfume balls she is passing through are her precious sisters or her precious friends. Madam never seems to learn her way around, forgetting everything she needs, or tossing a few things into the baskets of the Filipinas in the grand carved food halls – dates, candies, maybe marzipan fruits. And this is how madam floats through the Harrods food hall every afternoon – sadly, sadly – as the Filipinas are rushing around their madam, gently guiding her, watching her, crossing the paths of the Arabs who walk with their black man slaves, who always walk three steps behind, as the rules say they do in Doha.

And the Filipinas, their hearts are beating in the gold of the food hall, as they rush, rush, rush past those scores of fish prostrate in those cabinets on those crunchy beds of ice; their hearts are beating as they try and catch the eyes of the Filipinas who are shopping alone for their madams, the white madams – 'Hey, hey, hey, are you Filipina, hey, hey I need to make an escape' – and their numbers come quickly.

The Filipinas in the hotels, they have it easier than the Filipinas in basements. They still get slapped, cursed and bitten, but they see other Filipinas, there in the hotels: the Filipinas that belong to the French, the Russians, the Italians – 'Hey, hey, hey, help me I need to make an escape' – and they are soon texting, texting, to make this escape, to help make this sister a runaway.

The Filipinas all help each other: the word goes round, someone needs to make an escape; and they message and message until they have it all sorted out. The Filipinas who are in the mansions, they escape like this: taking big creeping steps, creeping to the doors – Hey, hey, master, madam I am going to put the bins out – holding two big bad crinkly bin bags; and when they are out the door they make a break for it, running, running, running, down the mews, round the statues, through the garden squares, with two big bin bags full of Filipina clothes, until they find them, the Filipinas who swore in Harrods to help them – and then they run for the bus, out, away, deep into north-west London where the Arabs never ever go.

The Filipinas who are kept in the hotels are not so lucky, they have to run away in the evenings, when the Arabs take them to Hyde Park; when it happens, it happens on those evenings, those cool September evenings, the ones the Arabs love, with the drizzle and the damp spreading grey. Those are the evenings when the Arabs walk slowly, slowly around the grey waters of the Serpentine – because this is their park, the park they love, the park they talk about on dog days in Doha, the park they think about when the grinding traffic of a thousand Land Rovers in Dubai grinds to a stop – the park where they feel happy, and cool, and watch the grace of the swans.

This is the moment, this is the moment, when the Arabs are walking at dusk, when the Arabs are happy, breathing in the thick damp air of a sudden shower, breathing in the light as the shapes of the trees turn black, and foresty, this is the moment, this is the moment, when they see other Filipinas, as master and madam and his other madam walk on ahead smoking, smoking, always smoking – and go, 'Hey, hey, hey, I need to make an escape.' And the Filipinas shout back, in their language nobody understands, that

nobody would ever bother to learn – 'We'll help you, we'll help you, sister, come back tomorrow, walk through here, in there, yes, there, the Rose Gardens, they'll not know where to run, if you run away in the Rose Gardens.' And the Filipinas hope, and pray, and ask Mary, that the Arabs will wander into the Rose Gardens, those walls of dying flowers and creepers and benches and haunted stone cherubs where the princes with secrets go furtively to hold hands and wait, excitedly, for it to get dark, and touch, the way in Doha you never could.

And the next day, they follow monsieur and madam into the Rose Gardens, round the corners, besides the spurting fountains, and then they run, they run, they run . . . and they run through the gardens, and round past the huge columns at the edge of the park, and through the gates at Hyde Park Corner; they run through the traffic, and they run through the giant arch under the winged demonic angel of war riding her chariot of trampling victory.

They run through Hyde Park Corner, that huge traffic island, that huge traffic island with the feel of an incomprehensible ancient ruin; that one where only the tourists linger, surrounded by the walls of names and the sculptures of soldiers that the English are very respectful to. Like they are tombs or something.

But this time the Filipinas are not looking – they are running, running, running, through the tunnels, to the bus stop, where they jump on any bus – and they are crying, crying, as the red double decker bleeps and rolls away, round the walls of Buckingham Palace, all blinking with hidden security and barbed wire; the most beautiful of all the parks in London that nobody is every allowed into but the Queen and her strange little dogs.

This is how a thousand Filipinas escaped, this is how a thousand Filipinas arrived as runaways in London – with nothing but a bin bag of clothes, or nothing but the phone number of Auntie Mia. This is the number they shouted across the food hall. This is the number they memorized from a whisper in silvery hotel lifts. These are numbers of their escape. The number of the mother of Filipina London.

Auntie Mia was once a music teacher at a school in the stucco of St John's Wood. This was a little school where the children were mostly little Jews with little twitches and little black curls. Auntie Mia would teach them piano and rush, rush, rush out for something to eat at McDonald's or a KFC at lunch – when in the nineties the runaways started to come. Auntie Mia would be in there, chomping, chomping, chomping – with her burger, with her wings – when the first girls started coming up to her. 'Auntie Mia, they told us about you.' 'Auntie Mia, they told us you were good.'

Auntie Mia would never forget the first hundred runaways: their names, their eyes, their villages. How the girls first heard of her having lunch in the McDonald's or the KFC in St John's Wood (she liked to alternate) she was never entirely sure. Auntie Mia would never forget the way they walked up to her – they were shaking, they were crying – and they warbled that many Filipinas had told them Auntie knew many rich Jews who needed many servants for their big houses that shone like sugar cubes.

Auntie Mia never rushed the girls. Auntie Mia always let the girls cry. Auntie Mia always held their hands: as in the corner of the McDonald's (or the KFC) it all tumbled out – how madam had thrown boiling water at her, how master had raped her, how madam had whipped her, how master had not paid her for nine months. Auntie Mia hugged them – Auntie Mia loved them.

A thousand Filipinas thank Auntie Mia. A thousand Filipinas came to Auntie Mia hoping for a new home. At first she ran around the playground asking the lady Jews who were so proud and so concerned about their how their babies were doing on the piano, whether they needed some more servants – and how many homes there were for them. And there were so many homes that needed servants that Auntie Mia stopped being a music teacher and became an agent for finding homes for their Filipinas.

A thousand Filipinas call her Auntie Mia. And every time they come to see her they laugh about the way they use words here in London. The Filipinas only snigger. They were called servants in Doha and Dubai. They do the same work here but master and madam shiver and shake when they say they are servants. They cannot use that word. They want them to call themselves domestics or household managers. They are still masters and madams but they shake when you say that: here, in London, only first names are allowed between a master and staff.

And every weekend the Filipinas come to see Auntie Mia. They come to relax, they come to laugh, they come to make noise, they come to bake frenetically, they come to be as loud as possible. They love karaoke. They love hysterical laughter: mocking, mocking, mocking their master and madam. With Auntie Mia the tension shakes out into hysterics – unstoppable hysterics. Because all week they are hidden, cowed, silent little women. All week – they are frightened of the line.

All the servants in stucco London are frightened of this line. But nobody knows where it is with their master and madam, because the Filipinas who have crossed that line have been fired on the spot. All the servants have their own ideas. There are some that say the line is speaking when not spoken to. There are some that say the line is speaking like a master: questioning, criticizing, even asking. There are some that say the line is being seen: a good Filipina is an invisible Filipina.

And every weekend they tell Auntie Mia about their new homes – as they bake banana cake and rice cake and cocoa cake and make non-stop Filipina happy eating. Auntie Mia knows the truth about being a servant. A servant is never only a servant. A servant is either a member of the family or a slave. And she knows what it means for her thousand children: the Filipinas are either very, very happy; or very, very sad.

Auntie Mia lets them relax. The spring uncoils. They are laughing, laughing – a thousand hours of tension has become a little fun as they mime out master or madam in a strop. And as they keep on eating their wonderful warm cakes tumbling out of the oven one by one – the gossip comes out. This is the highlight of the week in Filipina London: the upstairs, downstairs stories that only the Filipinas know, and only they can tell.

And every weekend Auntie Mia hears about affairs. There was a Filipina in a crooked old mews off High Street Kensington who was receiving hush money. There was a Filipina in Hampstead who had been handed five thousand pounds to lie. There was a Filipina in St John's Wood who refused three weeks' paid-holiday hush money because she was a Christian and ran in a fury to Auntie Mia to find her a new home.

And every week there are the tears about the children. A few years here; a few years there. And the Filipinas become mothers a dozen times. And they pass around their smart phones – there are my two Jewish children, these are my lost Arab babies, and here is my two, back then, Italian twins. And they cry, and cry as they pass around their smart phones with the smiling backgrounds of little ones. They made energy bonds: and then they were culled – move on Filipina, move on.

And they ask questions. 'Please, sister, please – you are now working in the big house in South Kensington. Does my French baby still remember me? Does he still put his head like this? Does he still remember who taught him to brush his teeth? Does he still read *The Very Hungry Caterpillar*? Does he still cry a little when he laughs? Please, sister – ask him if he remember me. Please, sister – kiss him for me.'

Auntie Mia is very strict with them. Things can go very easily wrong when you love the little rich babies. There is to be no talking in Tagalog to the little babies. There is to be no Tagalog lullaby. There is to be no Tagalog cuddles. Because one day when madam comes home the baby will start talking a little bit in Tagalog and madam will throw you right out. But this is very funny when it happens: when the Filipinas see the blonde Russians' babies, running, round and round in the private gardens, behind the railings, shouting like a Tagalog baby, 'Nanny, nanny – you can't catch me, you can't catch me.'

And then they tell the brave stories. And everybody listens and cheers. And everybody says, 'Next time I will be a brave sister like you.' And this is something they never expected to see: the punching, the kicking, the swearing – the men, the rich men, the men who have everything – they are hurting their women like the men who have nothing. And they hide this from everyone: apart from their Filipinas.

There was the millionaire in Hampstead that punched his pregnant wife. There was a drinker banker in Notting Hill who would come home and smash his cutlery and hurt everyone – the banker would even hurt his children. The beaters and the drinkers: they were no different from the beaters and drinkers in the shacks of Manila. They are cowards. They are always cowards: these men who lash out at women.

And they never bother to hide it from the Filipinas. The way their eyes bounce off the Filipinas. They don't land. The ways their eyes land on the Filipinas is how they bounce off the fridge. They have as much fear of the Filipina calling the police as they have of the fridge dialling nine-nine-nine. Well, it happens. A lot. And the millionaires, they are speechless, frothing – shouting, 'Who the fuck did this, you fucking fuck,' as the police cuff that bastard in his corridors hung with mirrors, and the Filipina walks up and looks him in the eyes and goes, 'Remember me, it was me.'

And every week they come and tell Auntie Mia: 'Auntie, Auntie, they treat us like appliances, like one of their appliances, which are made of metal, and even these sometimes break, and what about us, us who are made of flesh – we are the ones who are never allowed to have a breakdown.' And Auntie Mia hugs them.

And then they laugh again. About all the funny things about the masters. At first Auntie Mia only found the Filipinas homes with Jews. But the Jews, they love business, even a business that is not theirs – and one of the Jews recommended she create an agency and now she finds the Filipinas homes with everyone in London.

And the girls love discussing them. The Russians, they say, they pay the best. But they have this angry streak and their women are very sad. The Russians, they say, have too many staff and are very erratic: vanishing for nine months at a time, leaving them clueless, cleaning and cleaning away, in case they suddenly barge in. The Russians, they say, they are not very concerned about the clean – they never seem to notice the dust, they never seem notice the shine. And you can slack a bit for them.

The French, they are so different. They are not like the Russians at all. The French, and all those other peoples who come from countries like Belgium or Italy who are really just another kind of French – they are obsessed about the clean. They become angry with dust. They shout at a smear. But they are very regular. They are mostly here all year round. They are reliable: and payment it is always in full.

The Africans, they are so lovely. They only have a few Filipinas who live in the mansions of the Africans but they are very happy. The girls say they are kings. And they come very rarely, once or twice a year, but when they come – they are jolly, happy fellows in red, yellow and purple robes who are full of laughter and a love for girls. They have an eye for the cleanliness: but they are not as bad as the French.

All these people are so strange. All these people have such strange families. All the Filipinas want is to be together and eat cake together and laugh together. But not these people, the people who can do this right now. All the time they are thinking of the family they left behind – mummy, daddy, baby – and how they would give anything, how they would stop at nothing, only to live with their families, the way master and madam can. And this is why it feels so strange to watch these white people. How they do not love to be together, how they do not love to cook and eat together: inside those stucco mansions they talk to one another like they are passing guests in a hotel and hurry, hurry, out to do whatever they have to do.

The Jews, they say, they are white but they are very strange. They are like poor people back on the islands. They love to be together. They love to sit together. They come close to each other on the sofa and they talk, and talk, talk about everything and nothing to each other. They are rich people, the Jews, but they are very strange. They have huge long tables and grand silver bowls but when they have their special Jew dinners with all their chattering families they love to eat only the foods of poor people.

The Jews, they have this soup which is very precious to them. They teach the Filipinas to make this soup very earnestly, this is something serious for them, because this soup is very special for them. Of course, they serve this to them, this chicken broth with strange bready balls: and the Jews, they call this the soup of matzo balls. They serve this horrible thing to them on their huge tables and they eat it with their huge silver spoons. But why, why they are so smiling and happy – rich people eating the food of poor people – the Filipinas simply cannot understand.

The Jews, they are strange people. They like to talk to the Filipinas. 'We are an immigrant family like you,' they say. And when the Filipina goes, 'Oh, when did you move to Britain,' the Jews say, '1880.' And the Filipina is stunned and confused. The Jews, they only ever talk about Israel – Israel, Israel, Israel, all day Israel – and it is as if they are living here in St John's Wood but they are really there, in precious Israel.

Sometimes, the Filipinas are invited to come to Israel for the special Jew days. The Jews they talk about Israel always, like a land of gold. And the Filipinas they are excited to come because they are sure it must be a land of diamonds. And all the Filipinas are bragging when they are about to go: because this is where the Jews come from, and everyone knows all Jews are rich. And they are in shock when they come back: that is most definitely not the case. And they watch the faces of these rich people. They are so happy in this rundown, dusty, clapped-out place of poor people that even the Filipinas can see is nothing special like Doha, Abu Dhabi or Dubai.

All servants wish they could sit down and talk to their masters. All servants wish they could for one day – ask their masters questions. 'What is this Yom Kippur? Who is this Rabbi Cohen you always moan about? Why always, always, talking about Israel when you barely ever go there?' But this is over the line. This is the way it is – the way it always was – that servants may forever listen but never ask.

And it is tough working for the Jews. They make many Filipinas cry. They are more likely than anyone else to bring the Filipina inside the family – but this is mostly a charade. They never, ever want to pay – as little as possible, as late as possible. And there are many, many Filipinas who burst into tears when they realize that

after seven years the Jews have been cheating them on their national insurance, their weekly salaries, or even more. And then they come running to Auntie Mia.

But mostly on those precious afternoons, when at last, at last – they are visible, they can ask questions, they can cut people off – they gossip about Filipinas. They tittle-tattle about the Filipina that became a girlfriend of a disabled banker. They tut-tut at a Filipina who let a mad lady Jew in St John's Wood throw knives at her for seven years. They seethe with jealousy at the Filipina whose madam threw her a birthday party at the Dorchester. And it is painfully clear for Auntie Mia, everyone telling stories, everyone eating cake – who is one of the family, and who is a slave.

And as the afternoon becomes dark and the lights are switched on and more secrets come out with Auntie Mia, the Filipinas start to talk about managing madam. About how sometimes madam throws out all her perfumes – hundreds and hundreds of little bottles – and they scrabble out to the bins when she is asleep to scoop these bottles up. About how unfair it was when madam threw away her Filipina for grabbing dozens of dresses out of the recycling bags, which she was supposed to have instead taken all the way to the charity shop on High Street Kensington.

But lots of Filipinas have nothing to gossip about. Not the Filipinas of Kensington, the Filipinas of Hampstead and the Filipinas of St John's Wood. They work for the French, the Italians and the Jews. But the Filipinas of Knightsbridge, the Filipinas of Mayfair and the Filipinas of Belgravia, they are the Filipinas of empty mansions that they have to clean, day in, day out – as master and madam ordered.

These are their mansions. They know every nook, every cranny, every alarm, every alcove. They know how the light falls in the master bedroom and where the chimney draughts rush across the living rooms in winter. These are the Filipinas of the golden cage, they are there alone, over and over, cleaning a clean house for ever – in suspended Sisyphean splendour.

But the Filipinas are not fools. They get to know everything. They get to understand the security. They spend time with the cameras. They come to trust the man-guards. And, of course, it is inevitable that every year, in the dead of winter, when the windows frost, when master and madam are in the warm islands – there are the Filipina balls.

Those nights in winter, the streets in Mayfair are silent and cool like an ancient tomb. The street lamps come on – one by one, clack, pssst, clack – but warm house lights and fireplaces do not follow them on. There is nobody here: only sensor security and Filipinas. And this is when the brave ones, the clever ones, they are the ones who throw open their doors – and they stand under those colonnade steps in white woman's clothes, and welcome the Filipinas into the warmth of the winter ball.

Walking up the stairs into the mansions of Mayfair, they look beautiful, to die for, the way anyone does, in those clothes as precious as diamonds which madam never wears. And inside they are singing, the curtains thrown open to enormous views of those huge mysterious parks. And the Filipinas are laughing – their smiles across the black canvas of the night.

CATFORD BRIDGE

The suits are pushing.

The train to Catford puffs with its pistons to a stop at London Bridge. These platforms of long and curving concrete are washed in a harsh and functional light. This is a whiteness that bleaches out our make-up and brings out the lines in a human face. Commuters are jostling as the blazers and puffas are sucked into the battered carriage. I catch a glimpse of rising glass. The Shard. The glinting panes reach up, unlit, and dark, broken by some floors ringing it with light, over the heave of the stressed and tender.

I watch though the scratched window of the Catford train. Until seconds later the light is gone. This building is our new hierarchy, with its dim, sleazy restaurants in Imperial Chinese theme, with its menus for French bankers to slice their meat, with its apartments built for Russian oligarchs, with glass walls to press their fingers onto, with eyes looking into, but sealed away from, an immense vista of light. And like so much of London this huge, fragile piece of glass belongs to the Sheikh of Qatar.

Much of it sits empty. But it is never quiet. At night, these enormous open-plan offices echo with buzzing vacuum cleaners as African and Latino scrubbers do the work they must. And at the bottom, under the train bridge, Romanian addicts and Polish tramps sleep rough in the doorways that run to London Bridge. There are more and more of them. And in these streets around the Shard alcoves and doorways are fitted with metal studs to keep them away. The train rattles on.

I can see nothing in Catford.

The heavy train doors pull open. A sighing crowd flows onto the

concrete platform. Lamp posts stand guard over the clicking heels of the commuters scurrying away. I swipe out and follow them out onto the South Circular, glowing red, with hundreds of puttering, stalled cars. I walk through puddles along the engines rumbling in the traffic jam. I navigate the push buttons at zebra crossings and the big green orders from the traffic lights to find the Registrar.

She sits at the wipe-easy table behind the glass-wall windows of the Turkish restaurant. She is staring at a grey wall. This is covered in mirrors. There are big ones and small ones and each of them is in a carved wood frame. Some of them are even spray-painted to look like they are made of gold. I try to grin.

'I'm sorry for being late.'

The Registrar smiles, with puny toddlers' teeth, and with her bony hand, fingers the ends of her dyed blonde and abruptly chopped hair. There is something ghostly and pallid about her skin, so thin and white you can see little blue veins rushing into the corners of her eyes. And as the Registrar smiles again, with her slim lips, so slender they are hardly there, I notice how perfectly round her skull seems to be, with a fleshy button nose, and pink miniature ears. This is a face I have seen all over London. I think anyone could guess the Registrar is Polish.

'Hallo.'

The Registrar crosses her arms purposefully on the table over a low-cut black top that frames a cheap jewel. She talks with a rattle, a one-two-three intonation, that is fast but monotone. There is defiance there in that voice. But she wants people to listen to her. Because she thinks about her work – she has married so many couples, she has keyed in so many papers, she has spotted so many fakers – she is sure, she knows better than anyone, who the mothers of the new London really are.

'I want to tell you all about my couples . . . Nobody else but the Registrar in London sees how fast the city is changing.'

We are almost alone in the restaurant. But she is not interested in the food. She does not want a starter. She ignores the under-cooked kofta she eventually orders. She only wants to talk. Because the Registrar is in names and dates recording the new city being born. The new London where 57 per cent of births are to migrant mothers. And when the Registrar finds herself keying in the death notices of the old London, she sees how these names are old white British. This is why she is impatient to talk.

'I've married a thousand couples. At least. But there are always liars doing it for the passport to stay.'

She tells me how you can always spot a fake. How they always come in the same way. The one who has something to gain will do the talking. He is usually a Nigerian or a Pakistani male. The girl will sit there and smile with lip-curling strain. When they sit down, they hold hands like school children, not lovers. They sit there lying into your face that they are a couple. And when they leave they stop pretending immediately and the man walks out first, and lets the door swing back in the girl's face.

'That's when you know.'

The dodgy ones follow patterns she can scarcely discern. Every time there is a Nigerian man stumbling over his words with a grimacing bottle-tanned Portuguese she knows there is something dodgy. Every time there is a tense pound-shop-dressed Pakistani unable to answer her questions naturally – *where did you meet* – with a scowling Lithuanian girl in a puffa jacket she can tell they are making it all up.

'I don't know why these patterns repeat like this.'

But there are real couples she can hardly believe. There was the Nepalese man in the blue cardigan and the Spanish woman with thick black locks who rushed in like teenagers and smiled like children at Christmas when they got their paperwork. There was the Chinese man with a Pakistani passport who came in with this caramel-skinned French woman whose raven hair was tied up in a bun. The Registrar squinted and peered. But she knew instantly they were real: in the way her fingers played in the palm of the Chinese hand.

'You can feel them . . . The ones who are really lovers.'

There are some couples she marries, and she knows it won't last. She just types what she needs to into the system and thinks, This is like factory work, and never thinks of them again. But then there are the couples she never forgets, like the two Africans who married the other day, with the tongue clicks in their name.

'There are not many of them . . . the really joyous weddings.'

There were two huge crowds there for those two. They were dressed in swirling blue robes and sharp suits, and when the Registrar came to introduce their impossible tongue-click names – and stumbled – the crowds bellowed them out for her. They were not asked. They just did it. Not because they were worried – or offended – about the Registrar not getting those tongue-clicking names right. But because they were all so happy they were finally marrying, so happy they were finally doing it, so happy this was the day that they were all ready to shout.

The weddings she enjoys the least are the Pakistani weddings. Because with them they have already married in the mosque a few days before and they only come to the Registrar for the paperwork, like it is a hassle or a chore. There are a lot of quiet weddings. The Chinese come in small groups and they are quite subdued. The Spanish and the South Americans, or the South Americans with Spanish passports, or whatever they are, and some of them are very beautiful, they will marry mostly in small groups too, or maybe they are always faking it, she never knows.

The happiest weddings are the poor English and the poor Africans. The poor English come in on the discount day when a wedding only costs £49 and they are loud and noisy and when you tell them to move on they answer back and yap and bray and hoot their way out of the reception hall. The poor English are very quick to dance and jump around and they will yell, 'Yes, come on my son,' like they are at some football match and punch the air with their fists.

'They are so chaotic . . . the poor English . . . tumbling in and tumbling out.'

She thinks the poor look and sound so different from the rich even though they are both from the English race. They look cheaper. Their suits and dresses never really fit. But she notices the rich English marry with their women wearing little feather hats. It is very important to them everything should match: suit, jacket and tie.

But they sound so different. Like they are from another country. The voice is slower and slurs in very different places. They are not sounding so tonguey with that rat-tat-tat of a machine gun. They seem not to like shouting or bright colours or cheering. And they seem to pride themselves on clapping and crying with understatement. And they never answer back. Everything is 'excuse me' this, 'excuse me' that, and kept to time.

'They are very orderly people.'

The more she talks, the higher her voice heads into excitement.

The ones she loves best are the African weddings. They will not stop coming. These weddings are like sweet shops. The women will come in clapping in their wrappers like a singing box of Quality Street. The men will come in swinging their shoulders back and forth like exploded packets of Smarties and Skittles. They come in their hundreds, the whole estate comes, the whole area comes, and then there are people who come the couple doesn't even know. They shout out to each other, 'There is a party, come,' and the Africans will be cheering and dancing with people they've never even met.

She puts both hands flat on the table on the sides of an empty plate.

'I love the colourful ones. The people who are not scared of colours.'

And then there are the mixed ones. Polish nannies with Portuguese DJs. Lithuanian cleaners with Romanian builders. Ghanaian pickers with Colombian scrubbers. Nigerian drivers with Polish waitresses. These are the special ones. Because she knows these are the difficult weddings: the ones that can only happen in this city where love is really free. But there are more and more of them. She guesses maybe a quarter of the Polish girls are marrying something new.

There is a break in her voice and a thrill floods in.

'This is impossible in the city in Poland where I come from.'

This I guess is what the Registrar really wants to talk about.

'There was this couple that I cannot forget . . . Because they were so beautiful to me, because they were like the future to me . . . They had come to our office and they had to fill out the form and I noticed they were getting married in the Polish church . . . and I looked up and said, "Oh this is my church," and I saw there was this very tall guy standing next to this woman . . . But he was black, an African.'

I watch the Registrar as she thumbs a corner curl of hair.

'And there was this very beautiful, very pale, blonde Polish girl standing next to him . . . So I took them upstairs to the room where we decide everything. And I saw how the African he was saying nothing, and the Polish girl she was the speaker. They told me they had met in the mega-mart in Catford and that he was the security guard and she was the checkout girl, and they had fallen in love, and now wanted to marry here and never have to leave Catford.'

She pulls herself a little closer to the table.

'But I saw he was saying nothing. And when I finished the con-versation and went, "You are getting married on this and this day," I saw the relief on the face of the man like he had been under the water and was coming out and breathing. Because when the Polish girl was talking he had looked so worried, he had been so silent, he was so hunched. He looked hunted, like he wanted to hide. His body language . . . The body language of this big tall proud man was the body language of fear. He was scared of me. He was coming to me to get married but he was trembling . . . like he was going to be arrested. But I gave them papers.'

The Registrar ignores her plate.

'And the couple, they thanked me. They were so happy. They were flush and they were laughing. Because they said what I had done was miracle for them . . . to help them, to make them safe, to allow them to love. And the Polish girl she said, "Thank you . . . thank you for not taking the police on us . . . because we thought we were going to come and get married . . . and he would get arrested and the Home Office would come and take my love away from me to their concentration camps . . ." because the lover of the checkout girl, the security guard, he was here illegally.'

The Polish girl looked at her with watery blue eyes. Then she spoke to the Registrar like a friend might – 'Please, come to our wedding.' That was why four weeks later the Registrar arrived at the Polish church. The checkout girl was all in fluffy white. The security guard was in a tailored black suit. But he was not the man she remembered. His smile was over half of his face. His back was as straight as a lamppost. His voice boomed with laughter and he hugged everyone with both arms. The church was packed with Polish and Nigerians and the close ones, those who knew the story, they rushed up to touch her like the angel. The Nigerian mothers in shiny blue head wraps dashed up to her to bless her. The Polish cousins in polyester suits and fresh buzz cuts rushed up to thank her – for not taking him away.

The party took place that night. It was in the pebbledash house of a rich man. He owned it all. He was the only one living there. He even had space for a car out front. He was the cousin of the security guard and the manager of the Catford mega-mart. He had covered his whole house in plastic sheets so it would not get dirty. But when the guests arrived they rushed to the garden. There was even a marquee out there. But when the Registrar went in it there was nobody there: just an important chief sitting there from Thamesmead in crimson robes and a red brimless hat like a fez.

The guests kept arriving. The food kept being served. There was whisky and palm-oil wine and red rice with plantain and Tyskie beer and sour cream soup and whole trays of cassava fufu and amala. The builders were laughing and the security guards were coming and the cleaners were starting to dance with the pickers and the plasterers were moving closer to the carers. There was one song – then another – Polish rock, then Nigerian dance, as everyone became light-headed, and lost themselves in the swirl of smiles, where your heart flutters, and you might meet someone.

The evening turned very slowly into the palest blue and this colour hung there glacially fading for hours over the semi-detached where everyone was clapping and dancing on the clumpy lawn boxed in by the wooden fences and untrimmed hedges. This was one of those lingering and beautiful fallings of the light there is only in England in the early summer. When the light clings to the city and the air becomes muggy and the midges come out and something strange happens to all of us who have chosen to make our lives so far north. The colour over everything becomes lilac then pink and the moment came when the mommas in wrappers began arranging the plastic garden chairs in one big circle. This was when the couple came out.

She is no longer really with me.

'They were so bright, so bright.'

They were wearing orange robes that were covered with patterns of black circles that meant unity and round their necks hung pink coral necklaces in a huge lattice that draped over their shoulders. They wore crowns of coral beads, sewn together out of hundreds of tiny shining orange carved pieces. And they danced between the garden chairs. The security guard, he thrust his shoulders out so proud, and the checkout girl, she danced with her hands in the air and twirled towards him. And for a moment the Registrar wanted to cry.

She thought about what she wanted most of all in the whole world, she thought about the man she slept next to, she thought about the man who had given her a son, she thought about the lovers she had found and lost in this city, and she thought back in memories and voices how she had ended up here, in this un-imaginable place.

She had not always worked in a suit dress, of course.

The first job she ever worked in London was with her hands. She was a kebab girl. She had come for two months from Poland and she had found work for £50 a week in some kebab shop. She didn't really care about the money. She was overwhelmed by it all. Not by the fact that when she stood to catch the big red bus all these Syrian men would come up to her and go, 'I like you, let's have a coffee, now,' but by the fact that all these men were not Polish.

She would come into the kebab shop at 9 am and that was when it would start. She would take the chicken pieces, one by one, and rub them gently into the masala, and then skewer them onto the spinny thing. Then she would pull up the tall soft mush they used for the lamb. And he would be there, talking to her.

The Kebab Man was also around twenty-two. He was beautiful.

But his skin was cracked and aged by the heat of the grill. This made him look leathery. Older than he was. But this boy was the colour of ivory with stubble that bristled charcoal. She knew he was looking at her as he shaved off the doner, as it became hotter and hotter, and she hiked up her skirt to stop the sweat running off her face, in little drops, into the naan.

He would talk to her about Islam as she squirted this and that into the kebab and wrapped it for the drunks. They would be coming in all day, even in the afternoon, and their faces were pink and lined, especially at night, when they seemed so exhausted by the alcohol they could barely speak. They were Polish and English mostly, and some of them ate this like it was the last food in the world. Like they were animals. Or tramps. The builders, the Polish ones who told her they were builders, they became angry with her – 'Kebab working is not for a woman, get out of here,' they would hiss at her with their change.

When they were not there the Kebab Man would talk. His eyes would never let go of hers. They would look into her with everything he wanted. But then he would toss on the coal and fiddle with the gas and begin talking again about Islam. About how Islam was the best religion because it was against the drunks who ate this shit and about how Afghan men were the best for Polish women, because they didn't drink.

The Kebab Man would drive her home. He would pull out his baggie and crunch up the skunk and keep talking about Islam and the war and everything until it was rolled up and it crackled as he blazed the best toke. Then they would be laughing with the skunk. They would be laughing about the kebabs and the customers. And then with a little force he kissed her. And they fucked in the car.

The Kebab Man knew she was going home. And he began skinning up and imploring her in the haze and the skunk not to leave. 'London is the land of opportunity,' he said. 'You can be anything here,' he said. 'You can be with me.' He would lean his head back on the seat and breathe out so the smoke bounced back from the roof and made him laugh. He kept telling her London was a

country where if you worked you really could make it cool. But if you didn't, or didn't know how – you were screwed.

The Kebab Man did not speak English very well. He had come from Afghanistan too late to lose that da-dat-dat accent and he had screwed up learning because he was too busy rolling and beefing people at school. He told her these stories in the car at night with his grime tunes gently pumping out the stereo. He talked to her with his hands, about a London she could hardly imagine, of hoodies and mandems, and postcodes and guns.

The Kebab Man had a father. He was the one who owned this grill and the other two kebabs his brothers worked in. He would come in sometimes and scowl at her. Because the Kebab Man was married. His wife was beautiful and religious. And she was going to be the mother of his children. But she thought little about her. There was something she almost wanted, watching the hijab, and the veil, and the way she lived: but she was never sure what it was. She was not in love.

The Kebab Man could not convince her to stay in London. Nor could Kingsley the beauty man in a doo rag who claimed to be from Sierra Leone but only spoke French. Nor could the fidgety Lebanese guy with glasses who invited her round for dinner and mushed hummus for her. She had already decided. This would be her last weekend. That was when she went clubbing. It was one of those migrant places. Where they only sell beer in cans and the Romanians and the Poles go to dance. The lights had come on after the music when she went outside on the street and saw him.

He claimed he was Italian at first. But he was a Romanian of course. He was wearing blue fashion jeans with fashion stripes and a white shirt. But she could not remember the colour of his eyes. She never approached men. But for some reason she went up to him and started talking. She smiled with her eyes and made him know she was interested with her number. And then she left London goodbye.

But he kept calling her. He called her twice, three, four times. He called Poland. He told her who he was. He told her about his building site. He told her how his sister had died and he had been unable to return to Romania to bury her. And they started to fall in love over the phone. They would keep going even when they had nothing to say. They would talk for hours and it would seem like minutes.

Suddenly everything seemed shareable. There were no more secrets. There was his voice every day. She would tell him how there was no future in this industrial wreck. She would tell him how her father had died and the pain crept up on her when she least expected during the day, like in the supermarket, or the shower. She would tell him the only foreigners she had ever known growing up were the Vietnamese who sold vegetables in the market or her school-teacher married somehow to a Cuban.

And then they began to talk about the future. They made a house out of words. They imagined boys and girls. And they talked about what would hang on the walls. And they talked about London. Because Romania and Poland no longer mattered. And slowly one hour after another he convinced her to come back.

This was how she came back to London. First one weekend. Then another. And he would be there waiting for her at the cheap airports an hour away from the city where the builders and the cleaners fly in on the 4.30 am. They would lie in his sheets and have the same conversations. They made children out of words. Then they made their London. They never wanted to live anywhere else.

Then one weekend she came to his room. He held her and looked at her – *You've met someone* – and she didn't know what to say. She talked to him like she talked to herself – *Yes, I have* – and she watched his face whiten and sink. The Romanian pulled himself closer and said, 'You are in London. We are going to have a wonderful time. You can go back to him. But if you want . . . you can always come back.'

She had not really met someone. She had taken her phone to a repair shop and the boy, in that company logo polo shirt, had looked at her in a way that made her wonder, and she let him talk to her long enough to ask her out. And nothing came of it when she came back to Poland.

She felt the Romanian inside her. She knew he was sitting on

02 August 2014.

To the handsome Polish man who was talking to me in front of a restuarant in Brook Green Hotel Hamersmith, Me black woman & was waiting for a Ambulance for someone. When the Ambulance came you had gone without giving me your mobile number. Please let's meet again in the same place My name is Maria 077███████519

02. Sierpień 2014

Wiadomość do przystojnego Pana Polaka z którym rozmawiałam przy restauracji Brook Green Hotel Hammersmith, ja (ciemnoskóra kobieta) czekałam na karetkę dla kogoś. Kiedy ta przyjechała ty odszedłeś a ja ci nie dałam nr tel*. Proszę o kontakt. Maria 077███████519 his bed smoking and crying and drinking and not eating. She knew he was hurting. And she realized she loved him in the silence. There was something funny and no one to text. There was something sad and nobody to call. There were hours when she looked at his number. She would repeat it to herself like a magic code before falling asleep. Then she would begin to type it and then throw the phone into her pillows and gasp a little at what she'd lost.

Then he called. He called again. He told her about the building site. He told her about the plumbing course. He told her about the forklift-truck problem. He told her he thought of her every single day. He told her he avoided the places they had kissed. He told her to come back. That was when she came for good. They rented a little flat. This was not really a flat, more half-converted attic with a shower and kitchen space and a double mattress on the floor. This was where she held him.

She took the bus home one evening and there was no answer. The phone went through to voicemail. Then no longer even that. She did not find him there. She called his name. She called their special name. But his clothes were gone and the TV was gone. The Romanian had disappeared. And there was only £30 and a note in biro on the bed.

She picked it up. He had tried to write he could no longer trust her and that was why he had to disappear. But she ran out to look for him. She walked up and down the high road, coming in and out of the Romanian shops. She went into all the pubs and she started asking for him and calling for him but he wasn't there.

She called and called. But the words were gone. She shook in that mattress on the floor and dug her fingernails into her palms and screeched. But that was it. She worked at first in the kebab shop again. But it wasn't the same. And then she found a space as a shop assistant in a Sports Direct. But she couldn't let go.

Her face prickled with tension when she arrived at Heathrow. She knew he was flying to Bucharest this morning for good. This was the ticket they had booked together. This was the ticket she had booked to meet his mum. She breathed in and out and tried to see him in the crowds of wheelie bags and backpacks.

'Where are your bags?'

He smiled. He would always smile in that way. And he said he would call her. And he said he knew she loved him and he would call her and see if it would be the same. And then he waved at her through the passport line and she never saw him again. She left smiling and happy. But she didn't know he only had her old Polish number. The number which she no longer had. The Romanian called to no answer.

Over and over.

This was when she met the Blonde. She came from her Polish shithole. She was tall and so enamoured that she was friends with someone who read articles on the internet, and spoke English so quickly, and with such confidence, it made her smile wryly. She had baby skin and she was thin. She had a nice body and thin blonde hair. But she was very clingy. She was always calling her. She was always messaging her. Sometimes she would tell her that she really loved her. After three months of waiting for the Romanian to call, and cracking up in tension on the bus back from Sports Direct, the Blonde invited her to come to a Polish party in Hounslow. There would be joiners and fitters and fitness instructors with great bodies there, she promised.

'Wait for me at your station,' said the Blonde, 'and I will pick you up in the car with my boyfriend.' It was a hot grey day. Maybe, she daydreamed, the sky had been blocked out under a steel pressure dome. Perhaps, she waited for an hour there until they arrived. When they finally did, she opened the back door, and there was the Blonde yapping, and yapping, and she heard this man with a very mellow and deep voice. The Blonde was squawking at him for being late. That was when she noticed his black hand in a white shirt on the wheel.

There were lots of people at the party, and the Blonde went from the kitchen to the living room, and onto the patio, smoking and laughing, and taking shots, and gossiping with the cleaners, and the other girls she said also worked as receptionists. That was when the Nigerian came up to her on the sofa. 'How long have you been in London? What are you doing here? What would you like to do?' The

Nigerian was working as a policeman and his smile was broad and proud. There were carpenters in tight sports shirts, cracking open cans, trying to impress shop assistants in pleated skirts around them. He looked into her.

'Don't go back to Poland. You can be who you want to be here.'

She left him that night.

But the Nigerian kept calling her. 'I can find you work in a bank,' he promised. 'I can find you work in a hotel,' he claimed. 'I can find you work as a registrar,' he said. He kept trying to see her. He kept coming round for coffee, for a chat, and calling. Telling her that his friends thought she was beautiful and his cousin wanted her. This charade went for two months before he told her the truth.

'I want you.'

'We were waiting to buy a ticket or some popcorn in the cinema when I knew that I was in love with the Policeman. We were standing there and he just hugged me . . . and he just held me . . . and I just felt that I can let it go . . . and that I can let my guard down. My dad had died a few months earlier . . . And I needed someone to really take care of me . . . and I held him and I felt I can let go . . .'

The Registrar is talking when I notice it come over her face. The more she tells me about what passed through her mind in the beautiful wedding in the singing garden the sadder her face becomes. The prettiness drains from it. Her eyes become a little bloodshot and lips become pinched and cheeks wan.

'But *she* couldn't let go. And she kept calling him.'

She flinches. The Registrar suddenly notices the restaurant is empty. The owner is mopping up the floor. She looks at me. Confused how we have got here. For a moment she stops speaking. And then when she does her voice begins to wobble.

'She tried to commit suicide.'

Her flow stops. She has to force her words out.

'She swallowed some pills and she tried to cut herself.'

She looks at me, begging for something, with a little shaking in her voice.

'She told me . . . She had been working as a receptionist in the private hotel.'

Her voice has become fast. Almost rambling.

Then it stops.

'But she was really . . . a prostitute . . . She was not his girlfriend. That's how they really met . . . When I went to him, "Why did you . . . why . . ." The Policeman said to me men need things and they need to have it sometimes . . . and he didn't want to just go to parties and take some girl home and then have to explain to her the next day it was only for a fuck . . . And he thought it was better to come to a girl like her, do it and go home afterwards. And I thought . . . fair enough.'

But the Blonde would not stop calling. She kept sending texts. They both changed their numbers. The Policeman delivered her the job he promised. More time passed. And the Registrar moved in with the Policeman somewhere in Catford. There was a month gone by. Then another. She realized not too long after she was pregnant.

The glaring Turkish restaurant owner is impatient to lock up.

'But she kept calling . . . Going, "He's still using . . . He's still coming . . ." And I would start to have like panic attacks when she was calling and my heart was pumping and I was shaking and it was horrible . . . And then one day I picked up and I went, "If you keep calling I will tell your mum what you really do."'

The Registrar has lost the emotion in her voice. It is monotone again.

'Every now and again I hear she's around . . . She's around . . . She's somewhere around . . . She's still calling him eight years later.'

She falls silent, and grabs the side of her hair.

At the wedding of the checkout girl and the security guard the Registrar watched her and the Policeman's son the colour of caramel running between the jeans and the wrappers. He was shrieking with laughter. It peeled. It rushed off him.

She watched him running between the garden chairs and wiggling his hips trying to dance and with her heart she tried to tell him not to be frightened because tomorrow London looks like you.

The Registrar does not know the statistics. She knows the

couples. She knows the names. She knows the faces. The census reads there are now more than 405,000 mixed-race people in London. But she was not thinking about anyone else that night.

The night had finally crept over the garden.

The dancers were clapping and the music was becoming louder, and not slowing down, and the Registrar felt there was a trembling in her lip. The Policeman had bundled up their son. The engine had revved. He was driving the little one back. She was alone in the singing garden and she ached, as she knew – all she wanted in the whole of London was for him to propose to her.

FORE STREET

I am on the last train out of Liverpool Street. The booming echo calls out the names of the suburbs. We clatter through tracks into jumbled estates and aluminized hangars. On the line out to concrete platforms, deserted cul-de-sacs and rent-a-van forecourts. Tracksuit whites next to me speak in a language I cannot faintly place.

I get off at Edmonton Green. It is almost summer. Cars pass by, their windows down, tinkling out beats. Hoods hang around the newsagent hassling the Turks. You can hear the pubs emptying. There are shouts and the smash of a glass. A puffy, white-haired Irish woman is blubbing at the bus stop.

This is late. There are night birds. And still lights on in the vast yellow-brick estates. But not in every room. This is when the girls come out. When the work picks up. When the men get loud and want it bad. When between the street lamps there are no other women walking the street.

Officials estimate there are at least seven thousand prostitutes in London – and 96 per cent of them are migrants. These are mostly girls from the east: Romania, Slovakia, Lithuania. But also girls from the south: Brazil, Thailand, Vietnam. There are at least two thousand of them every night on the street. Talk to the police. Talk to the shopkeepers. They tell you there are many more than that. More and more every week. Most of them from Eastern Europe. Especially Romania.

There are less and less streetwalkers in inner London. There used to be a lot of women of easy virtue in Soho. But they have mostly gone. Sex shops are for the tourists. Brothels morphed into

TV production suites. Neon porno signs kept ironically alight over lunch bars for the boys from Channel 4.

You now find them at the fringes. Places like Edmonton. Places that were not meant to be ghettos. But economics slowly made them. Places like the strip between the petrol station and the estates on Fore Street.

I walk past the chicken shops onto the strip. There are quite a few things happening. I overhear a row. Then I look around. The Nubian Barber is locked up behind a clinking grille. But lights are on. Naked lamps that give a bluish glow to white tiles. This is 1 am. But the barber is at work: carefully trimming the chin of a serious-looking black man. There is little air of friendship between them: this is surly power.

The girls are obvious.

'What have we got here . . . some mighty fine . . . *bitches.*'

Two hoodies hassle and chirps one in white trainers and ripped white jeans to give it to them for free. They are only joking. But the girls have a code. They whistle twice when they see a bad man coming. The smilers they know who like to smack them up and rob the thirty or fifty quid they have in their butt pockets.

The girls are nervous. The weather has been good, T-shirt weather, and the boys are raging. But these days the money gets worse and worse. There are more and more girls from the sticks and every week or two another comes to the strip and bites her lip and tries her luck.

The girls all take it differently. There are girls like Marguerita who work it as normally as drinking a glass of water. The kind of girl who walks calmly forward when she sees a man standing there: looking hungry at her. Then round into the alley.

There are the girls like Irina who are so sick they have to do it for that fix. The bad boys sometimes pay them in little wraps. Get them into it. Girls so thin they look like they might crack.

'So you want it . . . ?'

'I can see you like me . . .'

She whistles at me from the wall behind the bus stop. Her street name is Jenny. She is Romanian. Aged twenty-five. The other girls are somewhere in between. She is fit, and shivers: a pink corset under an undone brown jacket – sparkle make-up smeared round brown eyes. There is a smell of spirits to her breath.

'You think we do this job for pleasure? You think us . . . *bitches* . . . can think about anything else . . . when sometimes we get stab? Of course we are scared . . . We are scared . . . We are scared of men . . .'

Her blue lighter does not spark.

'Marie . . . Marie is a good girl . . . Hello Marie, nice Marie . . . she good with the boys . . . always speaking nice . . . *yes daddy, you big daddy* . . . The man . . . grab Marie like this . . . And he stab her.'

I spark it up for her.

'This man . . . Maybe a crazy drugs man . . . *But I confuse* . . . I no understand . . . This is Edmonton . . . nobody understand . . . But some people say it's Turkish man . . . a crazy Turkish man . . . maybe jealous . . . . . . But maybe it's jihad . . .'

She looks at me.

'We don't know . . .

'*We don't know* . . .

'This why we scare . . .

'Police come and give us this . . .'

She dangles in front of me a little red see-through bag: filled with Quality Streets and a panic button to the police station.

'Police say, "When you get scare . . . eat the chocolate . . . press the button and we come quickly, quickly . . ."

'Do you want one . . . ?'

We unwrap foil and sit on the wall smoking.

'The Edmonton . . . This is crazy area . . . black area . . . They are drug-taking crazy people . . . They are knife people . . . Too much black people here . . . The black come to me . . . Kiss teeth like this . . . and go . . . *Yes bitches* . . .

'The African black man . . . he is not violent. They pay . . . But the young one . . . The one who born here . . . Those blacks don't care . . . They sometimes hit us . . . They sometimes have a group . . . come in the group . . .

'One black . . . he come up to a girl . . . push her head down and

when he finish . . . He put knife to her neck . . . *Not to pay* . . This happened to a good girl . . . a nice girl.'

We sit on the wall and the cars pass slowly.

'Give me ten pounds . . . because this my work you stopping.'

Then she slips off the wall and holding the note out front begins to act out with both hands the grab and touch of them.

'There are also Turkish people . . . the old men mostly . . . They work in the shop and the kebab . . . and they smell kebab . . . they are coming the most times . . . Turkish pay the best . . . Sometimes the Turkish is gentle . . . likes the girl a lot . . . same girl every week . . . sometimes bring her flower, sometimes bring her kebab . . .

'There are very little English . . . this is Edmonton . . . English no like it here . . . This is place for the immigrant . . . and the drugs.'

She is still shivering.

'Zip up your jacket.'

She is not listening.

'What is your blood? You is a Jew? Hah . . . We get your fathers, many times . . . the Jew who come in the cars . . . the big family cars . . . the Jew in black clothes . . . with the beards . . . When they come to us they take off the little hats . . . The Jews they smell. They sweat in bad black clothes . . .

'They come in the big cars . . . the one they carry the children in . . . Were you in a big car like that, Mr Jew . . . ? The ones with all the food bits . . . everywhere . . . between seats . . . on floors. There are no children when your fathers come . . . we are in the cars with them.

'They are the hungriest ones.'

Two whites in hoods came up to us, look and bounce.

'The Edmonton . . . It's crazy hah . . . It's a wild . . . The blacks they always fighting . . . they walk along . . . with the phone giving the music sounds . . . And they fight . . . With knifes . . . likes Gypsies in Romania . . .'

We walk a bit. Into the lights of the newsagent. To buy Coke.

'I have nothing . . . I am here three months . . . I have no room . . . I have no fifty pounds for room . . . One night, one girl I sleep her bed . . . One night good girl she say, "You have my bed . . ."

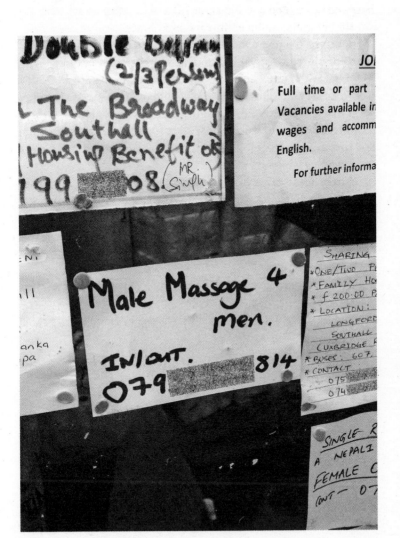

'I make no money . . . Want blowjob? Are you sure . . . ? Well, blowjob only twenty . . . But some bitches . . . they do for ten . . . I am angry them . . . I hate those bitches . . .

'Money? This is no money . . . one night . . . maybe twenty . . . maybe hundred twenty . . . next day . . . I have cigarette . . . I have make-up . . . I have Lebara phone credit . . . I have food . . . and money finish . . . I go back Romania with nothing . . . no money.

'I make no money . . . other girls . . . they speak nice . . . *yes hello . . . call me bitches, hit me yes daddy* . . . I don't speak so nice . . . I am not so nice . . . I don't go to apartment . . . I am scared . . . of apartment.

'I need make money . . . I need make money survive mister . . . Edmonton . . . I can make on lucky week . . . lots of Turk and lots of Jew . . . I can make five hundred pounds . . . In Romanian imagine five hundred pound . . . I could never imagine . . . never . . . In London five hundred pound is nothing . . . next day cigarettes and is finish . . .

'And I am here again going . . . *hey, hey* . . . to black crazy people.'

HANS PLACE

The key scratches behind the door in Knightsbridge.

I squeeze my notebook and ready myself: I am not entirely comfortable with the questions I have come to ask. What does it feel like to give birth?

The key scratches some more and then the creak.

It is not the face I am expecting, but a blubbery Russian maid.

There is no hello, only a head gesture to come in.

The room is a tight square and dingy behind drawn curtains. The floor is hogged with a fluffy rainbow rug. There is a baby in a blue grow wriggling in the middle of it. The maid scoops it up and takes me to a glass dining table.

This is where I wait.

I blink into the art on the wall: at a huge greyscale canvas – of a soppy pug, licking the pregnant bulge of a woman's body. The pug seems excited, a little unsavoury, and the toned small-breasted woman has no head, only a long, curving, ancient Egyptian neck. I try to fight it, but there is something hypnotic in the pug.

I tear my eyes away: into my notebook.

And I try and write down everything I know about the Russian woman I have come to interview. She is a mother, and I need to interview a mother. She was a model, who posed nude in furs on Red Square. She was a socialite, who sipped with the oligarchs. She was the wife of a minigarch, whose baby she bore in London. She is now living with another man, whose electric green scarf lies there over the divan.

I can hear her speaking upstairs, to the maid: a fast, unfettered Russian.

There is hostile, nasty art staring at me across the room: in red ink, in black felt tip, a sketch as intricate as a pulp cartoon is a monstrous vessel, tipped with the clock towers of the Kremlin, covered with the scales of a fish, commanded by a bear, winged like a Tsarist eagle, drifting between icebergs, its hull marked – OIL.

'So you want to know about birth?'

My subject has appeared somehow in the room.

Thin, a little skeletal in the cheeks. Skin a porcelain milk, with black, thin hair, the pitch of charcoal. She smiles with her teeth, trying to calm, or charm me. But there is something bashed about in her eyes.

'What story do you want me to tell you?'

I mumble something about female perspectives.

'What is the right story to tell you?'

This is the thing when you interview: some people take control of the play, others people want stage directions, some people start pushing, others confessing. Nobody ever treats you like a journalist: some talk to you like a friend, some talk to you like the state, others like a stranger on the train. I watch her sit down.

'I want you to call me Lena in your book.'

She sits there waiting for a command that doesn't come.

I smile a little risibly. And start the recorder.

Interviewing is a little like acting: and with my eyes, I want to seem a little wetter, a little more pathetic, than I am – so she takes control of her story. She snaps quickly, a little bored I see, and takes on the tone she uses to command the maid.

'My husband never called himself an oligarch.'

I note how her eyes swivel at the man's mention.

'He was a minigarch, to be accurate. There was a lot of millions, a lot, many of them. But it was not a billion. He was nothing really.'

The newly named Lena laughs, as if testing my reaction.

'I didn't live in a palace. I didn't have a pony. It was not like that.'

Her eyes scan me rather brutally for trustworthiness.

'But I did have a private plane.'

Lena makes another giggle.

I see a snap judgement pass over her face. And then she gets on with it.

'It's a funny story how I discovered I was pregnant.

'It was in Moscow. My husband always has a Christmas party at his company. And it was a crazy Russian party . . . with lots of friends, lots of bands, lots of stuffs . . . and we were supposed to go to Zanzibar for the Christmas holiday. And to go to Zanzibar you need to do vaccination. But I didn't ever do any vaccination.'

Her voice is very definite.

Lena sits at the table staring into the canvas of the licking pug.

'In my life I travelled all around the world for modelling, for working, and never anything happened to me. I tell him I don't want to do vaccination. And he says, "You have to do vaccination as I'm doing it. You have to do it otherwise you can't go to Zanzibar." And we are arguing at the party and this doctor lady, from his company, he pulls her over and she says unless you are pregnant then you must be doing it.'

There is a mimic coming into her voice: her pleads, his hector.

'I don't want do vaccination. And I went, "Well maybe I'm pregnant I can't take the risk." So my minigarch shouts immediately for his driver. "Go to the pharmacy and get the test!" Just like that. And think it's the night, and we are in the party, and with his men he can do that. And I just go back to the party. But soon, the driver is back for me. He brings these testers and my husband he goes – "Now go and pee on them and see!"'

Then she stops talking.

'And I am in the party, in the toilet, and I can see I am pregnant.'

Lena scrunches her face and looks at the floor. I can sometimes read expressions like this: when someone is hovering on the edge of telling me something. I smile, trying to fake the face of an old friend – I need her to trust me, to tell me all her story.

'He said I could have everything I wanted.'

Lena is not looking at me. She is playing with her rings.

'So he sent me to London to have Baby.'

In this gloomy room of Russian art I ask her to remember the takeoff in Moscow. Lena is talking slowly: the runway, the judder, the buffet in the ascent, how she gripped onto the leather arms of the seat, mumbling little charms, until her waxy valet came to escort her to the bed, in the minigarch's mahogany cabin behind.

I ask her about that space.

Again, she holds herself back.

'On that bed I was thinking.'

Her voice dips a little in tone.

'On that bed I was thinking.'

Our eyes cross: I hold them, still.

'On that bed I was thinking what they told me. I had been study-ing, in Moscow, the prayer books, in a small circle, and they had brought me to Kabbalah. They read to me from the Zohar. The most precious book. And they told me life is not the chaos it seems. They told me every soul comes back. That every soul is endless. That every soul chooses its parents for itself. That's what I was thinking.

'I was thinking. Why did Baby choose me?'

I have found my way in.

Tell me more: and she begins to smile vulnerably.

She tells me how she pulled the quilts over her head, and tried to sleep in this thin and parched air. How she tossed and turned on the mattress, the whirring and dinning grating her, as the baby was kicking inside her, more agitated than ever, and there was a buzzing hiss in her left ear. How slowly, she breathed: and repeated over, and over – the same question. Baby, why did you choose me?

'That was all I was thinking.'

London. Morning. Light.

Lena met the doctor the next day.

'How many women die in childbirth?'

That was the first question she asked the English doctor.

'Have any women died in childbirth with you?'

The English doctor laughed, as Lena noticed how green his eyes were, as green as a field in spring. They swiped across her swollen face like a scanner. There was something about his perfect, purring elocution that she did not really understand, that dimmed the tingle in her spine, as his black women scurried up, under the harsh examination light, with the paperwork.

'This is where my husband sent me.'

Her hands have fallen flat on the table.

Her bright eyes are digging for something in me.

'We had a penthouse in London, of course. One of the normal ones. It was all white. It was all marble floors. There was some art. Like some women's head and some shitty absurd art. It was a show-room really. My husband he just bought it on my birthday. We came, and he had just proposed, and he went into this one . . . and he went – "OK, I want this one." And that was that. And now I was here to make Baby.'

The way she is talking is changing.

'I had so many worries in this space.

'My husband he was not coming from Moscow so often.'

A few notes of a demented jangle creep into her voice.

'He had so many problems with the pipeline he controls.

'There was a legal case that came against his pipeline. There were fights. There were dangers. And I was worrying for him. And this worried me so much . . . as I didn't want Baby to get damaged by my worrying. My husband was fighting with the governor and the minister. I was worried he could be jailed.'

She pauses, and for a second or two, sucks in her lower lip.

'Always, always, I was talking to Baby in my head.'

Her weeks grew longer, and stretched into hours of tension.

'Always, I was asking this soul, that's come inside me, why. Why did you choose me? Why now? Why him?'

Anxiety only grew. The minigarch did not come one week, like he promised. She knew his case was progressing through the courts. She knew a weasel-faced governor and a veiny Tatar rat from the oil ministry were circling over his pipeline in the mining colonies: and the charge was political.

'He told me more than I should have known.'

But the minigarch did come back to London, as he promised. He looked slender, and like a monkey she picked the first grey hairs from the dome of his skull. He kept repeating in entire chunks of chronology the progression of the case, and the names of the officers, circling over the pipeline, who had snarled at him at the interior minister's estate, he was nothing more than a relic of a previous era.

'He was honest . . . and filled my small woman's head with worry.'

That weekend the minigarch barely left his apartment, the one he had bought her laughing on her birthday fifteen months ago. There was not one surface that neither gleamed, glinted, nor held some electronic secret – but neither of them, the daughter of a Soviet chemical engineer and the son of a Urals smelting manager, much cared, or understood, such things.

'He told me he might go to prison. For many years. He told how they were fighting with many things. They were fighting with mafia. They were fighting with courts. They were fighting hard. And that this was the risk: he would not see Baby.'

The minigarch's watery eyes had gone bloodshot, like he had swallowed a truth serum, or been force-fed in one of their wired installations outside Moscow, as he took her to the roof terrace and pointed to the garden square, and glowing lights of the red dome over Harrods, where they had once gone shopping. Would she wait for him? Would the baby know he was an honest man? Would the baby play in that garden square: hide-and-seek round those trees, in those bushes?

'This is what we were all the time talking about.'

And in the small mews house she sighs.

'All the time I was talking to Baby.'

Why did you choose this? she kept asking the baby, wrapped in the sheets in the morning, in the hazy white light, after he had left in his private jet.

But the baby refused to answer.

'I had so many worries . . .'

She mumbled to the endless one, when she could not sleep, and she walked around, round and round Knightsbridge, the empty mansions, and the sleeping flats, of all these hunted Russian couples, asking him – who is my baby? She walked for hours, in those blue nights of summer, when the garden squares hold damp secrets, when time flows a little differently, maybe slower, and the Gypsies played the songs she remembered on a broken accordion under the triumphal arch in Hyde Park Corner.

She talked endlessly to the baby.

'I was talking, talking, always talking. Why did you choose me? Why did you choose this? Why couldn't you choose a mummy with a daddy who's not going to go to prison? Where did you come from? Who are you? Why me?'

The hours she walked grew longer.

'I didn't pray. I don't really know how to pray . . . I would let my mind flow into thoughts and walk around London. I just asked for light. I just asked for light to come. Sometimes I felt there was a light entering. And other times it would go away.'

She stops talking, and pulls herself from the table.

'I was walking wanting Baby to know this place, wanting Baby to feel home.'

And then she leaves the room.

Some minutes later, she comes back from the kitchen.

'Then my husband he came back to London. For my birth.'

My eyes catch her swallow.

'But Baby is not coming. My husband he had come from Moscow. But Baby is not coming on his due date. My husband he had planned his life, his business. He had a week for me. But Baby then is not coming. And he was annoyed.'

There was a buzzing in her ears at night.

The baby was not coming. There was swelling in her spleen and an acid retch on her fuzzy tongue. The hours grew longer: she wandered up and down the apartment, enormous, pausing to look at the art the designer had thrown together, but she had never bothered to listen to him explain. Who was this stone worn bust on a metal stick? Were these splodges of purple a mood or a warning?

'Baby was still not coming.'

She has crossed both her arms round her chest.

There is something wounded, somewhere in her voice.

'I had to organize him: tours in London, visiting museums, as he had come and I felt responsible for him. I had to make things interesting for him. But Baby was not coming. And I knew he was looking at me and going, "Where the fuck is it." And I was speaking to Baby. I was becoming very upset and sad. And he was becoming angry. Because he had to be in Moscow. And I was so sad and speaking to Baby in my mind. I was asking Baby, "Please come, please come, start moving." And that evening my Baby started to move. I had asked her and now the baby comes.'

And, over the table, she smiles a little, at someone – not at me.

'Slowly, slowly, Baby is beginning to come. And I remember we played cards until twelve or one o'clock in the morning. And I felt the contractions beginning inside me. So everything was working. And we slept until morning. But there is pain in the morning. Everything is working. And my husband he can have a massage he has planned in the house. And now the contractions they are coming faster.'

I scrawl into my notebook: how she bends closer, trusting me at last.

'And we decided, not to take a taxi, but walking.'

I scribble in my notebook: there is something frantic in her voice.

'I was walking and the contractions are getting bigger and bigger and I was already feeling more, and more, pain. And when we get to the hospital, and the nurses find me, my husband he goes back in the taxi to get some stuffs he is wanting.'

The pain was coming in waves as they took her to the white room.

'But now Baby is coming much speedier. The pain is coming now and it is the big pain. And I think I am handling the big pain well, and I am telling Baby the pain is not so great, and that I can meet this pain without the anaesthetic, and then no I can't . . . the pain is everywhere, and I shout to the big black nurses, "I don't want to make this all holistic and natural give me anaesthetic."'

Her nostrils filled with hospital smells.

Light glinted from the linoleum.

'And the black ladies, they say to me, "No it's little for you to suffer as in a few minutes we are going to have baby." And I went, "OK fine." And they started to check. They were very relaxed. And then the last few minutes they started to run, and go crazy, and check. And the doctor, who was very relaxed, like an English gentleman from a Russian movie, he is running round and round with the black ladies.'

But the baby was not coming. The pain built, and built, and built – and she began to realize it was she who was screaming – as the black women they were touching her, they were holding her, they were rushing her somewhere, as they kept telling her in their strange voices to breathe. The pain was building: a heaving, throbbing, searing, pain, as the one within her pushed with all her might.

'And all of a sudden I notice they are worried, and shouting, and running, and I now am in the big pain, and someone is shouting her heart is stopping.'

The black women had started buzzing like bees.

'My husband he has just got there. And I can see his face. And he is shouting. He is shouting very big shouts. "She's my wife!" And they are pushing him away . . . and the big shouting nurses they are moving me into the operations room, where husbands are not allowed.'

There was shouting. More shouting.

And the trolley rattled into the operating theatre.

'And now there are lights everywhere in my eyes, and I understand something is wrong, and I understand something is bad, and I understand I'm supposed to have Baby already ten, fifteen minutes ago, and something is wrong, and I'm going, "No, something is wrong . . ." spinning into lights. And then they put anaesthetic and then blank. Then nothing. Gone.'

At first she did not understand: she was groggy, parched, a crackling petered in and out of her ears. And then she heard the bleeping, and the gurgling pipes.

'When I wake up Baby was not there. I woke in the bed. There was doctor and wires and black nurses . . . And I felt, very, very, bad after the anaesthetic . . . because it was intense, to stop me dying. And I am shouting. "Did she live? Did she live?"'

The doctor cleared his throat.

'There were complications.'

She felt the puckering of tension in her skin.

'And I do not understand what this means. And doctor goes, "Congratulations. You were very brave. You went through some very big complications." And I shout at him: "Did she live?" And he went: "The baby survived."'

The black women brought in the baby.

'Doctor he says: "The baby is very nice."'

But as she held the baby she felt a watery pang of disappointment.

'Baby was ugly.'

'She was so ugly. She was covered in a black fur, a black hair. Not only on her head. But on her shoulders, and over her back. The first time I saw her, this tiny little girl, she looked like a monster . . . with big purple veins. She had the face of a monkey. And the eyes of a fish. Her face was not beautiful.'

Her face crumpled in the white hospital glare.

'And so many people are coming to me and going, "Oh my god what a beautiful baby." And my parents, and my friends, they are all there, all around, all making the same voice . . . "She's so cute . . ." And I looked at her and I wanted to cry and I thought, She's so ugly. Why are they all lying to me?

'Why are all these people lying?'

That night she lay there holding the baby in the bluish light.

'I looked at Baby. Very tired Baby. And I thought, This soul has travelled so far. This soul might be an older soul than you are. I looked at Baby. I thought, This looks like a helpless baby. But it's not. The soul inside Baby is old.'

She was frightened she would break it.

'I took the baby and held it up and I said, "Hello. I am your mummy." I was not sure who Baby was. I am thinking, Why did

Baby choose me? I look and tried to imagine her soul coming through tunnels into the world. I said, "Baby, maybe we met as souls before in a previous life. You could be my sister or me your mother, some times ago." Baby said nothing. Baby only looked at me with the hugest brown eyes.'

An ancient thing.

PLAISTOW ROAD

The bell clangs once, then louder.

Then the children come out. Some run, others push. A few are lonely. Boys with half-undone ties run after girls with uncertain grins. Some are more welcome than others. Two girls in hijabs move off from the rest and gossip, furtive, clutching something, under the school wall. There are yelps and shrieks. A football match has started on the pavement. There is a haze in the air. I am waiting for their Teacher.

'There are not many whites, in my students.'

She has a soft, soothing voice, the Teacher.

And I instantly want to trust her.

'There were more whites, when I first came to Plaistow . . . twenty years ago.'

The Teacher is Nigerian, in her late thirties, with a rounded face, under a black wig. She has promised to tell me what the schoolchildren are like in Plaistow, where almost 80 per cent speak English as a second language and less than 10 per cent are white British. This is an area where the majority tell the census they have no British identity at all.

'England is not what it used to be . . . y'know.

I begin to walk and talk with the Teacher.

'There are so many migrants, so many. The children. They are maybe 10 per cent . . . of white. They are all Asians, so many Asians, Africans, or EUs, from the East Europe. I remember when I first came twenty years ago from Nigeria . . . I was the only black lady in the area. They were all white English then. Now all the whites you see they are not English. They are EUs. The children they call them "freshies". They muck about and push them, laughing they can't even speak English.'

Plaistow is one stop further along the Hammersmith and City Line from where the fictional tube stop Walford East from *East Enders* is supposed to be. But this immense demographic change now makes the grand old show look like creepy racial nostalgia. The white British population of old cockney Newham is now 16.7 per cent.

The Teacher hovers, her eyes on a troublemaker, picking on a small black boy. But she keeps talking.

'From what I hear, the white people they are moving away, when they hear the migrants is coming. They went from Plaistow to Canning Town. Then they heard Africans is coming. So they went to Barking. But when they heard we is moving there . . . They went out into the Essex. They didn't want us there.'

The troublemaker sees the Teacher and stops yanking a sports bag.

'Why did the English leave?'

She shrugs, and glances back at the bully.

'They just didn't like it. People don't like change, y'know.'

The Teacher is very dark, with small, affectionate eyes.

She lugs a huge handbag, and is dressed all in shades of grey. Her voice, the way she answers questions, or moves her hands, are on a soft, lullaby frequency. She talks about herself dreamily, with disinterest, as if she is discussing somebody else. She resists the questions as I try and make her tell me the very basic plot line of her life.

'I worked in McDonald's, first. But when I went to see my friends . . . I would go straight and play with the children. And they went to me, "Why don't you become a teacher?" When I came for the first time to a school, for work, they said somebody without the certificates can only become a midday supervisor. So that's what I did.'

We stop for a moment, watching the uniforms stream home. Some cluster, others gaggle, one runs wildly in a circle. This is a secondary school, and as we watch the boys kicking a ball from a distance, I note down how some of the children have the heights of men, and others the frames of boys. The friendship groups, some laughing, some vicious, in little groups of two or three, are mostly ethnically mixed.

Her voice skips, upbeat.

'The school they told me to get a certificate. So I did. And now I'm a teacher.'

I ask more questions as we walk, inviting her to reveal herself, or confess little things, to let out her life story. But she's not interested. Her mind is with the children. And, she wants to tell me what others never want to listen to – the stories about them.

'All of the time, I am dreaming about the children . . .'

We are now moving away from the school gates.

'I'm waking up and thinking, Is he OK? Is she going to make it? The faces they come to me in the night. And some faces they stay with me. They haunt me a bit, y'know. Sometimes, I'm like I wish I could see that boy again . . . Because, we are teachers. And we never get to see the end of the story.'

The Teacher smiles, and adjusts her wig, waiting for me to ask. So, my questions change track. 'Which are your favourites? Who was the worst? How are they different? Who are you teaching now? Are there Nigerians? What are the Muslims like?' And in an instant the low frequency in her voice is gone.

'Most of my girls they are Muslims.'

We are a metre out of earshot now, and we can begin to talk about race.

'They are very used to hiding, the Muslim girls.

'Most of them they take two bags to school . . . with two clothes. The Muslim girls in the school, they always come really holy in the morning in their scarfs. But then they go into the toilets, get changed, put on miniskirts . . . And walk around the school in make-up, high heels, and they take the scarf off.

'They take it all off.'

The Teacher giggles a little: and looks at me, as if betraying a little secret.

'And you see them kissing boys . . .'

She points at two hijabi girls gossiping, a little angrily, by the wall.

'And then they go home, rub their make-up off, and go back as the holy ones. So many are like that. Majority of the Muslim girls are like that. Most of their parents don't speak English anyway, so they have no idea . . . And after school now the make-up is already gone. Look at them . . . those girls are already all washed off.'

We are walking round the back of the gleaming new building, to talk quietly. The school buildings glint bright like Playmobil toys behind double-mesh green fences: a huge spaceship box of a building, clad in bright, happy, grinning orange plates. There has been a state-funding injection here.

'They say this is a multicultural school. But it's not. The school is dominated by Bangladeshi and Pakistani Muslims, with some blacks, a few whites and EUs coming in. I went to a Muslim school in Nigeria, so I can recognize this.'

The Teacher peers through the fences into the classrooms.

'But I am watching their religion, it's beginning to break a bit down.'

The Teacher waits until two Asian boys have passed us.

'They confide in me, the Muslim girls, but they can't tell their parents.

'Some of them tell me, oh miss they are religious, but I can't do anything about it, and I just have to abide by the rules. Very few talk to me about escaping later in life. But they end up having crushes on black or white boys . . . And they find it so difficult . . . They find it very, very difficult. They confide in me, y'know . . .'

The Teacher begins imitating them a little, with their whine.

'They are like, "Miss, Miss, don't tell anyone . . . please, don't tell anyone . . . Oh, Miss, I love that guy . . . Oh, Miss but he's cool, but promise you're not going to mention this to anyone." And they are like, "Oh please, my mum would kill me, my dad would kill me." But some of the girls they get aggressive. They shout at the ones who are taking it off, "We don't expose ourselves like a piece of meat. You are being like fresh meat in the market. Put the scarf back on!"'

And with that the Teacher pauses. And looks at me. 'So many girls pretend to be so, so, holy.'

We are walking past the broad glass windows of classrooms where the national flags of the students hang drooping: Albania, Nigeria and Romania.

The Teacher is still looking at me, trying to work out why I'm here.

'They hide a lot, y'know.

'The Muslim girls hide so, so many boys, in their phones . . . They go, "Oh, isn't he cool in that pic." And they go to me, "Oh, Miss, promise you're not going to show it to everyone." Y'know they like Justin Bieber. They talk about him all the time. "Oh, he's cool. Oh, I wish I could get married to him . . ." But I know they have a lot going on.'

She looks away from me, and at a piece of gravel under her feet.

'Because of the religion they are scared. They tell me, "Miss, Miss, if I get married to a Christian, if I get married to a non-Muslim . . . My dad will kill me." The Muslim girls get emotional, y'know, and they try not to cry. I see them all the time getting red in the face and then stopping keeping eye contact with me.'

The Teacher has been here for years.

She has seen it all. And now she has begun to see it on a loop. These days she teaches language support for the children who struggle with English. She runs the 'Show Me Your Homework' club at lunch. And she teaches general classes. She has had hundreds of students. But teachers always gets a few stuck in their minds.

'Let me tell you about some of them I'm teaching.'

Rakia is thirteen. Already she never wears her hijab inside school. The Teacher, and everyone else, thinks she is one of the most beautiful girls in the year group. Rakia seems to know this too. When she comes in, she puts on make-up in the toilets and undoes the top buttons on her uniform to make it a little bit more revealing. Her headscarf stays shoved in that second bag until she walks home with her little brother.

'But one morning I came in and I see Rakia, in the front row, she has a ring. I know what it is. I just know. And I went to Rakia,

"Are you engaged?" "No, Miss . . ." But when I had a closer look I saw it was a very expensive ring . . . twenty-two-carat gold. And she went to me then, "Miss . . . Miss, my mother had an arranged marriage."'

The Teacher speaks openly, quietly, now nobody can hear us.

'This happens so much to our young girls, really young girls. And I go to them, "Are you engaged?" and they go, "Miss I'm not." But I strongly believe they are. They are twelve to thirteen. The Asians in Plaistow believe in arranged marriage. The girls, they know it's wrong but there is nothing they can do about it. They go, "You lot, the government, think it's wrong, but our parents, and we think it's right." Most of them say that.'

A tremor of anxiety is now in her voice.

'In the classroom they go, "Miss, Miss, my mum had an arranged marriage, so we believe we have to have an arranged marriage." The girls they do it secretly you know, behind closed doors, they are not allowed to report on anything at all. They go, "Oh, Miss, I'm not allowed to talk about it sorry." And they marry their cousins. In Africa we never, never do this. Maybe a tribe, but a cousin. We believe it's wrong . . .'

The Teacher lets out a sudden sigh.

'Some students I trust, and some I don't.'

I look into the gleaming school and know I want her to tell me a positive story.

'There are some who come and talk to you, and some who don't.'

Amina talks. She looks much older than fourteen. With a longer, more drawn face. She never wears make-up but she uses Facebook. This is one of Amina's secrets. She comes up to the Teacher and tells her little things at the end of the lessons. "Miss, I have a boyfriend. Miss, this is his Facebook. Miss, he's at another school. Miss, I'm not allowed to have boyfriends. Miss, I'm not actually allowed to be on Facebook."

'Amina, she's . . . so clever she's actually got Bs.' The Teacher lets out a sudden, sharp sigh. 'And one day she went to me, "Miss, when I finish I'm not going to do any work." I went, "Why are you not going to uni when you've got high grades?" And she went to me,

"Miss, don't tell anyone about it, Miss, but my mum got married to her cousin." And there was this English girl who heard and went, "Yuck! How could your mum get married to her cousin? Miss, I wouldn't get married to my cousin." And then she went, "Miss, would you get married to your cousin!"'

A quiver comes into her voice. 'Amina told me again two weeks ago, "Oh, Miss, I don't have to do any work."' And then the words come with a little anger. 'And I went, "Why?" 'She just said, "Miss . . . when I finish I don't want to work." "How come, you are a very intelligent girl?" "Oh, Miss . . . I just want to stay at home. I just want to be like my mum." She says her mum is not allowed to work. So it's like the Muslim men are domineering. But I don't think Amina was happy when she said it. She looked sad.'

We are right behind the school now, where the new basketball courts are, through the tall mesh of green fencing. And there are cigarette butts everywhere. I can hear my questions become leading: I want optimism, progress, success.

'They don't have a chance, most of the girls.'

Aisha is the class clown. She is the loudest girl in the class. The brashest. Who always changes into a miniskirt when she comes to school and sits at the back putting on make-up with her friends in Maths class until it's over. Aisha is already having sex. She is fifteen and wants to make sure everyone knows she does it.

'She is always talking about that every time.

'Yeah, and I believe she is doing it. Aisha is talking like she knows. Not talking, like telling us . . . But shouting about it all the time. One day we had an outside speaker who came in to talk about sex education. And this woman she said, "Make sure you always use a condom." And Aisha she started shouting, "Miss, what's better using a condom or not using a condom? Miss, with or without! You know, Miss!"'

Then one day Aisha came to school depressed.

'And she went to me, "Miss, I feel like committing suicide." And she went, "Miss, do you know how to commit suicide?" And I went, "I don't want to know." "Well, I'll tell you . . ." And before I could rush to the child protection officer, Aisha said, "Miss, it's easy you sit in the bath and put in a hanger and maybe attach it to something electrical . . . and you sit in the bath and its kills you." And then Aisha she looked at me and went, "Miss, Miss, because sometimes I get fed up with my parents."'

I try and think of an optimistic question to ask.

As we stand and talk behind the basketball courts, there is little hint at where we really are. There is a little more rubbish overflow in the terrace running ahead of us. The bay windows are a little grubby. But otherwise, there are no more clues that over a third of children live in poverty, and a quarter of all households are over-crowded. This is a story hiding behind closed doors. Here in Newham we are in one of the poorest boroughs in England: out of 354 in the country this is the sixth most deprived. But in a city with industrial, organized street-cleaning, this is always obscured.

The Teacher sees little signs every day.

'Most of them, the girls don't want to go home. They are very poor, you see. When the girls go home all they do is domestic work. They have to help their mums in the kitchen, so they have no time to read. Some of them they come in stinking and go, "Oh, Miss, we don't have showers. We are only allowed to have our shower once in a week." As they have turns and they are not allowed to waste hot water. And some they cannot afford even the school meals. Others they come in ripped clothes. They are very, very poor, especially the Bangladeshis and Pakistanis.'

A lone white boy runs across the basketball courts.

'They live so many, all together, the Asians. The blacks they are living a bit better. But the Asians, they live with their grandparents. And they have babies in the family, and they are sharing beds. And they can't even sleep throughout the whole night. And they come in the morning without sleep and they can't concentrate. The parents still believe there is nothing wrong with it.'

I decide I have to switch the topic.

Maybe if I ask about the boys she will give me something positive. But the Teacher suddenly becomes anxious. Her eyes squint. Could we be reported for hanging around the school? What will the children think of her being here, in the smoking spot?

There are a lot of cameras watching: to stop the strangers coming into the school.

She wants to go to the McDonald's in Canning Town.

And we begin to walk to her blue Volvo.

'One of my old boys, he was called Mohammed. And this little boy he came in and he told me he'd never had McDonald's . . . "Miss, what does it taste like?" Mohammed, he told me, he came here when he was eleven. And he told me he's gonna start having McDonald's when he's working. He's one of the boys I'd really like to see. He's gone now.'

We get in the car and she keeps talking as the engine comes on.

'Mohammed, he would come up to me and tell me things.'

I strap in and hope for my GCSE success story.

'Always the same things. Mohammed he said he left his two years old sister back home. And three young brothers. They were so poor in Bangladesh they lived in one room, he said. In Plaistow he said he lives with his really, really wicked auntie. And he doesn't eat at home. He only eats once per day. It's evil, really evil. But the auntie didn't want him to come and his family they just immigrated him like that.'

Mohammed was a small boy, with bright brown eyes.

'He told me his auntie maltreated him. She didn't feed him in the mornings and sometimes nothing at night. And, y'know they can't really report it to the authorities, to the school. Coz they will get into more trouble. He said if he reported it to someone else in the family . . . they would hit him. He got proper beats from the uncle. They were beating him for little things. They made him do all this housework. The kinda person he was he just couldn't be bothered. He just thought, one day he's gonna leave.'

The Teacher grits her teeth. 'I wish I could see him again.'

The car swerves round the school.

There are still teenagers hanging around: smoking, squabbling, flirting.

'He's very ambitious. Mohammed got very good grades at school. But I never saw him again. I don't think he went to university. He said by the time he leaves school, he will go back home, and look after his brothers and sisters. And get a job to go back home. But I never saw the end. He's probably working in his uncle's shop.'

We drive along the old cockney cemetery towards Canning Town. The tombstones seem ever so slightly unkempt. The plants ever so slightly overgrown.

'One of the boys I am teaching now, he's ambitious.'

I relax a bit, now she is going to give it to me.

'Ahamed. He's a black, but also a Muslim. He comes from Sierra Leone. His English is getting better. I think he felt out of place when he first arrived, as he was black, and Muslim, and he began to tell me, "Miss, my mum says, 'Don't attend the mosques of these Muslims, as these Muslims, they don't teach us Arabic well. They preach not well.' So it's difficult to pray."'

The Teacher smiles and looks in the wing mirror at the car behind.

'When Ahamed came in I think he had mild learning needs. He's fourteen now. He comes for support during the homework time. He definitely wants to go to university. He said he wants to become a doctor. So he can wipe out Ebola completely.

'He's very bad at maths, though. He's really quite awful.'

The car stops at the lights.

I ask, 'So what do these stories say about the system?' The Teacher doesn't respond to the question. I ask again, 'Since you came and transformed into a teacher, and they have come and you are teaching them, do you feel the immigrants are treated well?' The Teacher sits thinking, chewing the question.

'I think the immigrants are treated . . . OK.'

Two African women are crossing, chatting, tugging blue wheelie bags.

'Y'know, black children in school are different from the Muslims.'

She is not interested in my questions. She knows what she wants to say.

'I see the new generation of black people. Our kids we've had in this country they are beginning to think like English people and their skin colour it might not really be mattering. Maybe. The

blackness is fading away. The blacks are trying to stay black . . . but there's no glue, no proper communication, no bond.'

The lights turn green.

'I ask myself, the children, are they becoming English?'

The blue Volvo goes.

'With black children they do. But with Asian children they try not to. The Muslims I don't think they will ever be English. They don't want to be at all.'

My eyes fix on an anti-odour yellow sun dangling from the mirror.

'I've got a skinny boy. Let's call him Mohammed the Second.'

I continue taking notes, hoping for a success. There must be one, statistically.

'He's an Asian. Always in trouble. That's why I'm not sure I should take him seriously. He's always in detention. He has no white friends. He's got Asian friends only. You can tell even when he's having a discussion his facial expression shows . . . he can never like Christians. He goes, "Miss, Miss we're going to go to jihad." "Miss, Miss we're gonna fight for our country!"'

The Teacher giggles at the steering wheel. '"Miss, Miss we're gonna fight," they say during break time or lunchtime. "You watch, Miss, I'm gonna go to ISIS." No seriously he says that. But the ones that speak like that, I don't think they speak very seriously. As they are only thirteen years old. But many of them do. Many.' The car is driving round a tight bend in an estate. 'I went to them, "Why would you want to do that?"'

The Teacher has her eyes on the double decker turning ahead. 'And they say, "Miss, I'm gonna fight for my country, I'm gonna fight for my religion! And that's what Allah says we gotta do." And I go: "No, that's not what Allah says." Some of them go, "Miss, I'm gonna kill all the Christians," when they are discussing. I hear it. In the break. "Oh, Miss, I'm only joking," they say when I catch them. But it's hard for me to know when the joke ends and it becomes real. I'm worried about religion. You should see the way they fight on Facebook.'

We park outside the McDonald's in Canning Town.

'When I started I knew there would be migration, but I never thought there would be this, this much, so much migration, that there would be barriers like this, between me, and the children . . . and a lot of barriers that affect students' learning. I never imagined it. I never imagined the barriers.'

The McDonald's is full. We move through the noise and the people with chicken burgers and sit at the back. The Teacher eats quickly in a sloppy mess.

'I want to tell you this story.'

I am no longer asking questions. I am only listening.

'This one really beats me each time I think of it. His name is Tunde. Nigerian. He came in a really bright boy. But he started mixing with the wrong group . . . And I went to him and I went, "You're in the wrong group. I want you to change . . ." And he went, "But, Miss, there's nothing wrong."'

The Teacher swallows, but she has finished her food.

'Tunde was following this particular boy who was always getting around fighting in the streets. You'd see him in his school uniform at ten at night fighting. I heard he's in prison now. He was black, from Congo. He was this Congolese boy just running around beefing on the street . . .'

She swallows again.

'Tunde has a lovely mummy. I met her at the Students' Achievement Day and we kept on running into each other in the market. And since then I see him. I'm like, "Are you OK?" And he's like, "Yes, Miss." But on this fateful day in the staffroom the head teacher called a meeting. An emergency meeting. And he sent us emails to say this boy is on life-support machine. And I'm like, "How did it happen?"'

Suddenly, she is speaking faster.

'I just didn't want to believe it. His mum's number was calling me. She was trying to get hold of me. And I remembered her talking in Plaistow market, being like, "Oh, don't mind that boy, he's really a naughty boy." And I'd be like, "Oh, don't worry, he's in good care." Tunde was a really handsome, nice-looking boy. So we heard the

news on the day. So I called the mum. And the mum, she's like crying by the life support.'

The Teacher's eyes seem a little glazed.

'She said on Saturday night . . . He said he was gonna hang out with his friends in Canning Town. And they all went to Beckton. To all have a fight. It was a postcode war. He went to beef in Beckton. He went to fight in front of another gang member's house. And then other gang members came to attack them for being in their area. They were not supposed to be there. So they stabbed him in the heart.'

Her eyes fall into the empty McChicken box.

They stay there for a while in the splodges of mayonnaise.

'I went to visit Tunde there. He was pale. He couldn't even talk. He was on a bed. I didn't know if it was a life-support machine he was on. Oh . . . I'm like, "Tunde, what went wrong . . ." He couldn't speak at all. He's lost his speech. He still can't speak. When he came back to the school in a wheelchair I couldn't look at him.

'The boy had a bright future.'

Around us is McDonald's.

An Arab man in a leather jacket, with nuggets. Two Nigerian men in Day-Glo, with cheeseburgers. A tattooed white man feeding his mixed-race daughter a Happy Meal. The Teacher ignores them as I try one last time for a success story.

'There's this boy. A black boy from Jamaica. His name is Dwayne. When he first came in I knew, yes, this boy looks really promising. Y'know the way he spoke. He spoke about his school. How he enjoyed his transition. How he enjoyed his induction day. Dwayne is thirteen now and he's quite grown up. Most of the time we use Dwayne as a role model. Because when he comes into the classroom, his eye contact with the students, who are doing stupid things in the classroom, he just looks at them and then they just respect him . . .'

She is looking at me fiercely.

'I know Dwayne will succeed. It's the way he carries himself. Him stopping children, telling them off, "You haven't got the right equipment. You haven't got the right shoes. Pull up your trousers."

Correcting the students. He reads. He's always in the library. Reading all sorts of books. He's scored a lot of points and getting awards in assembly. And trophies. He's a reader. And he is . . . he's a natural leader. Dwayne walks around the school. He picks litter from the floor. He's like a mentor. And the teachers love him. I think Dwayne could be a teacher. A lecturer, actually. I can see him attending Oxford, or something. Because, if you're intelligent – there's a future.'

I grin with satisfaction. I got it: Dwayne is on his way.

We say goodbye by the Volvo.

But before we can, something snaps.

'I used to know him.'

A black man, with gold teeth, limp on both knees, is gabbling to himself.

'He must have got into drugs.'

The Teacher hides her eyes from me, with her right hand, and gasps.

'Sometimes, I think this country's not designed for black people.'

HARLESDEN ROAD

I blink.

Thousands of vibrating little houses cling to the motorway. The static hiss never stops. The glass in their craggy faces quivers as the circular curves from the river. Their gables tremble with millions and millions of hurtling cars a year.

I drive north.

But these bad-luck strips keep on coming. Their trembling bow windows are caked in thick soot. The blown air tastes of burnt toast. These are where the worst doss houses are. Here sleep is only shallow. The white noise and the rumbling lorries never cease.

The orbital dips into a concrete gulley. Here the train bridge hurtles over. The noise reaches a scraping pitch in this cavernous space: and with a burn on tyres the car swings upwards and turns off into Harlesden, with a sudden glimpse of the white-painted arch of Wembley Stadium.

The metal commotion vanishes.

I turn, and turn, into this higgledy-piggledy little town of faded ghost signs for stout and ale, painted onto the sides of lintel-topped red-brick parades with all the feel of a hardened Northern mining town. But these are pound shops and halal butchers trading under their skirts. Box signs stick out hawking Islamic media and the citizenship test.

I park behind the pawnbrokers.

A balding, small-shouldered Romanian with pouch-like lids and a pointed belly leans on the wall, as a black man with a smeared face in a blue tracksuit and hunted, puny eyes saunters up to him and pushes him crack.

A tense Somali with a wispy flame-dyed beard comes out of the pound shop clutching six notebooks and a packet of screw-in bulbs. A Brazilian man with fluttering eyes and a huge peak of a nose steps out of the Afro Hair Shop, looking smug. And like scampering demons, savage little cats shriek like sirens over the gothic eaves and encrusted windowsills, right above their heads.

Harlesden is poorer than most Northern mining towns. Once there were enormous industrial estates, along the thundering lines into London, thumping tracks wider than the Thames. Railway cars would unload ton upon ton of Sheffield steel and Durham coal. These were the big mass jobs, where in the 1950s the Jamaicans and the Irish became British: working on huge lines in the plants with other men who got you into football or the pub.

But those industrial estates have almost all shuttered. There are no more production lines in Harlesden now: Poles, Somalis, Nigerians – these men work alone, atomized, as pickers, drivers, cleaners, builders. Marks and Spencer closed in Harlesden in 1984 and never came back.

We are now in the poorest 10 per cent of the country.

There is sweat in this air.

This is Sunday morning.

I stand outside Bilal Halal and try and get this down in my notebook: the heat, the commotion, the up and down roads meeting at the winding crossroads, the buzz, the Pakistani lovers at the corner, the Indian magic shop flogging sprays to De-Demonize your house, the bookshop All Eyes On Egypt selling black conspiracy theories, the cracked stucco, the warren of wrinkly bedsits in the terraces, grilles over their curved doors to keep the crack addicts out, and mattresses everywhere – mouldy, yellow-stained, singed – leaning on lampposts and walls, from the coming and going in this unfixed, undetermined point of arrival.

There is heat and bright golden light.

And everywhere sound: vibrations tumble out of the black churches with bass and treble, fuzzing the pricecutters and the pound shops with hum and boom, as prayer halls echo out of every corner – over the veiled mummies outside Way2Save, over the shrieking couple under the We Buy Gold sign over TGS pawn-brokers, and the oily men slipping in and out, twitching whether they win or lose, from the betting shops. The heat animates, unsettles, and unnerves.

The hum of prayer is everywhere in Harlesden: the old brick chapels rented out from the Church of England are full, and the creaky little prayer rooms are overflowing, the brethren with no way of knowing they are there but for the Microsoft Word frontage hanging over the pound shops and the chicken shops.

I walk on into darkening light. Police keep maps of London parcelled up into gang territories. Harlesden is a kaleidoscope: at times the city's murder capital, at others its gun-crime centre. But mostly forgotten.

African men with serious airs sit out front of their shops on plastic chairs with prams playing cards. Tiffs escalate. Urban showoffs strip to summer chests. I glimpse a kiss at the bus stop. He begs her for a moment not to get the 226, his eyes narrowing to curving slits. Clouds are gobbling up the blue. The grey whispers about rain: the air heavies, as I wander through the warren.

I am looking for gamblers.

There are 1,773 betting shops in London. Their glass fronts are frosted or pasted in green or blue plastic from the street. These are heavily concentrated by design on the poorest clusters and ghettoes of the city, where they are the most popular. And as I move through Harlesden their machines pr-ring and chime like machine birds in the gloom.

There are thousands of gamblers here – frazzled Jamaican bums and owlish Nigerian security guards, whimsical Polish carpenters and pouty Irish soaks, but they are all gamblers, and one after the other they tell me to fuck off, until I put on a hoodie, come back with a clipboard and tell them I am conducting a survey from the William Hill experience – *I hate this, you hate this, let's hate this together* – and I need to quiz them about why they gamble.

I am moving through the gloom, trying to steal their stories, breaking the gamblers down with stupid questions. Do you think William Hill should serve beer? Do you think William Hill should

have more bets on live video games like FIFA or Pro Evo? And once they've sniggered they're mine. Because once you make a stranger laugh, he's yours, he'll tell you anything.

Mukhtar is staring at the dogs.

He is skinny, a little brittle, with an oblong Somali head that slopes down into thick lips, charred from weed and khat. And over them are the eyes themselves: dark, good-natured and pinched as if frightened.

Both are glazed and wired.

Mukhtar is in a blue T-shirt. He is cold in the betting shop, and shivers and shakes himself, rubbing his arms and elbows. He looks at me pleadingly. Like he doesn't talk much to people. Like he needs me to stay. And the faster he talks, without asking any questions about my supposed survey, without asking even my name, without caring who he is talking to, he begins opening up his head.

He flicks his head in jerks and shuffles. And I slowly realize: if he collapses on the floor I won't be surprised. Or if he suddenly rips out a knife, I won't be surprised either. But what he says breathlessly is weirder.

'Let me tell you something right now, bruva.'

There is a trembling quiver in his voice.

'The last time I ever gambled I ran out of a betting shop screaming . . . screaming . . . I was on the pavement just screaming. My whole life it's like flashing inside my head . . . I was covering eyes and digging in my nails, just howling, man. And y'know what I couldn't even hear myself screaming. Because losing all my cash that day was like drowning. I was staggering, sobbing, swearing. I could hardly even breathe. I never gambled again after that bruv, I swear on Allah.'

Mukhtar is fixed on the glowing roulette machine.

His hands shake slightly. His breath is short. But he is only watching. His pupils are black and round and filled with the luminous shimmer out of the Diamond Deluxe box. Mukhtar is watching the people. He likes watching the people: how they grit their teeth, and bite their lips, and breathe out, whispering to Allah for a Jack, and slap the clicking keys. He likes watching the numbers and the letters, the gawky emeralds and the red cherries coming up again and again, making or breaking gambling faces.

Mukhtar cannot pull his eyes away as we talk.

'Some people lose £1 and punch the machine. Some people lose £2,000 and they just walk away. Some people pick up the chair and smash up the machine. But some people only smile and turn round and laugh . . . Some people they start hitting, and screaming, going, the people watching was their bad luck. Some people, when they get lucky they are shouting and crying out the names of dem horses and throwing their winnings at the guys in the box and kissing the watchers.'

He clutches the table facing the flickering screens.

'Some people they have like a pound and it itches on them . . . When someone tries it once, they're hooked. When somebody comes through these doors and picks their dog: he's gone. Some people they have one pound and they have to get out of the house, to get here . . . And when the machine gobbles it up, they keep thinking, I gotta get my money back . . . I gotta get my money back.'

He abruptly swivels round.

'You see that young man who just came in? That kid, he came in . . . He had ten pounds in his hand. I don't know if you saw . . . He walked all around. But the machines they were all full . . . He was very anxious, very anxious . . . He couldn't wait so he went out to find another William Hill . . .'

He keeps moving too close to me, and I keep moving back – one step, two step, three step – as he eyeballs me unblinkingly. This is his way in the William Hill. Mukhtar comes up close to the men on the Diamond Deluxe. He watches over his shoulder. They hear his heavy breathing. They hear it almost trembling. They turn round and see his eyes swelling and full of cherries.

'I don't gamble any more . . . I don't gamble after what happened . . . I only come in to watch . . . I come in to watch the guys with the shopping money . . . who puts it in and loses it all, and are literally tearing their hair out . . . There was a guy a few minutes ago with a can . . . with a Red Bull . . . He came in here and now he ran out shouting.'

Mukhtar rubs his elbows with a shiver.

'I don't gamble. I don't . . . When I was young and walking past these . . . I saw them and I thought everyone in the gambling shop is a bum . . . I thought, If I come in through that door . . . and make those bets . . . that's my life away.

'I like watching . . . I like it . . . I like watching when they are like, "Yeah, I'm winning, excellent . . ." I like watching the more money they lose, the more they come in . . . They come in and they are angry, every day, punching that, betting those horses, shouting at dem dogs . . . Thinking, I gotta get my money back . . . I gotta get my money back.'

He pulls himself up and squints at me.

'Y'see . . . I don't gamble . . . Because before . . . I was coming in every day . . . Sometimes it was a pound. Sometimes it was a hundred pounds. Sometimes it was a thousand pounds . . . Sometimes I didn't care that I lost a thousand . . . But sometimes it was hell to me that I lost a tenner . . . Sometimes it was hell to me that I lost a fiver.'

Mukhtar loves watching.

He loves watching the Dogman. He is an old feller from Grenada. The Dogman comes in every day: every single day. Monday, Tuesday, Thursday – a pound here, and a pound there. They call him the Professor, the Expert, the Professional. Because he knows his dogs. He takes his time with the newspapers. He squints at them and circles the promising ones with the little gambling pens. He rubs his hands before the races. He is always sure he is gonna win, the Dogman.

Then there is Rouletteman. He is a black guy who was born here: a right joker. He is Harlesden made and raised and he likes to think he has it with these machines. He will come in and play whether he has any money or not. He doesn't care. Because Rouletteman knows better than anyone a gambler doesn't need to have some money: he only needs to be able to borrow money.

Today, like every day, the Dogman wants to win. He sits at the back, and folds the paper, and breathes through his mouth, as the racing voice comes on – *and they're off* – and there is nothing in

the world but the dogs and the odds, and the chance of winning and getting back like a prince to Grenada.

But the Dogman always loses. The bigger the bet the quieter he is. He grabs the paper sometimes. Once or twice he tosses it. Sometimes he will softly go, 'Fuck,' and walk out before the Rouletteman starts hooting at him – that he is a fucking unemployed loser – like he does every time. The Dogman is a fax-machine repairman, who is no good with printers, and regrets ever handing Rouletteman that fact. He is a gentle man and doesn't like no fights.

Mukhtar likes watching them two on Harlesden Road. The Paddy Power is where the Old Zoot Suits hang, hoping for some right winnings. That is where the Grand National gets rowdy. The old fellas cheering old Misty and the rest of them horses like their lives depended on it. Mukhtar knows why: their giro probably does.

Scruffy and stubbly, these are the Notting Hill refugees. The old fellers who still remember the fifties when black people rented right next to Hyde Park, and would walk along those carved metal railings, with the cool air blowing off the night-time trees, with sweet and playful girls, and called Bayswater the Water, and Ladbroke Grove the Grove, and Notting Hill Gate the Gate.

Oh, they remembered.

The white people, they would call those streets they were renting over the Gate the Mangrove. They would come and buy some drugs from the bad fellers or to follow the gay ones to a party and there they were: in these lovely tumbledown houses. They became greedy. They saw how high those ceilings were. And they knew how close they were to the right side of the park.

What happened for the rich boy whites was a fairy tale: of Princess Notting Hill. First the cool kids and the gays started renting, then the Cambridge kids, and eventually the Oxford types too. The black guys became backdrop. Then they were almost all turfed out. They were renters: and the rents are what did it. But they still let them back into Notting Hill for carnival.

Those streets, they are unrecognizable now. The concrete pavements have all been smoothed out, to the millimetre. The white stucco mouldings have been restored to a pastry-like perfection. The way it was before: the boys hanging out having a zoot on the step and joking with the ladies or singing on their way home – unimaginable. The only sound those streets have at night now is the bleep, bleep of the burglar alarms whose eyes flick back and forth off every corner of Princess Notting Hill.

They wound up in Harlesden. There is no difference, really, between here now and there then. The place is close and forgotten. These are old village streets, with proud red-bricks and knife bins, and dirty grocers and cramped bargain and electrical exchanges. The big men in Polish building always clatter round these bends and look greedily at the red terraces: this is the next frontier – all these bay-windowed terraces waiting to be flipped.

The Dogman remembers the Mangrove. But the Rouletteman doesn't remember none of this. He is younger – and a right yob. He brings slimy curries in and slurps them noisily, his eyes glazed to his dogs, or the football, or the tennis, he doesn't care. He'll bet on anything. He'll even bet on how much the Dogman will lose that week.

The Rouletteman only goes still with the Grand National. His mouth opens slightly. Something is happening in his head. There is a scratching. A tiny crackling. He is breathing faster. He is gonna win this time. He is going to make it back this time. And whenever he loses the Rouletteman gets angry and sometimes even grabs the Dogman in an arm grip and knocks over the chair and dusts his bald head with his bare knuckles for a pound.

Mukhtar watches these losers and listens: to the thunder of the hooves and the breathless Irish voice rattling off the names, the slides and the giddying chances of the race. These guys are losers. The old man slowly eating a bread roll out of a crinkled plastic bag as he mutters to himself in some kind of patois. He is here every day. He is quiet normally. Sometimes he goes into the toilet, comes out and talks about singing a calypso for the horses. But otherwise, he is quiet.

Mukhtar knows the likes of Dogman. These men relish control. They love their numbers. They love making up their own mind.

They love making decisions: they live for making their own little bet. They never get to make many choices otherwise.

The old Zoots go quiet when the fresh boys come in, rattling those car keys and grinning big to throw down some cash for their favourite team. This is what the young ones like to do. They aren't so much interested in the dogs and the horses: for them it's always the same – a couple of goes on the roulette or a tenner on the footie.

The old Zoots tease these youngers. 'You call yourself a gangsta but you don't speak no patois?' They chuckle and tease and suss them out for a good mood or not before asking for a quid for QPR.

Mukhtar has gambled all the way through Harlesden. He knows the islanders who hang out in the Paddy Power. He thinks the whites try and avoid it. He knows the crack addicts who all hang out in the slots on the corner. He knows the Chinese who hang out in the Ladbrokes. He knows the moans of the last old Irish who come in with their walking sticks and always lose everything.

The old Zoots spread rumours about the Irish. They kept a close eye on those fellers. As the Dogman says: he has only ever seen the Irish win the big money. They come in clutching those little supermarket bags, with the cheap butter and the bacon in it, or whatever, and their eyes glaze over as the commentator begins to shout, louder, and louder, until – no matter how old they are – they roar when they win and shout the horse's name, drop the bag, and rush to the drum. Then the Irish are gone. They are gone a week, or more sometimes, until bristly and yellow faced they shuffle back in: 'I gotta make my money back.'

The Dogman thinks they must have inside information or something. Those Irish, they know them horses well. That is not just luck. Those tips must be coming from the pubs. The Irish, they have their own pubs in Harlesden, which the islanders steer clear of. The kinda pubs the older fellers have told him back in the day – they went around carousing and singing and shaking little collection tins made out of baked beans or spaghetti hoops for the IRA or something. They are all there, the Irish. There must be some men from the stables tipping them off.

There must be.

Mukhtar laughs at him. The Irish are gone. Even the English are gone now. That was Harlesden twenty years ago now. When there were so many Irish and they used to all traipse into the William Hill all laughing and jabbering and poking each other in the ribs. Those poor wretches. Their boots would be all muddied and the bottom of their trousers would be tied with string. When he asked why they said they were working in drains and unless you did this right there and then in the morning the rats would jump up your trouser legs.

Mukhtar remembers the way they used to dress. They would buy one mangy suit at the end of the week with the money the old Paddy running them at the construction site would toss them. Then they would jump all spick and span onto the bus and try and chat up the ladies on their way to the Irish dance clubs across Kilburn and Willesden. Sloshed. They would get properly sloshed: until everything was light and funny and everyone was singing and there was nothing that tasted better than a greasy doner kebab and nobody was as beautiful as the one on their arm.

And those suits. They ruined those suits. There would be grease stains down the lapels. The arms stank of tossed beers and slipped whiskeys. There would be bloodstains down the trouser legs from the fights or when they fell over, in which case they'd always claim it was a fight. And those dirty suits, they would wear them all week, down the drains, up the scaffolds, waiting to buy a new one for the weekend.

'They shocked . . . at first, dem Irish.'

Mukhtar can't explain it, but the Irish have vanished. That accent: he hears it less and less. At first there were less and less of them. And now there are next to none. There are still a few water holes, but they are almost empty now because the Poles and the Romanians like street drinking, with can after can in the summer in the park. There are certainly no more dance halls: he heard they have been converted mostly into Turkish cash-and-carries, or mosques. The only Irish left it seems to Mukhtar are the ones in that William Hill he tries to avoid.

There are some betting shops that just get like this. Nobody can quite explain it. They let a few in a first because there's no custom.

And then they let a few more in to sit and watch the cars and the dogs and the horses and the numbers on the screens bathed in the bluish glow that bounces off the walls. And before you know it: this is where the crack-heads are.

Mukhtar loses his flow, and looks around us, paranoid.

'Harlesden has become a strange place . . . These people, I don't know who most of them are. I didn't go college with none of them . . . I don't remember none of them . . . They all come here recently.'

Mukhtar doesn't know the numbers. But they are stark. The white British population has shrunk almost 30 per cent between 2001 and 2011. And much of the black British have gone with them. Mukhtar doesn't know the numbers, but he can always tell from the front garden. The moment this becomes an unkempt mess he knows there are Romanians or Poles sleeping crammed into every room.

Mukhtar doesn't want to leave Harlesden. But that is the dream of all the other Somalis. Mukhtar doesn't want to leave the boxing clubs, the reggae shops and the mango stands. Mukhtar doesn't want to leave the butchers' shops and lose the smell of that sugary air wafting out from the McVitie's factory down by the railway line, smelling so close to Hobnobs.

Mukhtar knows it will all be gone when all the Somalis vanish into the suburbs: gone, all those stories that nobody will ever write power ballads about, gone, all those gangsters that nobody will ever make blockbusters about, gone, all those late-night ricochets, gone, all those corner-shop war heroes, winking like owls, laughing, their mouths full of khat, their pupils bulging, and wanting to tell anyone who would listen about jeeps of the Puntland front and the dust of the Ogaden campaign.

'Everyone's leaving . . . They want to go to Birmingham. They wanna go out to far East London. They want to go where it's cheaper. Where there are more Somalis. They feel we are being pushed out of London . . . definitely pushed out . . . They feel we are not being given a chance.'

Talking in the William Hill and waiting for the Grand National, we are surrounded by sounds. The drrring and brrring of the slot machines like a thousand new messages. The click and ka-chick of the pounds clocking in and the rattling shiver of the coins coming out. The fluttering brrring time and time again as the commentator's excitement breathlessly gallops out of the TV.

Mukhtar looks at me: his pupils have pulsed and swelled.

'There's a bad atmosphere . . . Y'know . . . There are lots of demons in the betting shop . . . There are loads of demons . . . I don't think the human beings are possessed . . . I think they listen . . . I think they are listening to the demons . . .'

Mukhtar has grown not to trust the gamblers.

'Even though I'm in a betting shop right now I'm not that person . . . I used to be . . . You'll be walking past, and you'll just have to come in . . . You never think you are gonna lose it . . . You never think, you never think the machine's gonna swallow it . . . Double it! Let's go double it! That's what you are thinking . . . You never think you are gonna lose. Never.'

Mukhtar is sweating, a little.

'Y'know what the worst day was? I'll tell you what the worst day was . . . My wife and my children they went back to Somalia. To visit my mum . . . And I was supposed to go to the money transfer. They are waiting for the money to support them for a month . . . £580. When they were away I didn't know who was going to look after them in Somalia. Like I had no fucking clue what could happen to them in Somalia . . . I came out. I was supposed to walk into the money transfer . . . But next door was a Paddy Power. I nearly . . . I nearly . . .'

He freezes as coins rattle out.

'I lost it on the machines . . . I lost it on the Diamond Deluxe . . . That game . . . I gave it £500 . . . and I lost £500 in twenty minutes . . . My first forty pounds was fine, after that I was like, "Shit what the fuck shit what the fuck," literally just feeding the machine . . . "Shit, got to get the money back . . ." That was the worst day . . .

'I ran out the shop . . . Right the minute I left there was tears coming down. And they wasn't tears of sadness, they were tears of anger. Anger at myself . . . Anger at my soul . . . What a dumb as fuck thing to do. I went home . . . and I didn't come out for a week.

I didn't go to work. I was cussing myself. I was crying . . . The fear was I was gonna lose my family . . . lose my children . . . lose my house . . . I was shaking . . . I was praying . . . Now I can honestly say I'm not that person.'

The words echo funny. The way he chews them. The odd ring to it all. I think his family has kicked him out. I think they are not family any more. Mukhtar is telling the first man in the betting shop who will listen all this because he has no one else.

'I'm not a gambler any more. I'm only here . . . *Looking*.'

But Harlesden is full of gamblers. They are everywhere. Like José the Brazilian postman. He gambles everything he has. His food money, he blows it in minutes. José goes hungry sometimes. He has no money for days. Mukhtar sees him sometimes on those days and goes, 'Come on bruv,' and invites him in and gives him some Somali food. Mukhtar looks at José and knows it is true.

'Your soul, it doesn't belong to you . . . That is why in my religion this is made forbidden . . . Your soul, it doesn't belong to you . . . You can't condemn your soul . . . Never . . . It leads to depression . . . It's you condemning yourself . . . How dare you. You are not your own. You didn't create yourself . . . No, God created you. You can't . . . you can't belittle what does not belong to you . . . How dare you . . . How can you condemn what does not belong to you.'

Mukhtar lifts up his shirt and begins showing me his scars. Then he pulls up his trouser leg. Those gnarled marks, he says, are bullet marks. The Grand National starts. Impossible to go to the cinema, he says, because he pops out in sweat. There are movies that almost give him a heart attack. There are flashbacks that could make him faint.

'My wife wakes up screaming sometimes. My wife she was more braver than I was . . . My wife she had more . . . She was more heroic than I am . . . Every once and a while, every month, she wakes up screaming and every once and a while . . . that same wake up happens to me.'

There is no let-up in the machines' fluttering brrring.

'My first memory, I'm two years old . . . It's with my sister. She's giving me a glass of water . . . and that's it. We lived in a city, then a war happened. Bombs were going off . . . war was happening . . . what you are seeing on TV now from Gaza, that's my memories . . . And lots of my community haven't been rehabilitated . . . And they are taking and doing things to try and forget somehow . . .'

Mukhtar sucks in his burnt lips.

'I'll tell you what happened . . . I was in a village, and I was by myself. I was with my mum and we lost each other . . . She moved on to Djibouti and then the British government gave her a visa to come other here . . . But whilst she was doing that I got separated from her and I was on my own in this village . . . I was twelve years old at the time.

'Now what happened was these war criminals – it's what I call them – they came into the village and they came in and started killing everyone . . . I took a little, y'know, a bottle of milk . . . that full of water, a blanket and some bread that was in a rack . . . I was in a little hut. I was staying there and I just ran out . . .

'Then literally as I was coming out there was this old man . . . About sixty . . . He ran past me. And I was running behind him. A bullet hit right above his neck and came out of his mouth. He fell down and I tripped on him . . . And if I didn't trip I would have got killed as well . . . And he fell down and his face was sort of lying towards his side facing me and blood was coming out of his mouth . . . And as I tripped, I slipped . . . and my face went right into his mouth . . . and the blood that was coming out of his mouth . . . glug, glug . . . went right over my face.'

He wraps his arms around his chest.

'I got out with blood all over my face . . . I grabbed the blanket . . . forgot the water . . . And I was shit-scared . . . I was crying . . . And all the bullets are coming hitting and some of them are hitting my clothes . . . and hitting the dust . . . And literally for like six hours I was seeing people getting shot . . . people dying . . . children dying . . .

'I took me six weeks' trying to get there from village to village and through the jungle . . . It took me six hours to get out of the village . . . I was covered in dust and blood that wasn't even mine. I'd literally gone white . . . And I didn't know but I'd also got shot.'

Mukhtar lifts up his shirt and presses the scar with his thumb.

'Then we set out to find the refugee camp . . . Geneva . . . And from there we got the bus to the airport and then . . . we came to Harlesden. I remember the bus coming in and seeing all dem little houses for the first time. And thinking how weird they looked. With all them little knobbly decorations on them and everything.'

There is a sound of smashing. The huge Pole with the silver chain has lost all his money in the Diamond Deluxe and is now punching it and kicking it and cussing it as he throws it over. The betting boys all go quiet. The sallow guys on the roulette machine next to him flinch back. The commentator races on with the horses, oblivious.

The Pole steps forward to the bleary guys on the roulette. They look ready for him if he is really going to take them on. There is a shuffling as the punters pull out of his sight. He begins shouting at the two boys on the roulette next to his flipped machine.

'You may be Russian . . . But I'm Polish.'

Then he kicks it and swings the door out into Harlesden.

'See what I told you? Stupid . . . Primitive animals.'

Mukhtar has forgotten about the war.

'Y'know, Harlesden has become a strange place. Everybody moved. Not just Somali people . . . All the people I had grown up with, they moved . . . The English people . . . Where did they go? I don't know . . . Some of them went to the South of France. Some of them went out of London. They were replaced by these Africans and by East Europeans . . . Most of the white people you see here they are not English. They are not British . . . I don't know them . . . I don't get them . . . I don't know many people here any more.

'Every community is to their own. Nobody communicates to each other . . . It's not like it was . . . I mean I had a white girlfriend, she was my first . . . They see each other as aliens . . . The Somali community is on their own . . . And the Polish community is on their own. When I came over here there were loads of West Indians and loads of Irish, and everyone would be like, "Hey what up man . . ." But now it's literally a minority of faces I recognize . . . almost no one.

'I feel very isolated. I feel like I don't belong in Harlesden any more. You see that black feller over there? Here's one of the few people I recognize from back in the day . . . One of the old faces. London's changing . . . and it's not all of London, it's only certain areas. It's become weird. People were friendly once. People were welcoming. They are not like that any more. Because they don't know anyone. Everyone moved.'

Mukhtar seems emotional, and tells me it is time to go.

EDMONTON GREEN

I walk down Seven Sisters Road to the hospital.

This is North London. The evening glows with light. The blue gives way to pink haze. I look around. Around fifteen Romanians in battered trainers and T-shirts hang around stooped and gnawed between the Ford Transits and the Nissans outside the builders' yard. Their faces say what they are not ready to admit: no vans are going to pick them up today for any stacking or hauling. They bite their lips, share cigarettes, trying to make eye contact with the last foremen lugging sacks of gypsum and crates of MDF into their white vans. There are more of them looking, always trying to make eye contact, as I walk past the jumbled strippers and slicers in the window of the glasscutter, as the shuttering comes down outside the motor-parts store. They are begging for work with their eyes.

I turn under the train bridge, and where a row of old plane trees turns the pavement into a dapple of shade I come face to face with the old priory, behind its cloistered brown brick walls. The windows are carved with gothic curves and under the peaking eaves rain-washed stone figures of the saints shelter in alcoves. The furthest wings are wrapped in ivy, which reaches for the stone crosses on the slate roofs. But square signs with curling Arabic hang over the windows. The building is ringed with a brilliant line of electric-green fairy lights. And the thick green paint job on the door says the building is now a mosque.

I stand for a moment and watch the kids. A white boy in a yellow Brazilian football shirt in an outraged of game of chase hollers after his black friend in an England shirt as they tear down the pavement on mountain bikes, swerving with rubber shrieks between the startled Turkish women in brown and grey headscarves, gripping their pushchairs and carrier bags, clipping the shoulders of frail men on walking sticks coming to the mosque. But I walk on to the hospital.

Its functional blocks are behind a low brick wall, and its buildings are laid out like a Lego set, around squiggling roads lined with privet hedges and bright double red and yellow lines. I am standing outside the emergency reception. This is S136. The glass doors where the police bring those they find on the street all over North London to be certified as psychotic. The cream-painted ward curves at its sides and is rimmed with red-brick bands. There is little attempt to disguise it.

I have a meeting with the Sectioner.

'I think of this as my missionary endeavour.'

His eyes are pinched and tiny and he wears a beige corduroy jacket over a crisp white shirt. He touches his Windsor-knotted burgundy tie and moves to throw the small bottle of malt beer he is drinking into the litter. The Sectioner greets me with a soft handshake and a strangulated Nigerian accent. I need to speak to him. He is the mental-health officer who sections the most people in London. And these streets have the highest concentration of the insane in the city.

'Mental illness can happen to anyone. But immigrants have a higher incidence due to higher overall life stress. It's the uncertainty of not knowing whether they belong, whether they can make it or whether they can even survive in this city.'

Swinging through the fire doors, we walk along the linoleum corridors, smelling of disinfectant and hand wash, into his cream-coloured office. The walls are bare and the room is empty except for a computer table and two chairs. There are two thumps and muffled shouting through the wall.

The Sectioner has seen it all in S136. The old man who screamed, and screamed, when they took him into the linoleum-floored corridor assessment office, that a huge ravine was opening up at his feet. The woman who sobbed and waved her metal walking stick at the ghosts hovering over the laminated tables and the paper trays. But that was not even the start of it.

The police, they pick up addicts, who get brought in and made to sit down in that simple felt-armed assessment chair in S136. But they only shout louder and louder, 'Stop touching me.' No matter how far away you really are. These patients sometimes break down from the pain they imagine the Sectioner is causing them. And then there are the tramps, who are too frightened to come in because they smell gas, in the hospital. These are some of the people he meets every day.

'This is why I call it a missionary endeavour.'

The Sectioner is exhausted by psychosis. He is drained by those who sob and shriek that he is taking them to some vile concentration camp. But those who are frightened are easy enough to deal with. They know something, on some level, is wrong. But the ones who are grandiose are painful. There was one man who called himself the Master of Creativity: he told the mental-health officers that everything in this world he had created himself, from the printer ink to the hospital trolleys, from the carriages of the Northern Line to the gurgling refrigerators in the corner shop.

The Sectioner rasps, exasperated.

'And there are even black people who are so floridly psychotic they think they are members of the Royal Family and they had a meeting with the Queen last night.'

The Sectioner has completed an assessment on one Jesus Christ. But more frequently those the police bring in are political. They are being pursued by the CIA or in regular communication with Tony Blair. The Sectioner sighs. The police have brought in another man for assessment. There is no time to keep talking.

We meet again, at a house in Edmonton Green.

I get the train out of Liverpool Street: from under glass and metal vaults. I sit back on the muffy seats as the screeching begins. We are moving. The sulking Latino woman opposite has fashion cuts in her jeans. I want to look at her, but I am ashamed of my eyes and turn away.

Sun changes everything. The estates that at night look like prisons shine like architects' sketches. Golden light makes the lawns in the small parks glow living green. Giant gasworks are black against the falling sun.

Yards line the railway: smashed-up cars and piles of black greasy parts. These are where the skunk factories are. There are a lot of things they don't tell you about drugs. The first is who the criminals are. Forget the hoods and the fading Rasta on the blocks. They only buy the shit. They don't make it.

The police explain it like this. If you want to make skunk you need two things. You need dark space and a lot of electric charge. But nothing else. Yards are the perfect places: those bankrupt garages under railway arches.

The kind of people who own these are the Del Boys. Geezers. White working class. There is no future for them there. These plots are too broken up to be bought up by the developers. This is where the Vietnamese come in.

These guys really know what they are doing. They know how to vacuum-pack. How to beam that blue lighting right – and everything else chemical about hydroponics. They mass-produce: give the Del Boy a cut and give the gang boys a call.

This is no legend. In 2005 and 2006 the police conducted 802 skunk raids in London and found over two-thirds run by Vietnamese gangs. The locations: suburban houses, railway lines and wreckers' yards.

At the first few stops, the white rich get on and off: wearing beards and purple shirts and normcore thick-rimmed glasses. Their girls wear long ethno-dresses: they talk about Hackney like they own it. But they are gone before Stamford Hill.

There are tunnels and long green corridors, wild bushes and nettles and outbreaks of daisies. And trees: crooked ones and slender trunks and the ones with frizzy leaves glowing with sun.

There are gardens and washing lines and the back rooms of houses onto the tracks. Their roofs are a parade of useless chimneys.

The train is mostly sports clothes now. The unshaven African man next to me plays with his phone. Both Lithuanian builders have crashed out asleep. We clatter past big red-brick estates.

Here it is: Edmonton Green. The light has come to the strange hour when it loses all colour over the horizon. Above that band of creeping orange haze. Headlamps are coming on. Traffic lamps begin to glow red against the pale blue. Faded plane trails have turned a dirty pink.

Lamps clack on over the platform at Edmonton Green, but they will not be needed for hours in the summer. It takes a few tunnels to get outside. Here the war memorial is a traffic island. Towered over by shabby concrete blocks and industrial-sized retail outlets.

I walk towards the green: the patch where the builders hang out. Beefy but balding Poles in flecked tracksuits flick open cans of Żywiec and Tyskie. They are here most nights. But this evening one of their guys has passed out face down in the grass.

Head-geared African women hustle husbands and children, slowed down by nodding and smiling at every Ghanaian or Nigerian who is walking their way. They love this: the catching up.

I can see that the Turks are the Kings of Edmonton: the Bo Peep twenties parade has been converted into Turkish cash-and-carries, the bombastic thirties library overhauled into a Turkish spiritual centre, the old timbered pubs renovated into much-esteemed Turkish eateries – those with the best bread, the choicest halal and that nod, nod, wink, wink to that sugary beer. These make money: blacks, whites, browns – this is their real fare of a North London weekend. They call them the juicers: always busy.

The kebabs look good, but I know the statistics.

Twenty-five minutes by train, from the suits coming in and out like ants from the glass towers along Liverpool Street, the information city is not working. The people who live here also work in the City: as scrubbers, haulers and renovators. But their streets and estates are amongst the 4 per cent most deprived in the country. Nearly a third of the workforce here is out of a job.

Edmonton is deindustrialized London. Here were the factories that made the radio transmitters for the BBC. The Lee Enfield and

Bren guns for the British army. No more. These were terraces of white respectability where Norman Tebbit grew up. The cabinet minister for Margaret Thatcher was born at the right time. Because Edmonton was not made for deregulation. The assembly lines along the railway shut: this was uneconomic activity.

The working class pulled out and cockney tones morphed into Street. Terraces turned into tenements for migrants pushed out of a gentrifying centre. They were the evicted, the booted-out tenants, the escapees from Hackney and Islington. But the jobs did not come with them. The workers who used to live here were unionized. No more. The workers here are the migrant underclass – and the English trade unions are alien and meaningless to most of the Turks, Poles and Ghanaians in Edmonton.

The terraces of Norman Tebbit's childhood have become a ghetto. Today the area is 18.8 per cent white British. The cleaners and the renovators who live here are only minorities: Turkish, African, Asian. Community-sized minorities: Nigerians, Romanians, Ivorians. And family-sized minorities: Tibetans, Haitians, Chechens.

I walk on. I need to speak to the Sectioner. They mock him here. They call him the Plato of Edmonton. Because he is writing a book about the two metaphoric buildings that he believes encapsulate the whole of London and the whole world. I need to speak to him again. Two friends swear by his wisdom. Three others speak rapturously about his speeches: metaphors strong enough to hold crowds of hundreds of Nigerians silent.

'This bruva knows the insanity from the inside, man.'

The Sectioner lives in a geometric new-build. It has taken ages to fix the appointment. But he ushers me in: wearing a bright purple shirt and a black flat cap. There is coffee, which his wife silently serves. He has a very big TV. But my eyes fix on a framed portrait of a little son of his in karate gear, one of six. He has almost finished the first draft of the metaphoric buildings. I settle into his puffy pleather sofa. But the Sectioner does not move from the computer table, crammed into corner of the wall.

'Are you by any chance . . . a Christian?'

He speaks in a strained voice.

'Oh . . . well if you are a Jewish . . . then still . . . well you must have heard of the Jesus Christ . . . who preached about the brotherhood . . . ?

'When I think about Edmonton this is what I see missing . . .

'And this is why I think multiculturalism is a recipe for disaster . . .'

He widens his eyes and raises the eyebrows.

'Even in London. Even in London where people are more enlightened . . . And now I will give you many examples . . . of how multiculturalism is quite dangerous . . .'

The Sectioner clears his throat.

'The trouble is human emotion has not evolved to the right degree. As what happens in multiculturalism is all OK when everything is going fine – if the economy is good, if there is no housing problem, if there is no major social issue, no political upheaval, no major trouble, it runs OK . . . But if it goes bad . . .'

He raises his finger, vertically.

'Right now it could be the minority ethnic groups who are responsible for things going well . . . It could be all these Asians who have opened all these corner shops who are helping to fastly push away the recession . . . But nobody will ever praise them when it goes well, but come to them when it goes bad.

'I imagine London as two buildings . . .

'The first building is the one that accommodates London's science and technology: in this building we have moved from gliders to supersonic. We have moved from typewriters to the most high-powered computer systems, even voice-controlled ones . . .' His hands make their shape. 'You name it. We have moved from animal-propelled wheels to unmanned automobiles. This building contains all sorts of chemicals and biologicals and weapons and everything. The building has become a skyscraper. We can see its glory . . . But now the other building.'

He clears his throat.

'This other building deals with . . . London's emotion. It controls the feelings. The emotion that makes up our social interaction.

But unfortunately this building is still at the foundation level . . .
They are working by candlelight . . . The building is staffed by cave-
men. In fact nobody has done any building for thousands of years.
And there is rising damp.'

There is a long, theatrical pause.

'But the biggest danger, the biggest irony is what is happening
in London's undeveloped building controls what is happening in
the skyscraper with all the chemicals and the biologicals and the
computers . . . filled with iPhones that can detonate bombs . . . I
imagine it – this is a very important point – I imagine it like placing
a fully loaded machine gun in the hands of a five-year-old.

'Unless we develop our emotions . . . London is very unstable.'

Two of his sons run out to find a football, breaking us off.

'You know history . . . When there is a bit of nightmare and
economic crisis everywhere, you will find that people are signalled
out as the reasons things are not going well. They may say the housing shortage is the problem of too much foreigners . . . And what
will happen? I will tell you what will happen.

'I am African. I know in places like Kenya and Uganda where
there were economic upheavals . . . of course the foreigners in the
land paid dearly. As soon as things went bad they were killed, they
were booted out, they were made to leave. The reality is, there is for
us old ones no real community called Edmonton: the Asians are
doing their own thing, the Africans are doing their own thing, the
East Europeans also. The children have some more contact, and
better emotions . . . thankfully . . . but the race is still there . . .
and their emotions are not so good either.

'I personally love the mix . . . But let's not be blind.

'Anyone who wants to sound politically correct . . . which I don't
believe in . . . is like, "Oh, Edmonton is great, you get the food you
want to eat . . . Oh, it's great . . ." But what matters for me is the
human interaction . . . Do you see yourself in someone else even if
they look different from you? Do you? Do you really see you in me?

'Do you see yourself in a black African mental-health officer?'

He smiles, rubbing his knuckles.

'That's the question. That's the critical question. Do you see bits

of you in someone else even if he looks totally different from you?
If the answer is yes: you are ready for the multiculturalism.

'But that is not happening in Edmonton.

'People are living exclusive life based on their families, based on
their communities, based on who they perceive as like them . . . OK?
It's only a few people who can interact . . .

'The Asian community is living here as Asian community in
Edmonton. The Turkish community is living as Turkish community. They are enclosed. The white community is living as white
community. The African community is closed here as African community. But who is trying to understand the other? Nobody.'

The phone rings.

Everyone apologizes and continues.

'You know why this is dangerous . . .'

His stare won't let go of my eyes.

'Believe you me if push comes to shove you will find people who
will be going the path of ethnicity and going the path of groups and
religions . . . and for me this is emotional underdevelopment . . .
all you need to do now is assemble the people of Edmonton in this
field . . .

'Go please assemble . . . and everybody gather . . . and as soon
as people gather . . . just watch the movement . . .

'People will begin to position themselves, and automatically
without being told where to go the women and the men will each
go into ethnic groups – or religious or cultural ones – and the
people will just immediately divide on those lines . . . Asian people
to Asian people, African people to African people, white people to
the white people . . .

'And we need to overcome this . . . Emotionally.'

He seems happy when I leave him.

But I keep thinking.

I walk on through Edmonton. Along the pebbledashed houses
with the plastic doors until they disappear. Then past long construc-
tions of nineties new builds. They give way to the motorway lands:
railway bridges, hundreds of metres of track, bus stations on A
roads. This is the edge.

I pass a Polish couple holding hands along the A1055.

The reservoir is close: it is behind the road flanked with hedges and through the hanging gates over the canal. But I cannot reach it. Only the canal. Earthworks block the water from sight: security further bolted with huge thickets and iron fences. Midges are everywhere, buzzing very close.

Turkish kids are braying and passing around a bottle of vodka in the half-light. There are whoops and bike races along the gravel canal path. The girls have taken off their headscarves. I look at the canal. Lattice steel pylons are black on the evening light, marching with their charge into the glowing towers.

CHESTER ROW

I meet Shehu in between things.

He is thin-lipped and an expert in smiles. And he knows exactly what they mean. How they can disarm and open people, even wound them on occasion. He always looks more or less the same, clutching a black briefcase, in a blue mackintosh. He is always busy. There are evenings when visiting senators from Abuja request his presence in their glinting suites with mahogany surfaces on Park Lane, who in their flowing proud robes tell him to finish with London and come back to Nigeria.

But he always goes to the Uncles, 'I'm not ready, not quite yet.'

Shehu is always in and out of these hotels. He is bored of the ballrooms where the whisky flows, the cut glass shines, and it seems half the House of Representatives is there, nodding and plotting in their red rounded kufi caps and flowing damask robes, clicking their fingers to the Italians and the Poles for the canapés. Those are the evenings where all over again he is made for the sake of the legacy to take the high table, clear his throat and welcome the guests. Because the Uncles will be there with the Black Label tut-tutting in their Yoruba caps that peak up like little cloth pyramids that he is needed in Abuja.

When we talk he always takes a triple shot of espresso, and complains every time he is on his way to some committee, or Lagos Island delegation, which he would rather not be at, since he will be compelled to spend the afternoon scurrying in and out of the curved oak doors of Nigeria House, where every floor of the embassy rises with sculpted columns and arches of stone.

He is bored by luxury. And that is why he told me his life story in the Costa Coffee in the crusty Waterstones, overlooking the cars swirling and the tourists milling amongst the pigeons on Trafalgar Square, where pink American couples in round black sunglasses and bum bags and Japanese groups with matching plastic sun umbrellas pick at stale croissants and raisin swirls.

He speaks slowly at first.

'We were one of the first families to arrive in Belgravia . . . I remember when we arrived these mansions were all old tweedy money. But after the coup kicked my father out of power it was Margaret Thatcher herself who recommended us . . . and wrote our reference to become . . . pioneer Africans into the imperial terraces.'

This is what he remembers. His first memory is the lap. The doors opening. The people coming into the open surgery. The chief is receiving. He slouches back into the Napoleon chair astride his gilt glinting reception room. He scratches his chin and listens. They come in and settle down on the divan: to implore him.

They swell their eyes, surrounded by the gold leaf and the lacquered wood. But they have come for help. They ask one by one. 'My husband is dead and we have no papers. Can you help with a lawyer?' 'My son was unfairly jailed. Can you help support his daughter?' 'My sister was diagnosed with the breast cancer. Can you help with a second opinion?'

The son sits on the lap. These are his memories. His father, the ageing Yoruba chief, listens. Beadily smiling at his pride and gesturing to his beautiful wife. The money is upstairs in suitcases. She brings it down. He passes it out in elastic-held packets to the needy. Morning is over and the open surgery closes for lunch.

The chief of Belgravia was known throughout Peckham and Edmonton as generous and wise to those Nigerians who needed him. Once a week he would receive them in his town house on Chester Row. Listening, and counselling, all those pickers and carers with problems from the estates.

The second memory is absence. No booming voice. No open surgery. No old man in billowing red fabrics watching the box. The chief of Belgravia was, like so many Nigerians, an exile. But he was not hungry and young like his ambitious tribe of immigrants. He was tired. A veteran of independence. The loser of a political roulette. The chief died before his son Shehu was a man.

The parties stop.

There is no more shining white Rolls-Royce of the King of Ashanti pulling up outside. There are no more security guards in shades at that slim and elegant door, checking the watermarked invitations of the Nigerian couples in the Jaguars and Bentleys, or the MGs with their drivers left to sit in them and whisk them away at a moment's notice, back to their town houses and hotels. There is no more white-glove service, serving everyone unlimited whisky and champagne, in cut-glass treasures in the lower ground dining room, converted into a complete, perfectly serviced bar.

Upstairs there are no more musicians in the drawing room, the entertainment flown in from Abuja, the singers lost in the rising drums, the calling saxophones and subtle keyboards, as the businessmen in tailored suits, their pocket handkerchiefs so perfectly pleated, dance with their wives under the chandeliers, as they smile with perfect teeth at the women in origami headwraps, and whoop and clink and spray the musicians, the way they always do at the best Nigerian parties in Belgravia, flicking with one palm over the other – $1 bills, then $10 bills – over the shoulders of the most exuberant dancers, and over the heads of the most beautiful girls.

That was over. Now his mother was on her own, like so many others. London is a city of confused African mothers. Often, they only learn too late it is too dangerous to play on the street. Often, they cannot read their daughters' school reports, or keep track of naughty sons. London is not Africa. There are no friendly neighbours.

'In Africa the whole town brings up the boy. They are seeing him, going, "Hey you? I tell your father . . . ! You stop that right there." In London? Nobody help you. You in the supermarket . . . You in the home cooking . . . You in the supermarket again . . . and when you cannot see your son, nobody gonna tell him, "Stop, bad boy!"'

The stillness of Belgravia was Shehu's playground. He opened the front door and ran out into the street to play football with his brother. They only stopped when a car passed and scampered off the tarmac until it had gone. Then the plump serenity of Chester Row was theirs again.

Belgravia, all white, all silent, was mostly happy memories. Shehu would dash out front for his mother, to grab things she kept forgetting in the dashboard of their long green Saddam Hussein family Bentley. Little black legs would sometimes stick out as he rummaged around. But only once did the prim and proper neighbour put him in a headlock, and start shouting, 'Stop it, you little thief!' until Mummy ran out.

His third memory is the toothless uncle in the basement. The old man in white robes. The hunched prayer man from the forest. He comes back from school and finds bananas turning blue in the corners of the living room. The prayer man is cross-legged on the floor. His fingers dabbing oils and water onto his mother's slowly wrinkling forehead.

There were more and more of them coming to Chester Row as she took over the investment portfolio: the working witchdoctors coming out of the estates in Thamesmead, Tottenham and Peckham. The wife of the chief could not cope. She had not been educated like a man. The investments were not something she really understood. The witchdoctors were the only ones she knew.

The most powerful prayer men are in the Senegal delta. They are the most expensive and also the most violent. The wife of the chief would call and haggle and heckle and make them sing for her. They were not cheap. But she was very desperate. At one point she had three working for her: one in eastern Nigeria, a forest seer in Cameroon and in the delta one menacing Senegalese master. She gave them one instruction: pray for an increase in the price of oil.

Then the memory that scared him. The night. Shehu is being shaken awake. His head flops down. But they are there.

They grab him. The two prayer men in white bundle him and his brother into a Volvo. Then hit the pedal. This is 3 am. The car

turns and turns, through empty streets onto the motorway. Shehu is with his brother. They are strapped into the back seat, shaking.

This is Brighton. The Volvo glides past the flecked white paint of the hotel parade. The prayer men have arrived. Out of the car. They are hurrying them onto the beach. The shingle crunches. The wind sounds like a cat trapped in a drainpipe. And they begin to undress them. The boys are shaking, whimpering, looking at each other. Their toes digging into the wet pebble shore.

'I was scared shitless . . . I mean . . . I was scared totally shitless.'

The prayer men are chanting. Moving round them. These are Yoruba verses. This is protection. They wet their hands. They wash the little boys in Brighton sea water. The chants become rhythmic. The boys can see through the faint mist the looming frame of the pier. Nerves choke them. The men pour the sea water over them. Then start to sing. Before too long, they hurry, it's time: the prayer men bundle the boys into the Volvo and drive.

The wife of the chief became distraught. She felt life in the November drizzle. What curse was following her? Was it from her sister she left in Nigeria? Was it that witch she had crossed on Rye Lane? Why? When she had little children? She kept taking the 436 bus from Marble Arch, over the tidal river, back to Rye Lane, to the prayer men there. But this did not calm her. None of the forms or promissory notes made a single bit of sense. Nor did the incense and the knives, cutting incantatory scars into her cheeks, make her feel any more at home.

I am listening to Shehu. We are now on the King's Road. This is one of the last very English streets in London. Red trousers push past us. The characterless stretch of cottages from here into Fulham is a ghetto of signet rings. But Shehu doesn't care. He has lately become obsessed about Saddam Hussein. Locking himself up in his bedroom skunked up with heavy Middle East reading. Whole biographies, by *Telegraph* or *Times* correspondents, about the Iraqi executioner.

'Y'know until I was thirteen, or thereabouts, I thought the natural order of things was this in London. The richest people were Nigerians, then Saudis, then Lebanese . . . because that's the way things roll in Belgravia. I thought the natural order of things in London was this: the immigrants – them boys got the money.'

Shehu squints at me, about to say something.

'Y'know, it was when I was about ten I realized I was black . . . Like before you are ten you got no sense, right . . . Baby kids ain't got no sense of race. There were hardly any pure whites around me . . . everyone was Japanese–Italian, Swedish–Lebanese, French–American . . . There was so much race, there was no race, and colour that had nothing to do with money . . . Then it started to hit me – I think race hits everyone at that age – y'know, that I was black. I was in this private school, little boys, little shorts, and there was nothing . . . y'know . . . black.'

Shehu stops to light up.

'Then this cousin came from America. His folks were minted, and he had these Puff Daddy tunes on a Walkman. He plugged me in. And I was like, "Fuck! This is black!" Puff Daddy made me black. Next day I was rolling up my shorts and walking . . . ah ah . . . side to side . . . The teachers were like, "What happened to you?" But I didn't care . . . Puff Daddy had taught me what it meant to be black.'

Shehu had it easy. He was a Kensington teenage schoolboy. The richest borough. The Royal Borough. This is an immigrant area – 52 per cent of those who live here were born overseas, and 40 per cent don't even have a British passport. And a third of them arrived since 2001. This is London: a little corner of Brussels, a little piece of Dubai, a little bit of Singapore in stucco.

But there are no immigrants here: only foreigners who say they are globalized, expats or whatever they mean by 'Europeans'. Their lives don't really play out in London, but one week in Kensington, one week in Abu Dhabi, one week in Knightsbridge, one week in Paris, one week in Belgravia, one week in Lagos.

These people only talk about planes. They love to talk about airport lounges and fully flat business-class beds. Because this

London is in a 747 in Heathrow Airport more often than it touches the Circle Line. These are not full-time Londoners – for all they know Edmonton might as well be in the Midlands.

Kensington, those sleeping beauty houses, those empty garden squares. This is now the least English borough. Kensington has the highest percentage of residents who describe themselves as having no British identity at all – almost 40 per cent – and is the only borough to have seen its population fall since 2001. Since 2001 the white British population has shrunk from 50 per cent to 39 per cent.

This was when Kensington became Shehu's playground. He and his boys had it all worked out. His teenage stoner crew would vault the spear-shaped railings into little private parks, skin up under the plane trees and crack up in a circle about the chase for posh, easy girls.

'The thing about the empty mansions is these garden squares are totally empty, but totally buzzed up with private security. This means for a teenage blazer, Kensington is paradise. You can wander round and round stoned and laughing your ass off and there is no one to see you . . . and all the criminals too scared to come in after you.'

Shehu knew all the bad boys. They were not really bad. They were more into weed and girls and things – and they had generous wallets and bare cash. Their parents were either so successful, or they were so rich, that they hardly had any time for them. These boys were free: they had keys and credit cards, and sometimes Eritrean maids. They never did their homework. They would spend night after night in these bijou living rooms smoking up. They would break into hysterics, fuck around playing FIFA, or mong out, get bromantic and talk about themselves.

'Y'see nobody wanted to be English . . . We all came from different places, but being . . . y'know, English . . . meant admitting no outside sources of cash. It meant like being . . . from Birmingham, or somewhere worse . . . Have you ever been outside London? So, what everyone wanted to be was Global. What that means is your life is making money in all these different places, the places you still can. Global means living like they do in *Monocle* magazine . . . it means fitting in on the slopes in Courchevel, it means fitting in at a party in Berlin . . .'

Shehu stubs out his fag.

'That meant bigging up the other side. The Africans, we were always telling people how sick it is on Lagos island. The Arabs, they were always bigging up what they had to do with Dubai, the Jews, they were always bigging up what they had to do with Tel Aviv, the Indians, they were always bigging up them and Mumbai . . .'

He looks at me apologetically.

'Y'see, what being English meant to us, well, it was uncool shit . . . like Ascot horseracing, the green benches in Parliament, or those real boarding-school loser boys we'd meet sometimes at parties who never had as much money, or coke, chat as us . . . Becoming English . . . like becoming a fusty Tory or something . . . That's not money any more . . . That's losing out on all that Russian, African, Arab paper.'

Shehu and his crew were like everyone else their age. London boys have a skunk problem. Chemically enhanced weed gets there first. The absolute majority know what it is to be really stoned before they have kissed their first girl. Skunk gets there first because London boys are nervous. London boys are awkward. Like all teen-age boys. And here all of sudden is something that makes the sunshine warmer and even the cool kids laugh at your jokes. That soft smoke with its calming lick round your head: making every-thing so much funnier, lighter, brighter.

This is the same for everyone. Skunk is what everyone urban has in common. Little baggies and red eye. Hungry hours waiting in line for fried chicken. Staring stoned into geometric patterns out there, carved between the steel railings.

'When I was that age walking around, cocky little teenage boy trying to chirps the girls in Phones4U, and I bopped down into Shepherd's Bush or up into Ladbroke Grove, those hoods down there would see me and think I'm from an estate . . . They would never, ever assume I was minted, worth at least six public-school boys a pop . . . And you want to know what used to happen? Any time the estate blacks and their mates would see me, they would start screw-facing me: "Which hood you from, bruv? Which fort you from, man? Who's your backup, bruv?" . . . !'

Shehu got to know this because London can't admit it is addicted to skunk, because London can't admit it is addicted to coke. This is a city that can't own up that so much cocaine gets snorted at weekends that the water authorities notice its presence spiking in the sewers on a Tuesday afternoon. This is a city that pretends this £10 billion industry does not exist: by leaving its on-the-go distribution to the people it gives the least of a shit about: teenage boys – especially black teenage boys.

Shehu got to know this because of his face. He has authoritative eyes from his father. He has the same sexy little chin beard. His look is softened with the baby skin of his mother. This is a hit with the girls: redheads, blacks, gingers, curlies. Because he always knows how to smile in all the right ways.

Shehu got to know about gangs because he had cash. The money for baggies and the money for drinks. He was decked out in tailored silk shirts. He had the best watches and the smartest phones. He was even buying his ladies fresh trainers. The school-girls, they loved him. They called him the Nigerian Prince – the lurer-in-chief. Always chatting up girls with milkshakes outside McDonald's.

Shehu stops for another triple espresso.

'This was my downfall. You see this was the era when Robbery Squad was becoming active out of the Grove . . . This was the beginning of the Moroccan immigration up there, and these Moroccan guys, they wanted money . . . So they linked up with these blacks and mocha blacks from those estates. And founded the Robbery Squad.

'Our generation was the violent one . . . The big mass generation of London blacks and mocha blacks – and Arabs and Kurds, who wanted to be black. The era when Murder Dem Pussies kicked off in Hammersmith, and Moses was becoming the master salesman. Every estate wanted in – gangbanging was the big craze.

'Boys our age, Thatcher babies . . . There was nothing on London estates back then. No youth workers. No place to chill . . . only a crusty ping-pong table or two. You see the Thatcher babies, they hit the streets when the music was garage . . . Those were some angry tunes. It was all about jacking, getting jacked, jacking back.'

He has downed the triple espresso.

'The era, man, the 2000s, was the era of the hoods on bikes . . . Patrolling the streets of London like the horsemen of the apocalypse. It was not too long before the postcode wars began, W12 versus W10, and the horsemen began to raid . . . The Bush and White City estates raiding up on Grove. Then Grove raiding back.

'This was an easy period for crimes . . . First, the cards with no security PINs. Second, the big expensive phones with no locks and no trackers and no nothing. Third, people just carried more cash. Boom. These rudes would rock up, bike tyres screeching, like they were Janjaweed – y'know, those hooded Sudanese horsemen. This was like a military operation: In, out – "Give me your phone."

'Kensington kids, they are always in contact with the urban kids, because they want that skunk. There are even some who think they can play it hard and get proper into it and start dealing. But sometimes those rudeboy friendships, like when Jack got tight with Moses, they can go fantastically, fucktastically wrong . . .

'Robbery Squad were the ones that came after me. The Arab–Black alliance. They were led by this kid called Marvin . . . He was a mocha black, I think, weak watered-down stuff, not a real swinging African like me. That kid was spitting lyrics. He was speaking in rhythms. All shit. Thought he was Doctor Dre or something . . . But you know what Marvin was? He was a thug.'

Shehu had it unlucky. Robbery Squad would find him in Kensington Gardens. Shehu was taking his blondies to the grassy knoll

under the plane trees, the ones with the huge leaves – the knoll that led right to the palace gates where Princess Diana once used to live. He would chirps them into kisses: rubbing into the mud cigarette butts until the lines made big scary animal faces.

Then, surprise attack: the four bikes in military operation.

'You thinking you're hiding here, nigga. Playing the white boy . . . Yah looking nice there . . . Come on, bitchface, hand it over . . . Or we'll deck you right here, Mr Premier.'

Marvin would throw his bike down for the surrender ceremony. Phones would be handed over: complete with wallet and skunk baggy. This was Janjaweed – over and out.

Marvin was the leader of the Robbery Squad. The sight of Shehu sent him apoplectic. He hated him. He hated him for the silk shirts. He hated him for those pink-cheeked little ladies. He hated him for his public school. But above all he hated him for being black. Marvin could not stand it: why did he live spitting lyrics on an estate and Shehu on marble floors in Chester Row?

Fuck that punk.

Marvin liked to smack Shehu once a week. He wanted him to feel council estate fear: like he too lived in that socialist Lego-land of misery bricks. Stairwells full of scumbags trying to rap. Marvin liked to hunt Shehu down everywhere. Tree-lined avenues of Edwardian mansion flats: the Janjaweed were there. Cupcake-coloured Victorian backstreets: the Janjaweed were there.

'Think you're P. Diddy, Mr Rich Nigga? Coz I'm Robin Hood.'

Shehu was driven off High Street Kensington. This was where Marvin wanted to play. But he didn't get it. Those blondies were not immediately back to his cotch spot. A few Robbery Squad Arabs had the charm: but Marvin couldn't pull it off. So he got into more fights with the Fulham boys. Those estates – the Clem Attlee and all – were mostly white boys back then.

Marvin hated them. They got beef. Especially Tee. He was a real white scumbag: Reebok Classics and a close shave. Everyone knew Tee was undefeated. Tee and his wide boys – Lonsdale was their favourite brand – would deck team Marvin in minutes in Fulham. This was not a contested frontier. But the Tee boys knew Robbery

Squad would thump them out of Ladbroke Grove in seconds. This is why Tee would come out of his principality to neutral High Street Ken. every now and then. He remained undefeated.

Then there was dusty Mo from White City crew. He was a skinny fucker. From those spindly but deadly Somali crews. Marvin hated dusty Mo too. This one was not so easy. He was a charmer, actually. Hanging around, bringing some weed to the posh boys. Talking with that wonky, halting voice about the Mogadishu master moves you were supposed not to mess with.

That made the Robbery Squad want to deck him out, of course. This charmer they would find skinning up by the motorway ramps, over by Shepherd's Bush roundabout, that unkempt, windswept traffic island, almost swallowed up by its dual carriageways.

Bikes are incoming: and the theatre begins.

'What you fucking doing here? You should be in an old people's home you so ugly. Your bitch is in there, go suck her off you Moga-dishu mugface.'

But dusty Mo wasn't London. There is normally a bit of theatre before a fight. 'Mate, mate.' Bit of chest-puffing: then a bit of strutting. But dusty Mo did none of that. Moment game was on, Mo would hit. And that boy, word went round, from White City and far up into Harlesden, had been trained to fight like that in backstreet Mogadishu by some terrorist or something.

Shehu hated Marvin. But what he hated more was Kensington. Those pink-faced kids on the High Street never believed him. Shehu was told again and again by them there ain't no poverty in Kensington. Tweed-wearers would chortle: rudeboys from Kensington? They must be sons of sheikhs.

Shehu had started reading *The Economist*. He wanted London to think about black men and think about him. He would skin up but also click up Wikipedia. Kensington was not only money. Shehu knew he had his Kensington. But Robbery Squad was also Kensington. Beyond the Westway, in the brutalist towers, in the concrete cubes, was the joint poorest ward in London.

Take the sandstone switchboard of the Henry Dickens Estate. These are five hundred flats with a 58 per cent child poverty rate. This was the hood. The concrete city: where Robbery Squad came from. Walk around, talk to people. They say the place is crawling with hoodies. But even the police have no idea how many. Probably London has more than twelve thousand urban kids working what they call 'the strip'.

But in Kensington this is over the Westway: the carriageways supposed to bring prosperity. The Kensington you never see. Where the superhighway slices through state high-rise. Bringing speed picked up on the road from Oxford right through Westminster. The motorway Conservative MPs use to shuttle back and forth to their constituencies, keeping their eyes fixed on the road. But look at the poverty map of West London: the motorway made things grim. These wards are indexed blood-red for deprivation: the kids here grow up counted as some of the poorest 5 per cent in England.

Gangs were going crazy those summers in the 2000s: that post-code thing was raw, E9 had gone to war on E10, Brixton was beefing with Peckham, SE15 was locked in a struggle with SE19 – and the big one, the great beef between Hackney and Tottenham, that broke out all those years ago, after the death of Popcorn, that was calming down up and down Murder Mile, round the Clapton Ponds.

Shehu's mother was having none of it. The moment she heard about Marvin, she hired him Igbo heavies. For the rest of that summer these two Lewisham muscles were always two steps behind him. His teenage freedom ruined: no more skunked-up munchies, no more little bottles of vodka, no more shrooms in the park.

Shehu would pace up and down the stumpy red brick of the King's Road with a black eye from Marvin thinking about the numbers. Eighty-nine, the life expectancy for a white woman in a Chelsea town house. Sixty-two, the life expectancy of a Moroccan man in the North Kensington estates over the Westway.

'That shit is always forgotten. First, them blacks are disenfranchised by the system . . . They need their own MP but hell no . . . They are gerrymandered, whatever, into something where they are never gonna get anyone in, so they don't even bother. Second, them blacks are disenfranchised by the newspapers, who can't conceive you can have rocket-high child poverty in a street next to the rich rich rich.'

Shehu heard four years later that Marvin had gone down. The music was beating into his ears and he could barely concentrate as they told him in the club. The bruvas were adamant. Marvin was spitting lyrics no more. The boys from Bush rattled it off that Marvin had been tasered when he rocked up at a party he shouldn't have been at and before he could yelp for his backup or make for his strap. Then the Peckham Boys started beating him. They kicked him for being such a fool to think Grove was even on their level. Then they stabbed him for his disrespect to South London and finished it with lead. Or at least that was what they said in Bush.

'You want to know what drives me mad about London? The English, they can't even talk about these problems. This is their superpower. Talking by the side, making indirect references, never saying what they mean . . . They can't even admit to themselves this exists . . . That's why I've written a little dictionary, in which I go out of my way explain it all to anyone visiting from Lagos. This is how it begins . . . .

'Urban People – Blacks.

'Inner City People – Blacks.

'North London Intellectual – Jew.

'Devout Muslim – Practically Fundamentalist.

'Practising Jew – Barely English.

'Migrant – Poor Immigrant.

'Expat – Rich Immigrant.

'Ultra High Net Worth Individual – Oligarch.

'Vibrant Multicultural Area – Ethnic Ghetto.

'Hardworking People – The Poor.

'Oh and of course . . .

'Disadvantaged People – that means you're fucking impoverished.'

RYE LANE

William Blake had his first revelation in Peckham. This strange boy was running through the common. He was playing with the flowers. Losing himself in oak trees and counting blades of grass. His eyes were wandering. Then he saw them. A tree filled with angels – 'bright angelic wings, bespangling every bough like stars'.

Rye Lane today does not hide its poverty. Shop fronts tell the story: Khan's Bargain. Mighty Pound. Budget Carpet. Victorian brickwork run down, with rotten window frames. Art deco halls chipped beyond recognition. Rye Lane has almost no corporate outlets, apart from the fast-food chains and the betting shops.

I am outside the train station. African fathers in suits rush with their children towards the platform. Thugs in gold-spray chains are loitering. Tunes playing, headphones free, in a sign of dominance. A sick white man is on the floor. He stumbles, collapses back on a lamppost. His eyes then close, smiling, reeling, from his hit. Minutes later he takes out a few coppers from his pocket and arranges them on the floor in front of him, staring at them inquisitively for a while.

I walk through a small arcade to Rye Lane. Pakistani fruit sellers hawk yams to African women in headdresses under the train bridge. Lahori love songs are blasting from their hi-fi kit. I talk to them for a little while. There is no love lost at the bottom.

'There is no order in the Britain . . . Nothing . . . I come here six months . . . Blacks beat me three times. For a lighter . . . Police they do nothing to control these blacks . . . Nothing.'

Rye Lane is like the old East Africa. This is a black African street: they are the ones shopping and the shops are made for them. But they do not own them. The parades belong to Asians. They own the wig-shops black women flock to. They own the cash-and-carry houses, filled with yams and the bags of fufu. They run the import–export. And they are the slum landlords.

There are tensions here.

'They don't have, you know . . . the entrepreneurial spirit . . .'

I am talking to Arif as he jangles his car keys. Arif is a slum landlord. This afternoon he has been out collecting rent. The cramped little shops along the parade are right out of Africa. Bric-a-brac: piles of plastic plates, stick-free pans, palm oil, stacks of rice flour and crates of pounded yellow yam. Everything that you can haul out of a cash and carry. Mothers guard the shops. They are playing Yoruba songs on YouTube to their children, who answer them back in English.

'The thing is you see with us Asians . . . We came here, we snapped up all this property, right . . . Understood the mortgages, the way dem things are working, right. Kids all growing up to be dentists, accountants, pharmacists . . . But the Africans don't seem to have worked out how to make it work here, I dunno why.'

Africans in South London think of men like Arif when they think of Asians. They think they are more racist than the whites. Like in old East Africa they experience Asians as the ethnicity above them: men they meet diddling their change in the corner shops, or knocking on their doors demanding rent. They know them because their children go to the same schools – but throw themselves into furies and even threaten their daughters when they kiss black boys.

'The most racist people down here are dem Pakis.'

Down Rye Lane you come to what the urban kids call Cracker Jack Alley. That's before you reach Front Line Peckham. They never use the full name. Ten years ago Peckham became Peck 'Nam. There have been more than ten murders round here since then. And now it's 'Nam. Like Vietnam.

'Because we're soldiers here, like on X-Box, innit.'

But I did not go that far. I was looking for the witch doctor of Rye Lane. Fabric-shop owners shake their heads. The women in the wig shop deny all knowledge. I sit and chew soul food in the patty shop wondering what to do next. The music on the radio suddenly stops. There has been a stabbing in 'Nam. Then the tunes come right back on again.

Like old East Africa, there are compounds of white privilege in Peckham. There are a lot of what they call pop-up restaurants and hipster bars. These are where the fashionable rich rent a unit in an impoverished area to invite their fashionable rich friends to test out a dining concept.

There are a few fashionable clubs: inside has an eerie colonial feel. Beautiful boys. Intelligent girls. Clothes that make you jealous. Chatting and smiling as they share little plastic baggies before they feel the music and can dance for hours. These crowds are all white, bar the token few.

These people tell you they like Peckham, that they love the ethnic colour. But this is an expat society. They love it like a prop. Like a stage backdrop to evenings that the Africans are not invited to. They claim they hate the crime: gang culture is what's worst about London. But they don't seem to understand that the Peckham Boys are the ones killing each other to be the ketamine and MDMA suppliers – for their graceful parties.

Night on Rye Lane in the rain. The orange lights up its fall and glints out the puddles running along the gutter. Posh whites scuttle towards the clubs. They have not quite come up. Through the steamed-up windows they glance at the African women relaxing at the hairdresser: a braid or a weave takes hours.

I am one of those posh whites, listening to my friend. The rich cannot bear to talk about race. My friend insists she loves it here, but has become unnerved by the shouting and the drumming she hears every night through the thin walls of her flat. My friend mentions a club night. Hipster organizers have rented out a hall that an African prayer group uses in the week, but they keep on finding little pieces of this voodoo-cult whilst setting up the sound system: pierced stuffings and oils and dark masks.

The spring rain runs in the gutter, carrying little pieces of rubbish away. The pubs have closed. And things are louder now. This is Saturday night. Rye Lane is now another street. There are white lines outside the clubs. But their faces seem a little frozen, and stretched, like they have never been happier. Their eyes are glistening, their eyes are so huge, their irises are gone – now everyone has come up. They clasp each other, but the volume control is fucked: men shout without meaning to, girls suddenly squeal and the Nigerians squint from the minicabs, they are getting tired, their eyes are bloodshot, they are blinking with exhaustion, but there is pick up work to be done here – hold on, hold on.

This is London: the conquest of one postcode by another.

These are slum streets for which they have dreams. There will be coffee shops where there are cash and carries. There will be cocktails where there are yams. There will be bicycles outside organic delicatessens. But hold on – it's not so simple. These whites are also mourning their postcodes. They are bitter like refugees. 'We lost Knightsbridge to the Arabs. There are no clubs there for us. The Russians conquered Mayfair. We can't afford that. Notting Hill was swallowed up by the French. We can never live there – in the stucco where we belonged.'

So why should here be theirs?

They weren't even born here.

But that was all another night. I am still in the patty shop. These streets are where the BBC set the comedy *Only Fools and Horses*. But Del Boy would be a stranger now in Peckham. Next door is a bric-a-brac mall. This was where Shehu had told me to look. Rye Lane calls this a shopping centre but it is really an indoor market place with units. Suspicious African women eye me from their clothes stands: wild fabrics in reds, blues, greens and yellows. There are a few babies, wrapped in white cloth to their mothers' backs. Everything is dimly lit. The feeling is isolated. Hardly out of West Africa.

I strike up a little conversation with the Sierra Leonean man running a printing stall. The mainstay of his little business is the excesses of Jamaican and African christenings and funerals. Popular items include the 'We Miss You' badge. There are a few on display: beaming smiles of good-looking black men – stabbed and gone. The printer leans over the counter. He has an unsatisfied demeanour.

'You know what shock me about the London? That you on your own. People not friendly . . . People not there . . . they are so individualistic that you could be walking down the Lane, some bad men come and mug you there, you be crying for help, screaming for the help . . . and they will walk right past you.

'Something about this is not right. They might afterwards be like, "We heard" . . . or "We saw" . . . But they never help the man in front of his eyes. Nobody ever looks up. You know what I think about London? If people here were more alert . . . less bad things would happen to people here.'

The mall is soaked in a dim yellowy light. I have found Ephphatha Store. The magic shop. The man sits at the till holed up on the phone. He is being shrieked at. 'Madam . . . you must understand. Everything I do is for your own protection . . . your own protecting.' But her voice squeals through the receiver.

I finger what he has. There are baskets of ritual loofahs. Glass panels covered in crosses. Ritual drums. There are beautiful dried gourds. Covered over with a mess of coloured buttons on string that makes a haunting rippling sound when vigorously shaken. The magic man is being firm on the telephone.

'A child is a human being . . . A human being. I know you confessed . . . I know you confessed . . . But I must be clear there are no delusions.'

There is a basket of nasal sprays. Whole shelves of holy oils. Varieties of eczema creams. 'Rabbi Solomon' prosperity salts. And a spring collection of voodoo candles with names like Controlling, Miracle Healing, Money Drawing.

'Madam . . . I will come urgently. I understand this urgent matter . . . I will come to say the prayer. I understand. I understand. But I must go now . . . Some mens are in the shop.'

The magic man is watching a horror movie on very low volume on his vintage grey desktop PC. His eyes are locked on the screen as we begin casual conversation about Peckham. How the rents are

ABBI SOLOMON

MAGNET - BATH SALT

Will attract Love and money as magnet attract iron, and as the moon attract the Ocean and tide is

POWERFUL INDIAN HOUSE BLESSING PENTACLES OF

BBI SOLOMON

SUCCESS - BATH SALT

You will be successful in whatever profession or business. Wash away bad luck, misfortune, trouble, sickness, rise and fall and

POWERFUL INDIAN HOUSE BLESSING PENTACLES OF

SOLOMON

NET - BATH SALT

Will attract Love and money as magnet attract iron and as the moon attract the Ocean and tide

SOLOMON

K - BATH SALT

You will wash away bad luck, you will turn bad luck to Good luck, you will turn your misfortune to fortunes and your disappointments going up. How the mall is doing. How his neighbour in the printing stall thought Britain was crime-ridden.

'What is he talking about? He crazy that man . . . people not doing nothing when there is a mugging? He come from Africa . . . In Africa there are dead bodies on the street and people not do nothing. That man, what is he thinking? A mugging nobody react? In his country, the Sierra Leone, they are chopping heads with machetes in the street. He remember that? Why he is here?'

The man at the desk is a minister at a celestial church. These are the places where West African Christianity mixes with West African mystery: robes of white are worn, children are exorcised, blessings are dabbed on the head with holy waters and ointments and spiritual guides are followed and worshipped.

These are what other Londoners call witch doctors: but for the rural, traditional, immigrant in Peckham they perform many roles the rest of London had split up – confessor, counsellor, psychiatrist, priest, remedy-giver, visionary, seer. These are the men and women who confused African immigrants come to when they are in trouble. The city is crawling with them. They even advertise in the back pages of the free-sheet newspapers handed out in the Tube.

Mr Madiba.
FROM BIRTH, A GIFTED AFRICAN
SPIRITUAL HEALER & ADVISOR.
Can advise on love, business transactions, exams, court cases,
immigration & relationship problems.
Tel: 07960 682175

I quickly learn that witch doctors are like drug dealers: you always gotta wait. The big man in the shop made it clear. He would consider. But the prophetess had just flown off into the spirit and would not be down again for a whole week. I lie about what I need: I am a Romanian immigrant. And I want to know whether or not I should stay in this country. Things are tough.

A week passes: I call and call, until I am told the prophetess has come out of the spirit. The man tells me the only available moment for a 'consultation' is the very next day at noon sharp. I drop every-thing. This is extremely unusual: white men, even Romanians, do not normally get consultations so easily.

Trains to Peckham leave from Victoria Station: a glass roof from the nineteenth century covers fast-food counters and sandwich chains. Commuters rush, push and look at the gigantic timetables. Three years ago, there was a gang murder in the tube station, in the evening rush hour, by hoodies wielding a Samurai sword.

I board and pick up a free newspaper. A witch-hunter from Nigeria has landed at Heathrow and is preaching in basement churches in South London. Hysteria has broken out in the commu-nity: she is hunting for possessed girls. The witch-hunter has now gone to ground. Possibly in Woolwich.

The train rolls out over the red and brown rocks that lie under the tracks, then crosses the river, passes the monumental hulk of Battersea Power Station, ringed by cranes and construction work-ers, pulling up luxurious glass towers for Malaysian investors. The railway lines speed past industrial estates and high streets, past terrace after terrace and dozens upon dozens of cubic estates.

The train moans and turns: suddenly the glassy trophies of the city of London are laid out before you between the imitation Corbusier blocks with their square windows, and concrete shafts. The rail then dips: boarded only by graffiti and then unkempt, wild overgrowth rushing along the line. Damp places where kids climb over the barriers and smoke skunk and daydream.

Peckham has an imposing train station. But I do not stop to look at the yellow stones and their decorative carvings. Rye Lane rushes past me in my hurry – Bim's African Cash And Carry, Abuja Restaurant, Big Girl Bags, Juliet's Wig Shop – until I find myself back in the gloom of the bric-a-brac mall again. The big man is waiting for me in the magic shop.

'OK . . . OK . . . Go into the back, make a left, then a sharp left, then left until the security box, and then a sharp left and then the door . . . You see it . . . You will know it . . . You open it.'

I struggle until a kind-faced woman in white robes carrying holy water guides me to the temple. The big man meant straight through

the emergency exit. Then past the hoodies hanging around outside the Southwark Payment Centre. The route leads into an old industrial yard. Where the woman in white robes waves me goodbye.

There, where it is supposed to be, is a small door in a red-brick wall. 'Ring Ring' is scrawled in white paint over the buzzer. I enter the Holy Emmanuel Church of Christ. Inside two plastic trees with white plastic leaves flank the fire doors into the main hall. I take off my shoes as requested.

The floor is covered in thin and used blue carpet, lined with little school chairs for the congregants. There is no altar. There is a crucifix between two drums, both upright and covered in mini mirror-tiles. I smell incense. The back of the hall is hidden away behind huge floor-length curtains with a brown floral pattern.

There is little light. Walking up to me is a woman in what looks like a simple wedding dress. This is white, sewn out of a thick material patterned with reflective shine. Her headdress looks like a chef's hat. Three pale thick scar lines run down both of her cheeks. Before she opens her mouth, her eyes begin asking questions.

'You have . . . come for the prayer . . . Go down on your knees.'

Behind us is a raised platform strewn with bedding: uncovered white duvets and tossed white sheets. There is a woman in blue wrapped up in the bedding with a dozen bottles of sacred ointment and oils in a line behind her on the floor. I watch her hide a little yawn.

'She is the senior prophetess . . . She has been flying for one week . . . For one week no eating, no drinking . . . She was seeing many, many thing . . . She was having the vision . . . She was speaking. She only came down yesterday . . . we were all here for her. It was . . . beautiful.'

Kneeling I have visions of this women in blue, writhing and speaking in tongues and shouting out on the white duvets behind us, watched over by the junior prophetess, who is now explaining how we are about to proceed.

'We have in this church a very, very high success rate with the Home Office in getting people's papers for their stay . . . We have many miracle testimonies.'

As best as I can, I lie, I am a Romanian immigrant: is it worth staying here?

The rent is so high. The pay is too low. The city is built on bubbles. There is simmering white anger. The senior prophetess rises out of the duvets and walks towards me clutching a Bible. She signals to the junior prophetess in white who moves through the room to switch on a ventilator. Incense spews out. There is a whirring sound. The soothsaying and ritual blessing have begun. The junior prophetess speaks:

'He is in this country . . . O Lord Jehovah Emmanuel. You know the reason for them to be here. You know O Lord Adonai what brought him here and why he is here in this country.'

I cannot close my eyes. The senior prophetess is twitching. Her eyes roll. Yoruba voices spew out of her. Her hands fling back. The senior prophetess is chanting in her language in a soft voice. Her slender frame rattles like electric charges are playing with her. Her voice gives way to those of others.

'God have paved way for the Israelites in the Red Sea into the Promised Land. God will pave the way for you now in this country. In the name of Jesus Christ as we kneel here before you I decree his name in your life. I decree his blessing in your heart. I decree his voice in your mind. I decree his spirit. Amen. It is done.'

Then she speaks: the senior prophetess.

The Angel tells me to stay.

ILFORD LANE

This night is brown-purple. The beat-up car hurtles round the orbital and for a moment I can see the glow from the flyover. I am tired. And the car swerves slightly. Over the motorway, I can see the city glows piling up, into red blinking, orange towers, and shards. And then, jolting, I turn off with a screech into Ilford.

There is a hiss and crackle in the night. The Diwali fireworks are sparking up all over East London. They hiss and crackle and pop over the terraces. And make the pattering drizzle smell sour, like gunpowder. The hoodies are gathering round the chicken shops, between the block and cube redevelopment towers, round Ilford hill. But I drive past them, thinking, into the backstreets.

Down terrace after terrace, hundreds of bay windows glow. These were once desirable suburban addresses: on Henley, Windsor and Hampton Road. But today these are where you find the immigrant share rooms. The ones they advertise on Polish websites, or in little cards stuck in grubby windows of the Pakistani newsagents. This is where England begins. And today the white British population of these dingy streets south of Ilford station is around 10 per cent.

The windows make me think. How these long net curtains, with their thickly sewn patterns of polyester flowers and roses, which glow yellowy into the night-time, were once a sign someone had made it here in these hundreds, thousands, of little houses, lined up one by one, with that little bay window, proudly out front. But not any more. The successful English hate these kind of curtains; they want either that bay window to glow out with cream, soft linen – or glint through wooden venetian blinds.

The Diwali rockets pap and clack. Blue and green flash overhead. Behind me squeal and spit a dozen Diwali Catherine wheels. But there is something different about Ilford, I mumble. The terraces here are so long, and so straight, that when you drive down them, the street lamps merge into one orange blaze – up ahead. The car follows the geometry, as my mind wanders, imagining, this illusion must be why architects, for so many centuries, have longed for streets to be straight like this.

The last fireworks crackle and sputter. As I slow down, I notice these terraces carry the sad names of the other, richer London – Richmond, Kingston or Eton Road. And they turn and turn, mutating between Pakistani homes and Eastern European tenements. But those net curtains, they are always the giveaways. These were left up when landlords turned this pebbledash house into a tenement, as the English pulled out or died. You can always tell a slum house, where four Polish builders crash in bunk beds behind that chipped bay window, by those very same old and floral singed curtains.

I park the car next to a huge, almost wild, privet hedge. I count cracks, running through the mock-timbered gable of its pebbledash. But this is not it. There is the address I want to find, the same one that Roma beggars across London always seem to leave when they need bail. They laugh about it in court – the police, the translators, the prosecutors – and call it the infamous 20 H—— Road, Ilford.

The lights are off. There are no cracks in this yellow-brick new build with a pointy wooden porch jutting out over its slender plastic door. But there is detritus everywhere: a car bumper flung on the pavement, an overturned fridge in front of the house and a popped cardboard television box in the middle of the road. I come close to knocking. But I turn suddenly, with the fright from a roaring car, as an Asian man swerves his Volvo round the corner. This guy is speeding, and his face is almost fully covered by a hoodie and a thick grey-blue scarf.

I walk onto Ilford Lane. The last pub was demolished five years ago. This is now a Pakistani street: one that glints with electric red lights, coiled round every street lamp, over a lane where the night flickers with fairy lights, flashing purple to blue, like a Christmas-time decking, curling round Zarqa's sari shop, and Gul's fashion, across the road from B+B's cash and carry. The night is full of colour.

Electrics bleep: 2 am.

This is where the whores are. Below the flashing purple and blue fairy lights over Chopra and Sons, where a Palestine flag hangs from the flat above, they stand in their leopard-print leggings. Across from the shuttered front of Islamabad Halal, whose plastic illuminated hoarding has a cartoonish chicken and lamb for illiterate women, next to the crest of the King of Saudi Arabia himself, they catcall and whistle, with the smell of vodka on their lips.

The whores shove their hands in their pockets, look this way and that, and kiss their teeth when you pass a little slowly – knowing you want it, but maybe not from her – between the glow of Tasty Chicken, where the hoodies hang out, brapping and bragging, and the shuttered front of Saj Travels, where the posters hawk package deals for Umrah and the Hajj.

The whores, in pink tights or white jeans, they cup their fingers at you, and wave, and wink – this way, this way – into my alley, as they lean back on the grimy window of the old boiler shop, that they say is the last English shopkeeper on Ilford Lane, who always flies a traffic-dirtied Cross of St George, and a fluttering, sun-bleached Union Jack, and who like all the other last English shopkeepers in East London has become so very nervous about being swallowed up completely.

They look rough. But they can lock your stare, and pout, then flick their hair – come on, come on – strutting late at night on Ilford Lane, when there are no other ladies, when it's really night, when nobody can see you, and the big glowing letters over Roop Jewellers turn a deep red, and those four lads outside Dixy Chicken, looking fresh in their crisp white robes, are cracking up, and back slapping again, over another sickly, pungent spliff.

You can always tell the heat on Ilford Lane. The chubby little fucker running in and out of the phone box: three, five, seven times. The posse looking over him, hanging outside the electrical yard, arms all crossed, eyes scanning, and scanning, as they keep chatting to the bruvas in the pulled-over Range Rover. And of course the crack addicts barging in and out of the newsagent, jingling with loud Urdu tunes, begging the pin-pim-pim boys at their jangling cash till. 'I promise, I fucking promise, when I got it, I'll give it.'

I try and get it down in my notebook: the two hoods trundling slowly up and down the lane on their bikes, those last two cockney crack-heads stumbling after them, shouting, 'Come back, slow down.' And then I begin to notice the strange feel. This is a low street, and as I shuffle under the stubby brick spire of the Tamil Church, I can see not one cubic high-rise, and no bullying towers ahead – and start thinking, maybe this is the way it was, when you walked in the Victorian sprawl.

'You want it? Or are you fucking gay, or something?'

The fireworks have stopped. The only sound is the whoosh of the cars. And this screaming woman. She is so sick I cannot really make out her age: twenty to forty – the shape of her face has been too swallowed up. The cockney crack-head lifts up her stained top, and gives a flash of shrivelled breasts, outside the shuttered front of Nikhar's Fashion. Her grass-green irises sit on eyeballs, bloodshot completely. She has scratched chunks of the skin from her forehead.

'Come on . . . or you Romanian or something, speak English? I fucking need a tenner right now.'

Her eyes keep flicking ahead to the chubby Asian teen slowly winding his bike up and down the lane, grinning, with a toothy snigger back at her. She hiccups. And I hand it over. And she lets go of a bloodstained roll of toilet paper.

'The Pakis got the money here . . . There ain't no fucking white people here any more . . . You'd think you're in bloody Pakistan or something. They've taken it over, and made it their fucking Romanian whorehouse and heroin palace . . . them Pakis have.'

Electrics bleep: 3 am.

But nobody hates this more than the red-brick mosque at the bottom of Ilford Lane. They were ecstatic when the youth, in puffa jackets, trainers and jubbah robes, organized a Sharia Patrol to march up and down Ilford Lane shouting, 'This is a Muslim area,' at the soliciting whores, at the heroin dealers.

But much to everyone's disappointment – the butcher, the tailor, the mobile-phone shop man, the kebab man, the minicab office, the fabric merchant, even the high street solicitor specializing in deportation cases – the lads' Sharia Patrol made no difference at all. The disgrace lingers. Because crime on Ilford Lane is multi-cultural, or so they say: the Pakistani racket hand over a few grams to the Romanian racket, who pay their whores with drugs, and then give the Pakistanis a cut of their profits for their spots. And, hated by everyone, whoring thrives.

'Ilford Lane is Punters' Lane, bruv.'

You can see the signs in the upstairs windows.

The red curtains, opened onto crimson-painted walls, these are the whorehouses winking over this scruffy pebbledash parade, with breakable plastic windows, and snappable doors, whose very scruffiness seems to knows its place in the system. And then you begin to see it, with every turn: in that wide open door, with a sign that bothers only to have 'Guest House' printed, round the back of the chicken shop, not to mention those hundred-odd mobile numbers for 'Massage' pinned in the glass-wall windows of every newsagents, all of those shops plastered up in advertising from LycaMobile, or Lebara, to call whoever you want, in Bucharest or Lahore.

'Ilford Lane . . . is just bitches making money.'

Her street name is Angelica and she stands, cold, in cheap boots and a black dress, outside B.B. Fatima Cash and Carry. And she tells me the same lies as the rest of them. 'No, we love this. No, we want to do this. No, we have boyfriends.' But her voice trembles slightly with nerves, the longer we talk, and the more hoodies pass.

'Ilford Lane . . . is bitches working for no boss.'

But who is that Romanian guy in the blue hoodie, built like a bumper pack of Chinese steroids, with that bobbing greasy ponytail giving me evils, marching up and down the strip, between Raman Jewellers and the Mahi Grill? And who is that fucker in a leather jacket, parked on the corner of Mortlake Road, eyeing me down, as he smokes one after another Lucky, and takes all these 3 am calls?

'Bitching is what I wanted . . . Nobody forces us . . . become bitches.'

Her little brown eyes screw up with something, I'm not sure what. 'Give me money': and when I pass her a twenty to explain how the whoring works, out of an alley trots a girl in leopard-print leggings, who brown eyeballs her, and whistles, two fingers in her mouth, that way which in every language in London means exactly the same thing – 'Shut the Fuck Up.'

You can see the heat on Ilford Lane in the cars. When the MG and the Porsche come down pip-ping at 3 am and the hoods outside the Dixy Chicken pay attention. When you notice an abundance of sleek black BMWs driving in and out of a boarded-off construction yard. Why is everyone here up and alert? And why is everyone here flicking in and out their throwaway phone? But that is none of my business.

'Look . . . This is where they killed Mariana.'

Not all prostitutes are the same. Those Polish or Latvian girls, that fresh, un-addicted meat, in those glow-light massage parlours, with the bouncers along the Romford Road, they will cost you around £100. But here on Ilford Lane, we have the skankier end of the market. These are the girls the punters call the roughest treats. And almost all of them are Romanian. They are London's most at-risk group for murder.

'This is where they killed Mariana.'

The girls all know their place on Ilford lane. Loredana sits at the bus stop. Diana hangs around the builders' yard. And Mariana stood across from Chunky Chicken And Pizza 4 U. After he stabbed her, with two knife punches to the chest, this grease shack was as far as Mariana made it, and where she collapsed, into shock.

'She wasn't screaming. She was only spasming – like this, like this . . . And then doctors came in the helicopter . . . And they took her to the hospital, in Whitechapel . . . But Mariana was already dead since the chicken shop.'

Tonight, churchy black women are moving along Ilford Lane, in a happy little group, silently praying for the prostitutes. They stop at every girl and smile and try to remember their names, as they pull

Strip Burger
2 Wings & Fries   2·99

Add 50p for   Fries

GO CRAZY OFFER

Cheese Burger	Chicken Steak Burger
129	129
Fish Fillet Burger	**Chicken Strip Burger**
199	149
2 Chicken Steak Burger (Reg. Fries & Can Drink)	**2 Cheese Burger** (Reg. Fries & Can Drink)
3·49	3·49
1 Pc Chicken (& Reg. Fries)	**4 Hot Wings**
199	£1·20

Veggie or Bean Burger

199

out cookies and a coffee thermos. They beam, motherly, and offer them each a key ring, and then a prayer. Some nights they all say yes – and when they did, mostly, they asked the black women to pray for their mums – but, sometimes, on other nights they tell them to fuck off.

Most are too far gone to remember.

'When he said, "I kill you," we thought . . . he was making joke.'

Loredana crosses her legs at the bus stop, with her blue eyes, and sallow sunken face. Sodium light rims the curve of her head. Nothing makes her more nervous than a man asking questions about the murder. She smokes, and drags it deeply, before pulling tight her kerchief – a leopard-skin pattern, in purple, yellow and blue. They call her a Gypsy. Loredana has a mole on her neck, smack-dead eyes, two gold-tinted hoop earrings and a stained pig-leather jacket. She costs twenty quid.

'We knew him . . . who killed her . . . Mariana, she was always talking about him.'

Her faint eyes look at me. Did you know him? Because all the Romanians, and all the Pakistanis, and all the blacks, all the way up and down Ilford Lane knew him as that rudeboy dealer, with his baggies of smack, coke and crack, one of those guys, always cycling up and down, working the strip, one night after another.

'We laughed at him. When he said, "Mariana, I kill you."'

There are always the innocent on the street, and now those passing us, talking over cigarettes at the bus shelter, they lock their eyes ahead: the Asian teen eating a packet of crisps, he does not want to see this, the African man with a rucksack, who shoots my way one long, searching stare, he loathes this, a man talking to his whore.

'I was at his trial.'

I tell her, as I look for a lighter, how I watched the murderer take the stand. I tell her, as I pass her the light, how I watched him wink at the black guards, like they would back him up in this, but they tongue tut-ted him to face those impossibly posh Asian lawyers, in those silly wigs, from prosecutions. They sounded like Oxford. But he spoke in the new cockney and they pretended, playing with him with their kitty paws, they didn't understand what he was saying.

'Who took these photos, Mr Farooq?'

'Da bruvas.'

'Are they real brothers, Mr Farooq?'

'No, like bredrin innit.'

'Are these brethren relatives of yours, Mr Farooq?'

'No . . . like bredriiin, innit, like a bredriiin . . .'

I tell her, at the shelter, as the seldom car swooshes, some slowing down, before speeding, how I watched him squirm, and sweat, that squat little man, almost a boy, his voice cracking up like he was being done for a suspension, whose eyes bulged when the CCTV came on, of him trundling up and down Ilford Lane, who looked at me with eyes going, 'Fuck these cunts,' like I was support back in a classroom, when the prosecutor produced an emissions map of his mobile data, from here to the end of the Romford Road.

'Nah, for fuck's sake . . . Wasn't me, it wasn't fucking me . . .'

I tell her, how I watched him lie – as the curls of dead leaves in the gutter catch the glint from the street lamp – how he had met some girl called Destiny, on the street, who had invited him to a party, in her block round Plaistow way, where he had drunk a bottle of Teacher's straight, then smoked a whole spliff, accidentally, become waved, then fucked completely, bought a stolen mobile off an unknown hood off the Romford Road going home, then wandered home to watch a few episodes of *Family Guy*. I tell her, as we watch the Polish tramp searching for chicken bits in the bins, that I watched his voice give way, almost to a baby sob, when the prosecution linked the CCTV of his punch stabs to the data packets bleeping from his phone.

He is Shah Farooq, twenty-one.

He killed Mariana Popa, twenty-four.

'Mariana told me that Muslim boy . . . He loved her.'

The girls have their stories all along Ilford Lane. There are some girls who claim Shah screwed up his face, and howled, and lifted her up, running over the road – holding her in his arms for a moment, in front of the glowing windows of the chicken shop – before he rushed back over the road, and dumped her spasming body between the shuttered sari shop and the Nagina takeaway.

'I didn't see that.'

Loredana looks into me.

'I only remember Mariana spasming.'

The drizzle is turning amber, the golden-brown leaves in the gutter have lost their crinkle and turned into mush, and every now and then the steamed windows of the night bus rattles past, as we share my cigarettes in the shelter. But the more I ask about what happened that night, the more nervous she becomes.

The murder in Ilford was a year ago tonight. But everyone is expecting another. Jack the Ripper killed his prostitutes in White-chapel. He stabbed up their sweaty bodies in the crooked backstreets of the foetid Jewish ghetto, which the police hardly knew from Warsaw, between the Yiddish stalls and the swivel-eyed Kabbalists. But today, our prostitutes get murdered here, in this decaying suburb, at the edge of the new Muslim ghetto, between the mosque and the chicken shop.

'We was sitting, here, always . . . at this stop. And Mariana, she would come to the bus stop . . . and she was telling us, "Shah he loves me . . . Shah he wants marry me . . . He wants me to come to him . . . But I won't touch him," Mariana was saying, "because when I go to the clubbing with him, I become sick, because Shah he mixes my drinks with heroin."'

I tell Loredana, I want her in my car, to talk quietly. And she looks ready. I can see the blue hoodie with the ponytail pacing a little closer. But she needs to wait for her friend – the young one on the lane. Three Pakistani boys come round the corner giggling, clutching milkshakes and burger bags, as a tracksuit paces, like a man, angrily away from them, as they whistle behind her – 'Come On . . . Super Tongue.'

'Here Diana comes now . . . Now . . . we can go.'

In the wing mirror, the face of Diana terrifies me. It is the face of a girl child, waxy, anything between fourteen and thirty-four, with hovering eyes, and a nasty blonde wig pulled so badly over her head you can see black rim hair over her forehead. As she begins to talk, her voice makes me shudder. This is the mumbling, or high-pitch, baby-talk tone of a girl.

'When he killed Mariana . . . Shah . . . he came running this way . . . towards the bus stop, and he saw me here . . . and that's when I ran . . . As fast I could . . . faster than even a cat.'

The car is parked now behind some estate. And the girls are sitting in the back, smoking. It will stink for days. And that voice, of Diana in the wig, that seems to gurgle, from that place right between her teeth, like she has barely learnt to talk, makes little bones in the neck-spine shudder. But I force myself: concentrate, write down everything she says.

'He looked at me . . . When he came running past the chicken shop . . . and he didn't even look human . . . His face was so scrunched up, he looked like a monster . . . And I thought he was coming after me. And I ran, into some street off the side. And I was so scared that he was coming, I was babbling . . . and frothing, and shaking . . . and everything started to go white. I ran, and I ran . . . until I fell over. I tripped, and fell into some bushes, in front of somebody's house . . . And then I fainted, into the white.'

The car heating puffs out, smelling slightly, as the engine vibrates, and while Diana is talking, I can see in the wing mirror that Loredana in the kerchief is covering her face, whimpering slightly. I know she does not want to talk about this. That she would rather I just fucked them both – or hit them, the way some of the men enjoy doing – than ask them about what happened to Mariana. But I don't care. And I gesture. I want you to talk now.

'When he stabbed her, she didn't make much sound. There was no screaming . . . She was there spasming, just spasming on the floor of the chicken shop . . . And her stomach, her chest, it was belching out this blackish blood, as she spasmed . . . and that's when I fainted.'

Loredana pulls herself upright, the night glinting off the hoops of her earrings. Was I really not from the police? Did the police, then, tell me about her? Because she was the one that fainted. Did the police still want her? Because she was the one who was too scared to make the identity parade. I say no: and for a moment, she breathes.

'Mariana . . . She was the prettiest girl in Ilford Lane . . . We

would go clubbing with her sometimes, and she would take coke with us, and go dancing, and she would tell us about Shah . . . and how he wanted to marry her . . . And we do not know if it is true, but she told us once she had a baby in Romania . . . and after it happened, we heard, she was pregnant . . . with another . . . And that *bitches* say . . . was what he was stabbing into.'

Loredana winces and covers her face, for a second, in her translucent leopard-print kerchief. But nothing crosses the face of the girl-child talking, and her eyes seem to wander away, somewhere strange, and very distant.

'This was when we began seeing her . . . we began seeing her, for forty-one nights, bloodied . . . in a wedding dress, on the corner at Ilford Lane, pirouetting, and pirouetting, up and down between the chicken shops and the cash and carries.'

Loredana begins to talk.

About how for forty-one nights, after the murder in October, she saw Mariana everywhere, rasping in her dreams, weeping at the whoring bus shelter, rattling at the shuttered newsagents, screaming out to her from the chicken shop, as the wetness of the mist hung in the lane, and her soul pirouetted in white and blood, round the fabric shops, the floodlit petrol stations and the builders' yards.

'I felt she was inside my head . . . I felt she was in here . . .'

In the back seat of my car the whore clasps both hands to her head.

'I felt she was inside me . . . that she was not letting me go, I kept hearing her shouting into me, "Why did Shah stab me, when he said he loved me, why did Shah kill me, when he said he wanted to marry, why did he do it, why, why . . ."

'I was shaking, I was shouting, in my sleep, "Mariana, I can't help you, Mariana, I don't know, I don't know. I fainted, I'm the one who fainted . . ." And I kept getting less, and less, sleeping . . . until I was shaking, and hitting, and panicking . . . and she was everywhere, and I was seeing her everywhere . . . She was every night at the corner, shouting at me, to come to her, to save her . . .'

Loredana became useless. Girls can work up to twenty punters a night: but she could take none. And when she began spasming, and freaking on the dingy carpets of the sharehouse, crying out that Mariana was inside her head, the man she called her boyfriend sent her to Leeds, where his mother worked with the deep-fryer in the back of a chicken shop.

'I was biting and shrieking when they put me on the bus.'

Loredana had a window seat to Leeds. But she could not sleep. The bus from under the scuffed concrete around Euston Station was stuck in traffic between big glassy blocks, at the start of the huge flyover, raised high on its pillars, where normally a thousand cars rush over West London, like a metal river. They had turned a film on in the bus.

But she could hear Mariana; Mariana was all she could hear. The bus, it was leaving now, leaving London, leaving this huge unreal city, mangled together like a fantasy of Babel, where every villain in the whole world has a home, and vibrating, as it glided on to the motorway, that like them all, made the rushing sound of a waterfall, but this one she saw, was all lined by a thousand dingy little pebble-dashes, the net curtains in the windows singed for ever with the exhaust of a million little cars.

Mariana was screaming. Loredana blinked, her eyes stung by the light. The fields gushing into her eyes, they were green, as green as saris she sometimes saw on Ilford Lane, as green as the lettering above the Islamabad Halal, a green she had never seen before, and the sky was cracked open, into grey and blue, and light.

Mariana was screaming when, her hoop earrings jangling from under her blue kerchief, the pimp's mother shook her awake on the bus – its engine off and cooling – in the car park in Leeds. Her eyes were green, and between her wrinkles, fine like cracks in paintwork, she squinted at her passed-out body in the seat, and then snarled.

'The priest is waiting.'

Romanians in Leeds were living better, much better than any of the Romanians in London. The rent was cheaper, there were very few shared rooms, and the dew shone on the thick grass, round the old stone nave of the church, the one the English no longer used, because here they no longer believed, and the Romanians now rented from them. Mariana was screaming, and Loredana was

fighting, biting, and dragging, not to be pulled into the cool stone darkness.

'You have become possessed.'

The priest looked like all other priests. But Loredana had not seen many. His eyes glinted a yellowy brown from the candles he lit for her, and his beard frizzed out in tiny coils of black and wiry grey. He began to sing, rocking, in his black robes, as the pimp's mother gripped her still on those damp flagstones. He closed his eyes, and the prayer, it hovered, it moaned. And his holy water flecked and trickled down the prostitute's blubbering face.

'And that was when Mariana was gone . . . When she was no longer in me.'

These two faces are framed in my mirror. The sunken, frightened, long face of Loredana, who talks so brokenly, her black, greasy hair tied as tightly as can be to her skull. And I keep noticing, my eyes fixed into the mirror, how the older whore keeps looking to her left, at the round, pale peasant child-face, next to her in the maladjusted wig, whose eyes keep rolling up slightly into her head, whose lips keep curling with such a strange, grimacing smile. And with, a gurgle, she speaks.

'Bless her soul. I came back to the house . . . And I went into my bedroom . . . and Mariana was there . . . Her body was there . . . on the bed . . . on my bed, and it was all bruised, with blood marks, and cuts and everything . . . And she was going, "Please, please, help me . . ." The soul was lying next to her body, and she was talking to me, going, "Please, please can you help my soul get back into my body . . ." And I went to her . . .

'"I can't help you, sweetie.

'"I can't help you."'

LAMBERT ROAD

Brixton is the end of the line.

Where the escalators are overcrowded. Where the tunnels have wind rush. Where the name hangs in the head. Where we all have to get off.

This is where I meet Femi, in the backstreets. His hands fumble as he unlocks the door. His eyes are swelling nervously as he takes me into his overheated bedsit.

'I never thought I could do this.'

He is skinny, in a grey jumper, and speaks, haltingly, in a kind of Americanish twang, like anyone who learnt English from TV. This room is painted a fleshy pink. The colour grins nastily behind three knick-knack framed prints of soaring Jesus. The pink reinforces and dims the gloom, spreading over the MDF shelving, the battle-hardened sewing machine and a confused ceramic chicken.

Femi sits on a kitchen chair. He crosses his arms tightly onto his chest. I sit on the sofa, an old brown leathery thing. Torn in places. The kind of sofa that is never going to be repaired. Femi crosses his legs and looks at the floor.

'I wanted to come here . . . and wear a suit.'

Femi wants to work in an office. He wants to sit back on a swivel chair, and peer into a screen and say things like, 'I'm in a meeting.' Femi has always thought about offices. He thought about offices as he stacked up piles of plastic saucers at his mother's market stall. He thought about offices as he watched her sweat, swear and screech at the top of her voice that hers were the cheapest. He thought about brogues when his feet slipped in the market swill and the muck from vegetable rinds. But most of all he thought about

London: and when he thought about London, he only thought about visas.

Femi was trembling as he carefully read the printout from the British Embassy. This was a temporary student visa. But he knew that once he got to London, once he got working in an office, he would never come back to Nigeria. He would never have to pick up crates of vegetables. Never again would he catch splinters in his fingers hauling crates. Never ever would he be Femi the market boy again. His heart was racing as he held that piece of paper. But not as fast as his thoughts.

Femi glances round the bedsit and tries to smile.

'I did not make it . . . to the office. That was how it started.'

He swallowed, as six months later he stepped into the agency. It was just like the rest of them, a shifty high-street recruitment bureau, sandwiched behind frosted windows, between corporate pawn-brokers and seedy betting shops.

'I can't do it, I just can't,' he mumbled, he whispered, as the Indian woman behind the desk explained to him what working as a temporary carer in an NHS trust or an old people's home really involved. 'I can't do this, I'm not able,' he muttered, as he bit his lip and listened.

The more the woman explained, the worse the tingling felt. 'The primary role of a temporary agency carer is assistance,' she explained, 'and this will involve washing, toileting, hoisting, shaving and monitoring those no longer able to conduct these tasks for themselves.' 'I can't do this,' he heard himself whimper, as his thoughts became flashing, clear images, of his hand wiping out the sludgy stool from between their wrinkled white exhausted folds of skin.

Femi never gets to know the hospitals. The agency daily assigns him shifts by text messages.

Quite often there will be no shift and no beep until the morning. Femi will lie there awake at 5 am no matter what: waiting for the hour to be out. Only then he knows he can sleep. One week, the

agency sends him over to the hulking tower-block hospital, up in Edmonton. This is a poor area. He passes through the fire doors and notices there are lots of black people in these wards, and in the intensive care unit, where the bays are full of the very sick. There are sometimes Indians wrapped in orange clothes who come to whisper to the patients, or they will request to see an imam, with their long frizzy beards, and wide toothy smiles.

Then the agency changes the rota: he will be sent to that meanly windowed brown-brick hospital in Orpington, where he will suddenly blink, and notice that everyone in the bays looks, troublingly, the same: blotchy, wrinkled, white, loose and grey. And again: he will wake up with instructions that the agency needs him in the iron-clad pipe-gurgling wards in Kingston hospital, or even sometimes in the low-grade metal and glass round the priggish old red-brick down in Hammersmith.

Femi turns up and on every new ward he feels the same sneering, hostile glare from the permanent workers. He knows they see him as an agency worker: a threat, undercutting their trade unions, their employment and their pay. He is on a zero-hour contract. But the moment Femi, with his faintly Asian eyes, his manly, thoughtful voice and worried, childish smile, has charmed them into sharing their tea – the agency wants him elsewhere. They need him in new hospitals, and they need him in new wards. They need carers on the cardiac units, in general medicine, on intensive care, in acute stress, behind the scenes on accident and emergency, or even, he particularly likes this one, helping out the doctor on outpatients. But mostly, and he does not like to brag about this, it's old people.

What Femi hates is doing special. This is what the ward sisters call special one-to-one assistance. He will come in the morning, into the space of humming and bleeping, hoping they will not give him a special. Femi wants to move around: hoisting them up, moving back and forth feeding them, rushing there and back with the bed pan, or even better, shaving the men.

'The thing with special is you have to be with the patient twenty-four–seven, one to one, throughout the whole shift. The thing when you are doing special is you have to mark them . . . sitting with them, toileting them, feeding them. Honestly, it is easier when they cannot walk, because when they can, they are often confused . . . and the special means you have to follow them, especially when they are at risk of fall . . . because the ward sisters need you to stop the patient from wandering out, or getting out of the ward, or escaping onto the streets.'

Femi hates those days when they get angry. He has been given a special, and the whole day is spent pacing up and down after a muddled old white man; they go up and down the disinfected corridors, and round and round those buzzing, incomprehensible grey machines. Femi hates it when they become stressed, when they forget who he is, and start shouting at him.

'This happens every week. I think, maybe one in two of the white patient . . . they is like this. The special was at risk of wander, and he was going up and down the corridor and turning to me going, "No, I can walk, go away, why you following me . . ." He wanted to get out, but he was weak. The patient did not understand where he was, really. He was becoming tired and stressed. And when I stood blocking him at the end of the ward, going, "Sorry, it's not allowed," and he become distressed, and started shouting. "Why are you following me, you bloody African. Get off me, you nigger, go back and follow your parents in your home country." And I was feeling . . . a bit harsh to him. Because that morning I had toileted him and I had given him a really nice shave . . . and he had been thankful to me.'

The ward sisters will take him aside, they are warm Nigerian nurses mostly, or little to-the-point Filipinas, and tell him, 'Femi look at me, we know it hurts they call you nigger, we know, we've been here many, many years, but you have to understand they don't know what they are doing. They are sick. They may say they are – but they are not fine.'

Abuse is as normal as rain for the carers of London: at least 60 per cent are migrants. They move towards the bedsides and find muddled, frightened old people they have to clean. They are too weak to understand the halogen lights and the catheter smells. They no longer understand where they are. They screech sometimes: 'Get away from me, you wog.' They howl: 'Leave my stuff alone.' They punch sometimes: they think they are being robbed.

The nurses say this happens a lot. The white ward sisters mention sometimes that round about one in ten will say things like, 'Excuse me madam, I don't want that coloured nurse, I don't like her. Thank you very much.'

Femi stops, and fidgets.

'The old people are not all like this. They are not . . . all shouting. There was this guy, I came in the morning, and you know there was gonna be handover time. And I thought, I don't want to do a one on one . . . that is the last thing I want to do. As I came in, I saw the patient. He was really tall, he was built, a huge white man . . . but he had bad hair, it had all gone. There he was, just moving and moving, and making sounds on the bed.

'I looked at him and saw he had not even been shaved . . . He was eighty, his eyes was white, like they had no colour . . . like grey . . . I could see him as I was coming in, the changing room was down the corridor, and I could see he had no bed sheet on. Because he was really agitated, he was groaning, moaning . . . on that rubbish bed. The handover went to me, "You are going to be with this patient," and I thought, Oh God . . . He was sweating, kicking . . . Oh God, this is going to be a long day.'

His cat-like eyes narrow and he crosses his legs very tightly.

'And I went to him, "Hello, good morning, sir," because I like to say good morning sir and shake their hands. Most people don't shake their hands, and the reasons I shake their hands is I want them to see me as a friend. Because at some time in their life they would have worked in an office, doing business or something, and it is like greeting them for the morning . . . This is my way of doing my job.'

Femi sits crossing and uncrossing his feet.

'The man didn't shake my hand . . . and he couldn't talk clearly. So, the nurse, she had been with him on the night shift, she went, "Look, I just changed him . . . that guy, he's really agitated . . . you got to keep careful, you gotta do this, you gotta do that . . . You have to change him every time, change him, change him . . ." and there was no sheet. You know how the hospital bed sheet is? It's like plastic. It was gone.

'So in my mind I thought, What I'm going to do for this man, is I am going to give him a very good wash. And see what happens. So, I gave him a wash. I gave him a really, really good wash. I took my time . . . I didn't care about taking my time . . . I didn't care about spending so much time with him. And the man was crying. He couldn't talk clearly. And he was only crying, and going, like, "Ohh . . . thank you . . . that's the best wash ever . . ."'

Femi goes quiet, and looks at the floor.

'And I . . . And I thought, If that nurse had given him a wash. He wanted to be calm . . . calm. You know water will calm you down, he just needed some fresh help . . . so I helped him out. And they told me to put him back on the seat, and then he sat for one hour . . . and then I went, "Yes, let me get you back onto the bed." And then he was yelling, and I couldn't hear what he was saying, so I come close, and I try very hard to listen . . . and what he wanted to tell me was he was a builder, or something. But he couldn't say that, he couldn't make those words, only groaning, "I make things . . . I make things . . ." I asked him, "Sir, what did you do?" he couldn't answer, he only went . . . "I make things, I make things."'

There is a shiver in his voice now.

'I thought, Maybe he's a carpenter, maybe he's a builder, or something, or craftsman, I dunno . . . So I went and found this for him. I gave him some white papers, to make things, and he was trying to make it fold, with his hands . . . you could see he was trying to make something, but he couldn't . . . He started shouting sticks – "Sticks, sticks" – and I thought maybe we can do something with sticks. But I couldn't find any . . . and he fell asleep, he was tired after that. Later that day, his wife she came, his son, he came too and . . . he couldn't really talk. But he pointed at me, going, "He's a good boy, good boy." And then he was gone, sleeping . . . like he had not for a long time . . .'

Femi knows these people are not well. The nurses have told

him about dementia. That they have this sickness that makes them become like children again. 'Femi,' they say, 'it's almost their time to go, they are not really here, this is why you keep hearing these things.' He had been confused at first, when the old man breathing through gurgling tubes had limply grabbed him and gasped: 'When will you let me see my lawyer, he told me to wait here, I have the documents, and I have been here for hours.' The ward sisters shook their heads, 'Femi,' they said, 'there is no lawyer.'

He strokes his head.

'They are always waiting for the bus . . . They are always saying things like, "When is the bus coming? Why have I been waiting so long for the bus? Excuse me, mister . . . do you know what happened to the bus?" They are looking at the clocks and thinking about the bus. "Mister," they tell me, "the time is almost nine, I need to rush for the bus . . ."'

He is not looking at me.

'The ward sisters, they told me, "When they are calling to you like this . . . they are becoming like children with dementia. And you have to start feeding them on the coloured plates that we have. They are like children," she said, "and they will eat more off a coloured plate than a white plate, because it makes them happy."'

Femi is happy when he is on his feet. What he likes best is moving down the bays, between the buzzing life supports and the ventilators, peeking through the curtains, checking on the old people one by one. They want something different every time. Femi might be running for the bedpan, hoisting them up, switching on the TV or looking under the bed when their newspaper slipped off. Femi likes to keep moving, answering the family questions, and hates nothing more than spending the whole day in one bay.

The more he works in the concrete-paste tower block in Edmonton and the tightly windowed wards in Orpington, the more he notices the difference between the black people and the white people. The white community will come one by one, or in twos and threes, when they came to check on their old people. They seem to worry a lot about their sick people, especially the white daughters. The sons are a little colder. They will come, often only for ten minutes, and not ask many questions, only say things like, "Oh, Dad, I have some forms for you to fill in," or, "Oh, Dad, did you see the news today." The daughters, they stay longer and they ask many things: "Can you shave him please, thank you, we are so glad you washed him, thank you, and please, please toilet him."'

The black people they come less often. Femi is troubled by this. He has decided it must be because their work is less flexible. They must be doing things like him: picking, cleaning, guarding, check-outing. They must not be working in offices. But when the black people come, they come with the whole family. There are grandchildren and aunties and cousins and neighbours, all coming in, with balloons, with bouquets – all chrysanthemums, dahlias, daffodils – until there will be so many of them the ward sisters will tut and go, 'No, no, we need to make them wait outside, the other patients are at risk of feeling crowded now.'

The black people are different. There are the ones who take the news more like the whites and the ones, the established black guys, the ones from the West Indies mostly, and the ones from Africa, who take the news the patient is not for resuscitation exactly the same way they do back home.

'When this happens I don't want to stay around them . . . You know when people get the news in Africa, the emotions . . . it's different. It doesn't mean they love their people more or less, it's just different . . . Africans would be crying and throwing themselves, jumping up and down and throwing their body everywhere, and scream and shout . . . And white people they will only cry softly, and be in the corner, or go, "Oh Dad, oh Dad . . ." The whites cry in the waiting rooms, I find, always, in the corner, always, behind the doors . . . crying, and crying . . . all red and everything. But even if you offer them a cup of tea they will still accept it . . .'

He looks at the drawn curtains, scrunching both hands.

'The first time I saw this, I was like, "Huh . . . do they not love their old people?" But then I realized that with the white people, it's more inside, they are more secretive with their crying . . . I think they are ashamed of it very much. The same happens before they die, with the old people, when they make their mess, they are always very, very ashamed . . . They are going, "Oh sorry I made a mess . . . I am so sorry, please, excuse me, I made a mess . . ." and they won't listen when I tells them, "It's fine, this is normal for your age, this is why I am here . . ."

He sighs, softly.

'They never listen.'

The old black guys sometimes croak at Femi, 'What island ya from, mon.' There are a lot of frail, frail guys in the Edmonton tower block, who asked that question before he understood what they meant. There are times when they could say things to him, like, 'Where are you from in Africa, bruva, hope it's easier these days, bruva.' They seem weaker, a little more beaten, than the whites.

Femi notices everything. There was one evening when he was passing through the bays with the wheels clicking on the feeding trolley when he saw an old Jamaican guy. He was almost passed out, and his family was there around the bed, going, 'We love you, Grandpa.' They had brought him what looked like a medal, and put it on his plastic bedside. Femi moved closer, asking the daughters, 'Would you like some tea,' and saw the medal was a little bronze cross with the face of two kings on it.

'"What's that?" I asked him . . . He was almost gone. He was breathing very softly, and his eyes were closed. But he whispered, "That's an OBE . . . it was given to me by the Queen." I looked at him, this old Jamaican guy, looking so bad, and I thought, He has met the Queen? So I went to him, "Sir, why did she give it to you? What's the story?" And the old Jamaican, he shivered, and went, "Son, maybe I'll tell you another time . . ." and he was sleeping. The daughters they told me he had done such great works, but not what they were . . . and then I went to do some feeding further down the bay. But what got me, was that in this country . . . this old black guy can meet the Queen . . . I thought, OK, this guy did it . . . I can make it too.'

On that day Femi made the handover at 8 pm, pulled on his hoodie and never saw the old Jamaican again. It takes him around an hour to get home. Most evenings, he takes out his thick, scuffed accountancy textbooks out of his bag, and holds them in his lap as the train pulls out of Edmonton Green station towards Liverpool Street. There are some evenings where he can read a bit, highlighting whole sections, for the exams he wants to one day take, to qualify eventually for office work.

But mostly, he is too tired. The little things are still niggling him: the unhelpful colleagues, the man who had vomited earlier, the women who had snapped at him about something that was not his fault. Femi stares lazily, wanting to forget them: the train windows are dirty, but the sun licks everything. Golden light shines round the thousand living leaves of the trees. Giant gasworks are black against the falling sun. And behind them, the offices, the biggest offices in the whole world, all of glass, all of them filled with light.

Femi gets off at Brixton and tucks his accountancy books back in his bag. There are Nigerian and Ghanaian people everywhere here. There are the bin bags and the rotten leftovers from the street market on the avenue. There in coloured African wraps are round Nigerian and Ghanaian mothers hurrying home from church. They remind him of his mother in Lagos. There are the Jamaican boys and the mixed boys hanging around the station, with their hoods and their bikes, trying to chirps the light-skinned girls that every-body adores. And there are a few white people these days, in office clothes, that walk very fast, where they need to go.

Femi walks past the preachers lining up outside Iceland. There are Jehovah's Witnesses preaching in Yoruba and there is an old homeless man who called himself the Messiah of Black People who will shout and scream that the white people are stealing Brixton and want to evict and drive them from this space. The two hurtling rail-way bridges behind him charge and dramatize the high road.

Femi walks past the McDonald's, the one that never shuts in South London, where the gangbangers and the hustlers come for nuggets at 3 am, and where some guys have even been sprayed for their disrespect, when some grinders just lost it that night. Femi continues up Brixton Hill. These are the hot days of summer. The old men are smoking in string vests, and nobody can remember the cold. The street lamps are coming on, hours before they are needed, and glow into that strange hour, when the colours seem to seep away. He looks towards the estates.

There are lots of rumours there amongst the black people. There are a lot of older guys from the islands, who are telling that the white people want to take over Brixton. They are telling that the white people have remembered how close it is to the centre, and how beautiful are its backstreets, grand old houses with solid bay windows and stucco moulded doorframes. They say they want to evict them, then bulldoze their estates, and build some luxury flats or something for the office people. Those estates, the kids there call them hoods estates, where they only talk about legends like Five Star or Rico Tracy and other street sensations, who had gone wild, or gone down for their crimes. Femi is not interested in any of this.

He turns onto Lambert Road. Femi had arrived in London when mostly black people lived on this street. The first piece of advice the old timers gave him was this – never wear a hood, because London is scared of young black men. But this street is changing now. Every time he sees a plastic sign go up outside white people move in. They are young professionals. They wear suits. And Femi will see them sometimes and pang inside that he wants to be like them. But it hurts him to walk past these people at night.

'Sometimes when they see me coming . . . and it is the night time. They see a black man coming . . . I see the boys they put their arms on their girlfriends, to protect them in case this black man in a hood approaches them. And I see the girls who are crossing the road . . . to be away from this man, and I see the girls who are a little bit braver . . . how they are walking past me, and the way they walk is frightened of me . . . because I am a black person and this is the night in Brixton.'

This makes Femi feel sad. This makes Femi feel he might never wear a suit. And sometimes when he unlocks the door he thinks of the story of Daniel. This is his favourite Bible story. He feels as if it was written for him. This is what he told his girlfriend. She is Nigerian too with a huge lippy smile. But she was born here. Sometimes he lies in her lap and she strokes his hair and they talk about Brixton.

'I don't believe you can have equal rights between black people and white people here . . . I just don't believe it's possible. Because, at the end of the day . . . this will always be their country. But she doesn't. She gets angry and goes, "No, we have equal rights, you have to believe that we can have equal rights."'

And then, sometimes, he falls asleep.

Femi lives with Grace in a house that looks like it had once belonged to a very rich man, or maybe even been a mansion, but was boarded up into damp, cramped little rooms. They are both earning less and less money. The rent is rising, and right along Lambert Road there are teams of Poles and Romanians throwing up scaffolding and smashing these boarding houses back into imposing family homes. They both wonder if they should move out like lots of other Africans. They are many; many have gone east to Woolwich, and Thamesmead is becoming more and more popular. They say the white people are leaving from there and the rents are low, even if in outer London it does take time to get anywhere, hours really.

Grace slams the door and moves quickly to the Underground. The light has turned a nasty cream colour under creeping fishbone clouds. She turns onto the main road as the headlamps are coming. Backlights begin to glow red against pale blue. At the corner she ignores the stooped twitching drunkard, murmuring savagely, and trudges on.

Grace is heading to the old red-brick hospital in Hammersmith. She is a hard, direct, even brutal woman, with very thin lips. She is around fifty, she thinks, though the people in her village don't really know. Like Femi she is also an agency carer, but she works nights. On Lambert Road, the fuses kept blowing, and in their two rooms the lights will often dangle dead. They are often too exhausted, when the bulbs hiss and clack, to rush out and replace them.

'How long will this take?'

That is her normal day. But today Grace is talking to me. Before leaving for work. She sits on the kitchen chair under the dangling dead bulbs and the gathering gloom and glares at me like a fool. She stares into me like I will never understand, and if it amuses me to ask her a few questions about working with bodies, I am welcome to it, as long as it doesn't take too long. And she crosses her arms.

'So what do you want to know?'

Her arms show she has dabbled in skin-lightening creams. Running over her arms, and onto her face, are tones that are blotchy, and ravaged, over her two tribal markings, like teardrops, cutting down over the top of her cheeks. She is wearing a traditional brown-and-yellow-patterned robe, and a pale-blue headscarf. As the house becomes gloomier, the pungency from her boiling soup in the kitchen creeps between us and the sofa, and the man she calls her boyfriend walks in unshaven in a stained wife-beater, unshaven, waiting to be fed, and looks at her plaintively.

'Wait . . . I'm giving this man my life story.'

She talks firmly, one sentence after another, like it was all those years ago, when she was a market trader in Lagos. Her stall had been piled high. She was screeching at the top of her voice to buy her gift cards, her pots, her plastics and her toasters. She had dreamed of setting up a business in London. But that was a long time ago now. She has been a carer now for almost ten years.

'There is no easy surviving . . . in this city.'

Grace never knows how much to budget – could she afford yet more bulbs, a new phone card or another sack of pounded yam – because agency work is permanently temporary. Grace will only know at the end of every week if they want her again. That is why she never knows how much money she has, or where she really stands.

She hates nights, and there is nothing that angers her more about the nights than the tramps. They sneak into the hospitals every night. They come in, all stinking, and sweating, and wail they have some sickness until the doctors at A&E admit them into her wards. They sob they are hungry, and demand feeding, before passing out, but the very next morning they pick up their bag and say they are going.

Grace is a strong woman but there are times when she will have to call the Ghanaians in security. There are tramps who they know instantly are not sick, and they will turn them away, but when they are desperate, the tramps will sneak back in through A&E and the

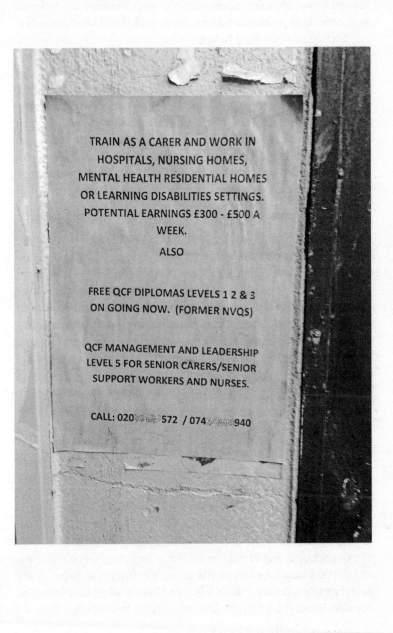

emergency exits and wrap themselves up in the empty beds on the wards. Carers will find them, men in women's wards, sleepers without any documents, taking up space in the cardiac, and have to try and chase them away.

The carers, they see something like this every week or so. They know there are people trying to sneak into the wards at all times, because nobody really knows who is who, and who will be there tomorrow in a hospital. The permanent nurses are stand-offish to the carers, because tomorrow they could be in Edmonton, not Hammersmith, so they are never really part of the team. They are only filling holes. And the carers, they sneer at the cleaners, slopping their mops and pushing foam up and down the linoleum. The regulations say they are not allowed to come near the patients at any time.

Grace gossips with the permanent staff only if they are Nigerian, and she finds across London, but especially in Tooting, they are bickering about the cleaners. They have been bringing Eastern Europeans in. They have been replacing the black people in charge of cleaning with Poles and Romanians, and they are bringing in their own. The nurses will come in and notice whole teams of Sierra Leoneans have vanished from the building. They have been replaced by white people, from Poland, Lithuania or other places they have never heard of.

They are taking over, these Eastern Europeans, the nurses sigh. They are coming in, more and more, and taking over all the cooking and cleaning jobs that the Africans and West Indians have been doing for years in these hospitals. The carers look at them jealously. They know they are more acceptable, because of the similarity of the race, and they are invited to come here with no visa at all. They see them becoming very quickly happy in this country, and settling in, feeling themselves more at home here, than even the Africans who had been here for a very long time.

The handover means it is time to be assigned new patients. And in the early evening it means talking a little to them during the feeding. Because they like to talk about who they had been. There are lots of things about these patients Grace does not understand. She sees lots of stupidity she cannot comprehend. There are many, so many, who come in alone, who whimper they were lonely and cold, and then tell her, when she asks when their visitors are coming, that they have no children.

'They are calling me, "*Nurse, nurse* . . . nobody came to greet me." And I say to them, "Nobody came to greet you? Oh, where are your children?" And then they say, "I don't have children." And I always go to them, "What have you been doing all your life?" I always ask this question. Some they say, "Because I don't want to have children . . . *I don't want to touch the stress* . . ." Some, they may tell you, "I got married . . . but there was no children." Some they say, "It's because I am having pets." And I go to them, "You are having pets? But your pet is not here now . . ." Sometimes they cry, some do cry, the ones who was looking for children . . . through their lifetime, they cry. They tell me, "*They wasn't coming* . . ." and I hold their hand, like this.' She mimes the pant in their voice.

Grace feels it is different in hospitals at night. They are mostly sleeping, but you can hear every sound, every buzz, every bleep. Grace will come to them with the bedpan, when they shout, 'Nurse,' and then watch them tumble back into sleep. But it is never silent. The machines whir and ching and bounce with blinking red dots, there are bluish glows and screens flicker with green electric lines. That is when Grace will hear the moaning. At night there are many, many dementias.

'The ninety-years-old womens, they are calling the names of the husbands . . . They are calling him . . . asking you when he is coming. "Why is he late?" And you tell them, "He is on his way." You see on their fingers, the white people, for them the wedding band is a very, very important thing . . . The ninety-years-old womens, they always have it on them . . . and they never let it go.'

She mouths their cries.

'They are calling . . . the husbands, even some they call their mummy. They say, "*Mum . . . Mum . . . Mum . . . Mum . . .*" They are ninety-years-old women. They are calling you nurse . . . "I want my mummy, where is my mummy . . ." *Mum . . . Mum* . . . and you tell them, "Your mummy's coming," just to keep them quiet.'

There are some wards where they keep teddy bears, for when they are really sobbing, but really all the carers know there is no cure for dementia. They are becoming like children, the older carers had told her when she first started, so you need to smile and talk to them like a baby. The ones without children are the ones she really pities, there are so many people on the ward that need her, thirty people for washing, feeding and toileting, hoisting and even shaving, that when she hears they are groaning, becoming agitated and moaning, she only has a few minutes for them.

'We have to pet them, to calm them . . . like they are cats. We put our hands here . . . and we press down, helping the patient to breathe . . . This calms them. And they are making a little less sounds then.'

Grace and Femi squabble about dementia. He has taken his training. They have told him dementia is a natural deterioration and can occur in anyone. Grace has never seen dementia in Africa, and she and the other nurses think they know why there are so many white people here, without anything left of their minds.

'When I see them, I think of Africa, where with the old people, people always come to them, no matter how old they are, and come and greet them in the morning. And talk to them and ask them, "Do you want us to do anything for you," so in the afternoon, they are looking, out the window, and people come and see them, if they have not seen them for a long time, "Hello, auntie, is there anything I can do for you," even if she can't go out, we will open the window, and the whole street will be greeting them . . . They have something . . . they share, their opinion, their spirit.'

Her knees tightly together, she peers into me.

'The English . . . they are not like that. The English are much crueller than us . . . They are much less advanced. Here they don't want to talk . . . They abandon them. And even when they have children, they lock them in the bedroom, and you are sitting watching TV . . . or send them to school away. And after school, they just throw out their children . . . and the children will go their own way, and the mother will go her own way. It's not like Africa, we love children . . .'

She will not let my eyes go.

'It's their culture . . . where they abandon their old people. They send them to places for them to die . . . The old people's homes, they call them, where they play them some music, to make them not realize they have been abandoned. And there is such sadness, such sadness, because they know . . . they know this where they are . . . and that is it. There is nobody that comes . . . There is maybe only once a year, some grandchildren that come for them . . . and you can see on their face . . . they become like wrinkled, because they are frightened of old people . . . and they leave after ten minutes sometimes. That's the problem, they are lonely . . . and because they are lonely and not talking, nobody is helping their mind to stay here . . . they are getting the dementia . . . and us, we are watching them and washing them and pitying them.

'Most of them die in pain. There are more that go on the night shift. The ward sisters will come to the carers and say, "This one is 'not for resus'," and they know the doctor is not going to be called any more, to breathe the air back into them. The carers are always so busy. They are rushing. There is a man who needs a toileting. There is a woman who needs a blood-pressure check. The bedpan is dirty and somebody needs to clean it. They are not there to hold their hands.

'There is nothing, there is nothing for us to do . . . We are for cleaning, washing, wrapping. We are hearing them, but are looking after thirty patients, we don't have time for that. They are not so much shouting like that . . . They are shaking, they are shaking like this . . . with their shoulders. And we are thinking maybe they need something . . . and it is only when they stop that we realize, that man he was fighting death . . . They always fight, and shake . . . and make a breath like this . . . *haaaah* . . . it's always very sharp . . . at that moment when the soul leaves the body . . .'

Her voice has become softer, more definite, and drawn.

'There are the quiet ones . . . they are not making sound, just looking, but at that moment . . . when it is trying to get out, they are shaking, moving . . . shaking like something electric, and breathe . . . *ahuh* . . . when it gets out. Then there are those that are struggling, and shouting . . . and crying out . . . You can't see it get out, it's a spirit . . . It goes out, and you don't know when it goes out . . . The only thing you see is that they move, they move, they move, and stop . . . and once it stops, the soul is gone.'

The carers know what to do next. The next of kin have been notified and they move away from the bedside. They draw the curtains round the bays, and then the curtains of all the other bays, so when they take the patient away they do not see it. The other old people are getting nervous, so the carers they come up, and they go to them, 'Would you like a cup of tea,' or, 'Would you like some water as the doctors and everyone is rushing coming in,' and sometimes, there are people crying.

This can take some time, but when nobody comes, it can all happen quite quickly. The carers and the nurse then take the body to be washed. They cross its hands and then they wrap it in cloth. The whole process takes around thirty minutes,

'So, so many have died . . . The first day that I saw somebody that died . . . I was shivering. The reason was that I was the one that saw him go . . . I went to his side, to his observations, and immediately it's coming, it's coming, its bleeping and whirr . . . the rota is at zero . . . and the man he is breathing . . . *haaaa*.

'Because of that I was shivering . . . and they ask me to wash him, but I can't . . . That was my first time . . . to wash the dead body . . . I have done this many times now . . . With the nurse I wash every month, maybe two, maybe three patient . . . now for ten years . . . And we wrap them, cross the arms, round the neck . . . in a white cloth.'

She is speaking much slower now.

'Most of them they die in pain . . . When it's better for him or her to die, when the pain is too much, too much . . . they have faces of pain . . . It's frozen, it's open, like this . . . Most they die fighting, the seventy years, the eighty years, the ones who die of disease . . . they have been fighting, fighting . . . The bodies, the ones who die in agony, they are warm, from the fighting, they have been fighting with the dead, struggling . . . and they are warm . . . most of them are not cold, immediately. Unless it's the very old one, the ninety years one, when we wrap them they look fresh . . . and happy, and cool, like . . . they are sleeping . . . '

Then the nurse goes, and the carers wait for the boys from the mortuary to come and take them away on their rattling trolley.

LEA BRIDGE ROAD

The imam pushes towards me a plate of sweets.

There are angels hovering over Leyton. There are thousands of angels trembling over the bus stops and the estates. You can't see them. But they are there. Sometimes you might hear a voice calling your name, then turn round to nothing. But they are calling you. When a man is dying the angels come. His two angels Munkar and Nakir have come to the ward and the hospital sheets. They whisper and with their hands begin to rip the soul out of his body.

'This is why a body trembles when it dies.'

I am walking up the Lea Bridge Road that runs from the ring road that crosses London's other river out east into Pakistani London. The traffic heaves. But the River Lea drifts sluggishly to the Thames through the remains of reeds and marshes. There are dog walkers who see crocodiles here. But the authorities have found nothing.

I keep walking. Tattered urban seagulls peck bins and caw. The fakely Roman stucco front of the old Regal Cinema is now an African church. The old movie hoarding stares blank and empty.

The mosque frowns into a dowdy terrace over the road. It's a huge red-brick box with stubby minarets dangling with unlit fairy plastic coils; the walls open into pointing window arches filled with rusting green fittings. Bus after bus clatters past, unloading a few old beards for the lunchtime prayers, or boys in tracksuits who shoot into the gym next door that advertises in Urdu with Arabic letters.

I meet Hajji in the entry corridor. We stand on the shine of the blue Formica between walls tiled in curling and pointing green

Islamic patterns, and walk past the green felted announcement boards covered with laminated charity appeals for Syria and the plastic boxes filled with leaflets asking 'Thinking Of Returning To Your Country?'. Hajji is taking me into the washing room. This is the mortuary where Muslims come for their last moments close to another human before they are buried.

Hajji washes sometimes one, sometimes three bodies a week. His lips are thin and pinched. His white beard curls and flares at the sides of his head. He has a squat, rounded nose and small brown eyes, which stay very still, and never stop peering. Hajji is bald. But he doesn't mind because his neck is craned with pride, under a crisp, finely patterned boxy white skullcap. This is the mark of a Mecca pilgrim – which is why he is called Hajji.

'This is how I wash the bodies.

'First we go to the hospital. To see that everything is done nicely. To see they are wrapped nicely. And then we take them here . . . Into this room for their washing time.'

The washing slab is raised enamel. It is grooved slightly with runs leading into a plughole. For a moment too long he stares at it.

'Here they are coming.'

Hajji points at the gently curved block of wood to rest the neck, and then at the cardboard boxes reading DIGNITY PRODUCTS. The naked light glints white flashes off the blue and white mosaic bathroom tiles covering the room nobody can bear to be in. He shows me the shower nozzle and his bright plastic buckets. Then Hajji taps his hands on a stack of three bronze-handled wooden coffins and a metal hospital trolley. There he begins to tell me.

'The bodies that I wash . . . all look different. The youngsters, they look different. The old men, they look different. Sometimes when they've had heart attacks they come . . . again very different. But you see mostly the bodies that come to me, they are cancer bodies . . . and when someone dies from a cancer . . . You can't generalize. They look very different . . . sometimes they look very emotional . . . Or sometimes they look very peaceful.'

Through the thin partition the imam is singing.

'When the bodies . . . are emotional . . . they look like they have

shaken. And I can see when I touch them, this body has been shaken . . . The heart-attack bodies, they look very stiff and emotional. But the old men who die from a brain tumour, they look different again . . . Those bodies . . . some are soft . . . This is all about the emotions, really.'

Hajji takes me through a gloomy, carpeted room. There are around twelve balding men sitting cross-legged in a circle in thick black parkas, with fur trims, or long grey woollen coats. There are some who sit with their legs tucked under their knees. They are arguing about politics: one phrase in Punjabi, another in English. Hajji ignores them.

'The bodies, they all come to me in different colour. Some people they come to me with a very green type . . . some bodies, they are a red type, and some body they are black . . . yes, the feet come completely black . . . especially the hands and feet . . . And then there is the light blue type . . . when the bleeding stopped.

'Everybody dies differently.'

Hajji guides me into the office.

Here we sit on low felt-covered plastic chairs in a cramped and cluttered space where the walls are shelved with a library of brightly covered books embossed in gold and silver. There is a crumpled sugar packet on the table in front of us. Hajji is sitting there, with his arms folded, but as he talks, softly, quietly, I sense he can never really leave the enamel slab behind.

'You see . . . The greatest difference . . . it's in their eyes . . . Sometimes they are a light yellow colour, just like an egg . . . It's a light colour, there . . . But most of the time, when we have a youngster, their eyes are different colours . . . red colours from the pain . . . because they don't want to die.'

The group outside is praying now.

'But mostly I wash the old men. They are very peaceful. They know they have to go now. Peaceful bodies are no problem . . . Peaceful bodies are lying there very gently . . . But some bodies they are very tight. You can't move them. You have to move whole bodies to move only their hand or leg . . . But mostly the bodies move gently

. . . You can move all the parts, everything, because there is no problem. The soul has already left this body . . .

'You see old men fifty, sixty, seventy, eighty year, hundred year, they are ready . . . The old man has a body . . . all in white colours and the normal colours of his skin . . . Only his feet and the head have gone a grey colour . . . But young man, a man before fifty, forty, before thirty especially, they look so different . . . They are very stiff. The body of a man who does not want to die is very stiff . . . it's not a soft body . . . because they suffer much . . . and it freezes them, the pain as they die . . . and their skin is all grey . . .'

The bodies are laid on the table when Hajji comes in for the washing. There is always singing. There, again and again, as his hand runs gently over with the soapy water, he will sing to the bodies in Arabic, the words of purity, that there is only one god, and Mohammed is his messenger. The words will tumble out of him, rising and lilting in verse, as he switches on the shower nozzle.

This will gently wet them and calm them for their journey. And then, always slowly, always calmly, Hajji will begin to sing the verses of the Koran, the song that there will forever be a sign of him on this lifeless earth, in the grains, and the gardens of date palms, that he has given us with his long breath.

The things that Hajji hates most are the tubes. There are sometimes thirty or forty cannula stuck into the body. They are bedded under the skin and when he unzips the bags he finds them puckered and punctured by needlepoints. But this is not the worst. Those are the pipes. The bodies who stare at him contorted and yellow with the corrugated pipe sticking out of their mouth: the one that they have run right through the gut.

'It's not easy to take it out . . . When you pull too hard it takes out the whole body . . . it comes out . . . because it's not an easy job. This pipe is very long. It's a two-foot pipe inside. So when I see like this, I tell parents out of the room . . . I ask them not to sing there with me. And I pull out the syringes, maybe thirty, forty, and then I tell the parents, "Please don't stay with me," because I don't want to have parents watching the pipe come out.'

The bodies come in many different ways from the hospital.

There was the nine-year-old boy who had been burnt alive. His face was knocked out from the fumes and colours of grey. He was burnt from the chest to the groin and the hospital had wrapped him in tightly fitting plastic bandages the doctors ordered him not to take off.

There were the bodies who had died from the terrible disease. These already came in the coffins and they were sealed in a tightly wrapped plastic. The mosque was forbidden to open these. That was when Hajji would do the dry wash. He would take the body into the washing room and then make the movement of washing with his hands over and around the plastic sealing as he sang. And he would finish with a tiny drop of water on the coffin top.

Hajji has seen death in all its forms: peaceful and contented, violent and struggling, but the ones that always shake him up the most are the Tube suicides. These are the worst bodies. The bodies that the doctors tell the mosque not to unzip. But they do. Nobody knows the pain inside. Nothing but a wash can calm the body that was smashed by the rails for the journey.

Hajji faints each time he unzips the bag. Not one time has this not happened. And then the mosque shouts, 'He's on the floor!' and a boy runs to get him a glass of water. The feet and the hands are gone, severed off. There are huge gashes of ripped flesh into the broken torso. The worst bodies are the ones where half the skull is missing. He begs the family not to come in. He blocks the doors pleading, 'Do not see this body.' But they always force him.

'Believe me . . . When you hear the sisters scream you never forget it.'

There is no shriek like it in this world. There is no way for Hajji to even describe it. But he comes for the washing. His hands are gentle. His songs close to a lullaby as he puts these bodies of young men on their sides and sings and binds them. There are some imams who say you must not wash a man who has thrown himself but he does not believe this. There is no way of knowing what made these boys jump with their pain.

'Sometimes the body talks to me as well. That moment when I see the person's eyes. Then I feel the situation. How bad it was . . .

It is like looking into the negative of a photo printed on the eyes . . . I see pain . . . It is telling me in this impression what he suffered . . . So that suffering I feel it all the time . . . This is what I feel in the washing room, when I sing to them, and I talk to them in Arabic.'

He rubs his right hand over his heart.

'A lot of people sometimes say when they come from Pakistan . . . The wife they bring her for him, and the wife she don't like him and they are fighting each other . . . Sometimes they don't like the parents. And the bodies they are telling me they were everyday going, "I have to go back . . ."'

'The bodies they are telling me they were fighting . . . and that he was mentally upset always, and his head put in the wall, that he was living saying, "I have done a mistake . . . I have to go back." They are saying . . . sometimes their work problem, sometimes their finance problem, sometimes he make some little mistake . . . and the police catch him. A lot of different things they tell me in the washing time.'

The prayers are over and we hear men leaving.

'So when the washing time is over . . . I ask some question to parents. "Who was this person?" "How was his behaviour to his wife, and his friends?" So afterwards when we talk outside, that moment which I saw in the washing time . . . I share with the parents. I tell them about this person . . . how he looked . . . And then they tell me who he was.

'And then I match that moment to what I saw in the washing time . . . And in 90 per cent of the time, I am completely satisfied what this person is telling me in the washing time was true . . .'

His pitch has fallen to a mumble.

'Whenever I am washing I am thinking . . . whatever I am doing . . . Remember yourself, one day you will be in this situation, so I never try and rush their wash, never . . . and if anybody wants their wash slowly, or calmly, I have to do it . . . Because I don't know when my time comes. Always I'm thinking, I'll be this one . . . I'll be here.'

Hajji talks in a rippling thick Punjabi accent. He sits with his back flat on the back of the chair and gazes not at me but past, into the glinting embossed gold and silver of the hundreds of shelved prayer books. He has moved his hands, and rests them on his knees. The old computers hum and buzz softly.

'One day, one body came . . . And when I touched the body, I told the children standing there, "The uncle is talking to me now." "What's he saying to you?" they asked. I said, "The uncle is saying . . . You give me wash . . . I'm happy you give me wash."

'I told them that. I don't know anything else about him. But when I saw the body I told the parents. And they went, "Do you know why? You are right. You know why?" One day before, he asked, "If I am dead . . . when I'm dead . . . I want Hajji to wash me."'

This story breaks into smile.

'But those are the old men. The young men when I see the body and I see the eyes . . . All of their face . . . and all body is stiff . . . I feel they died in huge pain . . . And they want to tell me, "Please give me a wash very gently . . . Because I already suffered a lot of pain . . ."'

Hajji feels happy after he has washed many old-beards. He comes out and there are his grandchildren. And his children and their wives. And they are smiling knowing he is ready to go. And they gather round in a circle and pray for him. These men are happy to go. But not all of them. There are the ones whose faces freeze like a negative into his eyes.

'One day I was brought a body from Bedford. And somebody murder him . . . By the knife . . . Seventeen knife stabs . . . seventeen time they hit him with the knife. The knife slashed here . . . three time here . . . three time there . . . into the stomach . . . and when he gripped that knife to force it off him . . . he cut all his hands . . .

'The body they brought me was a middle-age man . . . and after that somebody bury him one month . . . And after one month the police caught them and took the body out . . . When they brought me the body, his eyes were like this . . . open . . . and his mouth was open . . . And he look like he saw that person who killed him . . . and is shocked . . . his body looked very shocked . . .

'It was green, he was all green . . . And if he was alive . . . he would scream too much . . . His hands were like this . . . sticking out . . . He looked like he still shaking . . . Like he was shaking, "Allah, give me one more chance . . ." His body was not relaxed. His eyes look like he want to say something to me. "Please be very gentle."'

Hajji suddenly begins to move. His eyes look like he is no longer there in the office sitting in front of this huge laminated table covered in papers and brightly coloured folders. He holds his hands together and blinks. His voice is cracking.

'When this type of experience come . . . it is very difficult for me to sleep . . . sometime . . . for days . . . because when I sleep the body come in my eyes . . . and my dream and wake up . . . And they speak to me . . . Sometime they say, "I have two or three dreams . . ." One a young lad . . . I buried . . .'

Hajji stops. This is a face he remembers. A face he repressed. But his voice breaks into a strangulated sob.

'And he told me, "Uncle . . . somebody turns to me . . . very bad . . . I suffer my life very badly . . . And after that they kill me . . ." I went, "So why they kill you?" "Because they take my all property . . . They want to take all my properties . . . They want my inheritance as I am an only child . . . And they are very powerful people . . . So they already killed me . . . So I'm very happy I'm here . . . I'm very good . . . But I feel very much pain . . . at this moment . . ."'

Hajji slouches forward and adjusts his skullcap. The longer we talk the more I realize how he has been aged by the washing. His eyes are pinched without sleep and sunken into wrinkled brown skin. His exhaustion is eating into him.

Hajji has told the mosque several times, 'I want to stop. I can't keep going on like this. I'm a minicab driver. I'm sixty-four. I'm not a professional. I'm only a volunteer.' But the mosque says, 'You must. You are the only person that the families trust to wash with love.'

Hajji is tired. London has gone by so quickly. He remembers wandering the alleys in Whitechapel in 1976 for the first time, when the winter mist rose from the river, and the mornings smelt of tanning leather and the Jews, he had never seen them before, brushed past him holding their books, with those long black coats, in kaftans and fedoras. Those were the cold mornings, which pinched the skin, when the curl of Brick Lane echoed with the click of their heels, but the Jews began to disappear, and by the 1980s their strange alphabet that looked like flaming letters was gone from the brick fronts, all reds and browns, and some stained black by a hundred years of soot.

Hajji beat leather morning and night. He beat leather as the Jews sold the leaking domed building they prayed in to the Muslims, telling them that this had once been a church, this cavernous space, the light coming in, spinning around and leaving, so slowly, with the evening, the light rising and falling with the pale London sun down from those huge rounded windows of thin brittle glass.

Hajji beat leather until the last white-bearded Jew had packed up his string-and-box shop, until all the crooked brick parades bustled with the traders flogging their belts and fabric rolls and pirated cassettes in Bengali and Urdu, as over them plastic boxes with neon lights inside grew like toadstools, when he didn't notice, saying, 'This is a balti house,' and, 'This is an Indian restaurant,' until the whole of Brick Lane glowed with red and yellow at night.

This is all finished.

The factories had closed. The tannery had folded. The hawkers were shuttering up. And like the Jews, wherever they went he did not know, the Muslims were becoming the strangers, on the tight curve of Brick Lane, between the crowds of drainpipe jeans and bright colours and the whirr of the coffee machines and the thump and tinkle of the beats from the clubs, and his friends from the tannery, they no longer hung around smoking and laughing under the train bridge, fighting sometimes about the coups in Pakistan, but pulled out to Leyton, and Forest Gate to drive minicabs, one by one.

Hajji sits in the office. The door hangs open and outside the old men who no longer work sit on the fraying brown carpet covered in fuzz and dust from wall to wall breaking off and talking. Hajji feels bitter amusement towards them. The men who think they are holy here five times a day.

They are becoming frightened of him because of the washing time. There are men, the old ones, the ones who are almost a hundred, who become confused, and forget it is Ramadan or *Jumu'ah* prayers, and they have come to look at him, with colour-drained old eyes, trembling with the fear of a sacrificial goat after Eid, as he smiles to them, like he is really the Angel, who was sent for their end all along.

'There was one prophet. He went to a man after he died, "Somebody kill him . . ." And he went and saw his eyes . . . and when he saw the eyes he saw the person who kill him. The prophet he looked into the eyes, and he say, "I see this person and he is the killer . . . Because the eyes they are telling me a picture."

'I have seen many eyes . . .

'Three days ago I saw a twenty-eight-year-old man . . . Brain tumour . . . He was six foot two inch . . . Believe me I couldn't forget him . . . His eyes were open like this . . .

'Y'know, he was a young man like you . . . And you don't want to die. We have families. You have mother and father and sisters and brothers. You are doing very nicely . . . When a young man is dying . . . a lot . . . a lot of questions come . . . Why it happens only for me? Why is nobody else? I'm twenty-eight years old, why not someone else . . . So soon? His body was tight . . . Because in that last moment . . . you are filled up here . . . with all the questions and all that suffering and pain . . . it's here . . . here.'

Hajji stops speaking. His five fingers touch his head.

'So when you die, everything it hits here . . . So everything is left here . . . They are asking, "Why? Why me?" And in the washing time the man who sings to them sees it and he can be the judge . . .'

Hajji cups his forehead. The bodies. He has seen so many bodies. But he still goes cold like a damp old house around them. Hajji moves both hands to cradle his creased forehead.

'His eyes were asking . . .'

Hajji gulps.

'His eyes were asking . . . why he had a brain tumour . . . His eyes were totally white . . . They were speaking . . . They were so open even I couldn't even close them . . . And his eyes . . . they were telling me . . . They were telling me . . . "I don't want to die."'

The mosque finds every funeral different.

The most challenging are the Somali funerals. That is when the health and safety regulations go out the window. They come in their hundreds and they pray in every corner of every space. They are praying in the office and praying in the toilets and praying in the fire escapes and there is no way you can stop them as they are family united in their prayers. The Pakistani funerals, they are much smaller, but the mosque finds them much more emotional. The mothers and the sisters they cry and often so do the men. The Nigerians, they are the loudest. They will come in and begin ripping their clothes and jumping up and down letting the emotions grip and control them. But the smallest are the Arab funerals. This surprises them. There were Moroccans with only three or four relatives that had been buried here.

Hajji gathers his stuff to go. The door clicks behind him, gone.

I head to Hainault via Newbury Park. The Central Line shakes and its metal squeals on the lines with the friction of a furnace as those tight and narrow terraces that swallow up East London give way to golf courses and huddled suburban houses surrounded by shedding hawthorn, acacia trees and long lines of firs.

I trudge along the New North Road to the cemetery. This is the last walk in Muslim London. There is a light rain. The sky is turning from a slate grey into a bluish haze. The streets are strewn with leaves: whole, cracked, piled, alone, all orange, yellow or a light green.

I trudge past the bungalows with their garden gnomes and porcelain owls blinking from the windows and then the messy upturned earth of the allotments until I meet the playing fields. I trudge through the muddy grass till I reach the cemetery gates. This is the Garden of Peace.

Behind birch and elm trees the Muslims of London are buried. Their graves are neatly dug from upturned earth; a neatly placed plaque marks the name of the buried. There is a saying that flowers

are not meant to be brought into the cemetery because it tempts and torments the dead with their colours. But their English friends keep bringing them: lilies, posies and wreaths.

Two boys brush past me. They are my age. One is Asian in a red baseball cap, a grey tracksuit and a shiny black puffa jacket. The other is black and in blue jeans and pale blue padded light ski jacket with the hood up. The grave is under a baby elm tree. There, they pull out the scratched leather hide covers of the book, sling their arms brotherly over their shoulders and begin to sing. I turn to leave. The sky is a powder blue. Over the playing fields are the cones and cubes of distant towers.

Blinking bright dots of light.

NOTES

Victoria Coach Station

3 **at least 55 per cent of people are not ethnically white British**
http://www.ons.gov.uk/ons/dcp29904_291554.pdf

3 **Every week two thousand migrants unload at Victoria Coach Station**
https://books.google.co.uk/books?id=vcFoiYfXNxYC&pg
=PA157&lpg=PA157&dq=2000+migrants+a+week+victoria+
coach&source=bl&ots=O91Cs2etGV&sig=Sf2k9clAHkB-
g6WsbbSddrz9ThoQ&hl=en&sa=X&ei=rnyWVa2eFMiBU
6GClMAI&ved=0CCIQ6AEwAA#v=onepage&q=2000%20
migrants%20a%20week%20victoria%20coach&f=false

Peckham High Street

36 **There are more people in London with little to no English than live in Newcastle**
http://www.neighbourhood.statistics.gov.uk/dissemination/
LeadTableView.do?a=3&b=6275062&c=london&d=13&e=14&g
=6317304&i=1001x1003x1004&m=0&r=1&s=1435953045803
&enc=1&dsFamilyId=2500&nsjs=true&nsck=false&nssvg=
false&nswid=1366

40 **There is a whole African city in London. With more than 550,000 people this would be a city the size of Sheffield. And it has grown almost 45 per cent since 2001**
http://www.bbc.co.uk/news/uk-england-london-20680565

41 **Minorities make up 55 per cent of London. But they are only 10 per cent of its police**
http://www.theguardian.com/news/datablog/2013/jan/28/
police-force-ethnic-minority-officers

Neasden Lane

54 **The white British population is now around 18 per cent. South Asians make up 33 per cent. The black population, roughly 19 per cent. Between 2001 and 2011 the white British population of Brent tumbled: losing almost 30 per cent**
https://intelligence.brent.gov.uk/BrentDocuments/Brent%
202011%20Census%20Profile.pdf

Elephant and Castle

85 **Less than 2 per cent of the new flats will be rented out by the state to the poor**
http://35percent.org/
http://www.theguardian.com/cities/2014/sep/17/truth-
property-developers-builders-exploit-planning-cities

86 **The quarter of London that rents from the state**
https://www.london.gov.uk/sites/default/files/Housing%
20in%20London%202014%20-%20Final_1.pdf

91 **This is where 70 per cent of Britain's illegal immigrants are hiding. This is a city of more than 600,000 people, making it larger than Glasgow or Edinburgh. There are more illegals in London than Indians. Almost 40 per cent of them arrived after 2001. Roughly a third are from Africa**
http://www.london.gov.uk/mayor/economic_unit/docs/
irregular-migrants-report.pdf

94 **More than 95 per cent of London's thousands of underground cleaners are immigrants, and more than three-quarters of them come from black Africa**
http://www.migrationobservatory.ox.ac.uk/policy-primers/
migrants-london-policy-challenges

http://www.geog.qmul.ac.uk/globalcities/reports/docs/
workingpaper4.pdf

99 **There were 643 suicide attempts on the underground between
2000 and 2010**
http://www.standard.co.uk/news/tube-suicides-increase-by-
74-per-cent-as-recession-worries-hit-home-6366152.html.
The figure includes successful attempts.

Hammersmith and City

107 **a 40 per cent child-poverty rate**
http://www.londonspovertyprofile.org.uk/indicators/topics/
income-poverty/child-poverty-by-borough/

108 **The White British are leaving: their share of residents fell
35 per cent between 2001 and 2011**
http://www.lbhf.gov.uk/Images/Wormholt%20and%20
White%20City_2011%20Census_tcm21-73251.pdf

White City

127 **a gun is fired in London on average every six hours**
www.standard.co.uk/news/crime/shocking-figures-reveal-extent-
of-londons-gun-crime-9779349.html

128 **Scientists had tested the water, and found this city had the
highest concentration in Europe, higher than Berlin, higher
even than Amsterdam**
http://www.newsweek.com/london-does-most-cocaine-
europe-sewers-say-339393

North Circular

151 **As much as 40 per cent of new immigrants in this city have
been accommodated with an increase of persons per room**
http://quarterly.demos.co.uk/article/issue-4/london-all-that-
glisters/

160 **More than 60 per cent of Polish migrants working in London today now come from troubled small towns and the countryside**
http://www.esrc.ac.uk/my-esrc/grants/RES-000-22-1294/read

175 **London is home to more than 150,000 Polish migrants, probably**
http://www.migrationobservatory.ox.ac.uk/sites/files/migobs/
Briefing%20-%20London%20census%20profile_0.pdf

179 **The majority of tramps in the city are Polish and Lithuanian. There are at least five thousand of them. Over three thousand have been bussed home over the past five years**
Interview with Barka UK, November 2013.

179 **There were Polish tramps in north London who were forced to work unloading trucks for Turkish shopkeepers**
http://www.theguardian.com/uk/2010/aug/12/homeless-poles-
rough-sleepers

179 **Others were found roasting rats in back alleys in Tottenham and Haringey**
http://www.theguardian.com/uk/2010/aug/12/homeless-poles-
rough-sleepers

182 **There are roughly a hundred thousand people like Jurek in this city**
https://www.london.gov.uk/sites/default/files/llmp.pdf
http://www.theguardian.com/money/2010/apr/10/migrant-
construction-workers

183 **More than 30 per cent of the children here grow up in poverty**
http://www.londonspovertyprofile.org.uk/indicators/topics/
income-poverty/child-poverty-by-borough/

183 **Beckton is the ninth most deprived**
https://www.london.gov.uk/sites/default/files/Update% 2001-
2012%2001-2012%20Ward%20Level%20Summary%20
Measures%20of%20ID%202010.pdf

184 **less than 25 per cent white British**
http://ukdataexplorer.com/census/london/#KS201EW0020

184 **Eastern Europeans make up as much as 20 per cent of the
Beckton population, Bangladeshis and Pakistanis a further
13 per cent**
http://neighbourhood.statistics.gov.uk/dissemination/
LeadTableView.do?a=7&b=6114058&c=E6+2RP&d=13&e=
62&g=342854&i=1x1003x1032x1004&m=0&r=0&s=
1436103785830&enc=1&dsFamilyId=2477

N21

203 **Their population has fallen by 620,000 in London since the start
of the century**
www.bbc.co.uk/news/uk-21511904

203 **Between 1971 and 2011 the white British share of London's
population slumped from 86 per cent to 45 per cent**
quarterly.demos.co.uk/article/issue-4/London-all-that-glisters/

206 **17 per cent of the white British have left the city in the first
decade of this century**
Ibid.

206 **250,000 migrant cleaners of London**
news.bbc.co.uk/1/hi/magazine/4259608.stm

Knightsbridge

214 **Today there are at least fifteen thousand servants in Mayfair**
http://wetherell.co.uk/wetherell-blog/homes-in-mayfair-now-
employ-more-domestic-staff-than-in-georgian-times-report-
wetherell/

215 **In a third of London's boroughs half the population churns
every five years**
www.ucl.ac.uk/london-2062

Catford Bridge

236 **The new London where 57 per cent of births are to migrant mothers**
www.ons.gov.uk/ons/dcp171778_375070.pdf

253 **The census reads there are more than 450,000 mixed-race people in London**
http://www.thetimes.co.uk/tto/multimedia/archive/00364/Census_364748a.pdf

Fore Street

253 **Officials estimate there are at least seven thousand prostitutes in London – and 96 per cent of them are migrants. These are mostly girls from the east: Romania, Slovakia, Lithuania. But also girls from the south: Brazil, Thailand, Vietnam. There are at least two thousand of them every night on the street**
http://i1.cmsfiles.com/eaves/2012/04/Sex-in-the-City-1751ff.pdf
http://www.bbc.co.uk/news/uk-11012084

Plaistow Road

274 **almost 80 per cent speak English as a second language and less than 10 per cent are White British**
http://ukdataexplorer.com/census/london/#KS206EW0009
http://www.newham.info/research/CFProfiles/Plaistow.pdf

275 **The white British population of old cockney Newham is now 16.7 per cent**
http://www.ons.gov.uk/ons/rel/census/2011-census/key-statistics-for-local-authorities-in-england-and-wales/rpt-ethnicity.html?format=print

283 **over a third of children live in poverty, and a quarter of all households are overcrowded**
http://www.londonspovertyprofile.org.uk/indicators/topics/income-poverty/child-poverty-by-borough/

http://www.londonspovertyprofile.org.uk/indicators/topics/
housing-and-homelessness/overcrowded-households-across-
london/

283 **out of 354 in the country this is the sixth most deprived**
     http://www.newham.info/Custom/LEA/Demographics.pdf

Harlesden Road

293 **the poorest 10 per cent of the country**
     https://intelligence.brent.gov.uk/BrentDocuments/
     Harlesden%20Locality%20Profile%202012.pdf

294 **at times the city's murder capital, at others its gun-crime centre**
     news.bbc.co.uk/1/hi/uk/1169598.stm

294 **There are 1,773 betting shops in London**
     www.bbc.co.uk/news/uk-england-london-20997925

304 **The white British population has shrunk almost thirty per cent
     between 2001 and 2011**
     https://intelligence.brent.gov.uk/BrentDocuments/Brent%
     202011%20Census%20Profile.pdf
     Figures are for the borough, Brent.

Edmonton Green

313 **these streets have the highest concentration of the insane in the
     city**
     http://www.haringey.gov.uk/sites/haringeygovuk/files/south_
     east_collaborative_health_profile.pdf

315 **In 2005 and 2006 the police conducted 802 skunk raids in
     London and found over two-thirds run by Vietnamese gangs**
     http://www.dailymail.co.uk/news/article-488618/So-YOU-live-
     suburban-skunk-factory.html

317 **their streets and estates are amongst the 4 per cent most
     deprived in the country. Nearly a quarter of the workforce here
     is out of a job**

https://www.google.com/fusiontables/DataSource?dsrcid=
622724

http://www.theguardian.com/cities/2014/feb/03/enfield-
experiment-london-cities-economy http://www.enfield.gov.uk/
healthandwellbeing/info/13/enfield_people/151/employment_
and_unemployment

319 **the area is 18.8 per cent white British**
http://www.google.co.uk/url?sa=t&rct=j&q=&esrc=s&source=
web&cd=1&ved=0CCIQFjAA&url=http%3A%2F%2Fwww.
enfield.gov.uk%2Fdownload%2Fdownloads%2Fid%2F7228%2F
edmonton_green_ward&ei=-ouWVdu7J6W17gbr1oaIAw&usg=
AFQjCNFq_ptZIMPAyZh3RqvGUKWt_0cGRw&sig2=ZyMh52
HxoGxzQa59_qx0lg&bvm=bv.96952980,d.ZGU

Chester Row

334 **52 per cent of those who live here were born overseas, and
40 per cent don't even have a British passport. And a third of
them arrived since 2001**
https://www.rbkc.gov.uk/pdf/Census%202011%20-%20
December%20Release%20Summary.pdf

334–5 **Kensington has the highest percentage of residents who describe
themselves as having no British identity at all – almost 40 per
cent – and is the only borough to have seen its population fall
since 2001. Since 2001 the white British population has shrunk
from 50 per cent to 39 per cent**
https://www.rbkc.gov.uk/pdf/Census%202011%20-%20
December%20Release%20Summary.pdf

336–7 **the water authorities notice its presence spiking on a Tuesday
afternoon**
http://www.ft.com/cms/s/0/c55315d8-e696-11e3-b8c7-00144
feabdc0.html

337 **this £10 billion industry**
http://www.ons.gov.uk/ons/dcp171766_365274.pdf

341 **equal poorest ward in London**
http://leftfootforward.org/2013/03/the-tories-have-no-plan-b-for-kensington-when-the-property-bubble-bursts/

341 **These are five hundred flats with a 58 per cent child poverty rate**
http://leftfootforward.org/2013/03/the-tories-have-no-plan-b-for-kensington-when-the-property-bubble-bursts/

343 **the kids here grow up counted as some of the poorest 5 per cent in England**
https://www.london.gov.uk/sites/default/files/Briefing-2011-06-Indices-Deprivation-2010-London.pdf

343 **Eighty-nine, the life expectancy for a white woman in a Chelsea town house. Sixty-two, the life expectancy of a Moroccan man in the North Kensington estates over the Westway**
http://leftfootforward.org/2013/03/the-tories-have-no-plan-b-for-kensington-when-the-property-bubble-bursts/

Rye Lane

346 **There have been more than ten murders round here since then**
www.murdermap.co.uk/murder-map.asp

Ilford Lane

358 **And today the white British population of these dingy streets south of Ilford station is around 10 per cent**
http://ukdataexplorer.com/census/london/#KS201EW0020

Lambert Road

380 **Abuse is as normal as rain for the nurses and carers of London: at least 60 per cent are migrants**
http://www.newstatesman.com/2013/07/without-immigrants-our-country-wouldnt-function-so-lets-give-it-go

This book is dedicated to Lagun Akinloye and Matei Clej.

I want to thank the Cichowlas family without whom this book would not have got off the ground in Pimlico. I am deeply grateful. I want, once again, to thank Daniel Johnson for sending me to Beckton when I got back from Siberia. I want to thank Kris Doyle, on behalf of myself, this book, and the reader for being the most gifted editor I have ever met and Georgina Capel for making this all happen. I want to thank all my family, but especially my mother Rosie, as a life-line editor, my father Tim for encouraging me, and my brother Jacob for listening, to the earliest, roughest drafts. Esti, Eve and Ray thank you for being there for me when I needed it and putting up with these stories for so long.